Screenwriting
A MANUAL

Developed from a concept by
Jonathan Dawson and Ian Stocks.

For Felicity who made it all work.

Screenwriting
A Manual

JONATHAN DAWSON

OXFORD
UNIVERSITY PRESS

OXFORD

UNIVERSITY PRESS

253 Normanby Road, South Melbourne, Australia

Oxford University Press is a department of the University of Oxford. It
furthers the University's objective of excellence in research, scholarship,
and education by publishing worldwide in

Oxford New York

Athens Auckland Bangkok Bogotá Buenos Aires Calcutta Cape Town
Chennai Dar es Salaam Delhi Florence Hong Kong Istanbul Karachi
Kuala Lumpur Madrid Melbourne Mexico City Mumbai Nairobi Paris
Port Moresby São Paulo Shanghai Singapore Taipei Tokyo Toronto Warsaw

with associated companies in Berlin Ibadan

OXFORD is a trade mark of Oxford University Press
in the UK and in certain other countries

National Library of Australia
Cataloguing-in-Publication data:

Dawson, Jonathan.
    Screenwriting: a manual.
    Bibliography.
    Includes index.
    ISBN 0 19 550832 7.

    1. Creative writing. 2. Television authorship. 3. Interactive multimedia.
    4. Motion picture authorship. I. Stocks, Ian. II. Title.

808.23

Edited by L. Elaine Miller of Otmar Miller Consultancy Pty Ltd, Melbourne
Text designed by Derrick I. Stone Design
Cover designed by Propellant
Cover photograph from The Image Bank
Typeset by Derrick I. Stone Design
Printed through Bookpac Production Services

Contents

Preface   vii
Acknowledgments   ix

Introduction: Starting Out   1
Chapter 1: Getting Ideas   5
Chapter 2: How to Begin Your Script   12
Chapter 3: Behind the Screens   19
Chapter 4: Commercials, Corporates and Infotainment   26
Chapter 5: The Documentary   33
Chapter 6: Shorts, Soaps and Sitcoms   41
Chapter 7: A Short Course in Comedy   47
Chapter 8: The Pitch   59
Chapter 9: Creating Characters   80
Chapter 10: The Plot Thickens   95
Chapter 11: Writing Series TV   114
Chapter 12: Writing Feature Films and Television Movies   138
Chapter 13: Children's Television and Film   159
Chapter 14: Animation: Imaginary Lives   173
Chapter 15: Scripting Multimedia   192

Appendix 1: Legals   210
Appendix 2: Video Games: A Very Short History   215
Appendix 3: Gallipoli   218

Glossary   220
References   226
Recommended Reading   227
Index   229

Preface

Screenwriting: A Manual is a guidebook to planning and writing proposals and scripts for all the screen media. Whatever your ambitions or interests, you'll find guidelines for developing ideas and presenting them, along with examples of successful scripts in the many genres. Hundreds of movies are discussed for good reason. Watch them!

Here's a brief outline of what's covered in this book:

Before you start writing, you need to know your market and your audience. In Chapter 1 we move on to the basics of the scriptwriting business: building on an idea, and how that simple idea becomes a complex story.

From short movies to features, there are some principles that can help with the task of grabbing an audience and keeping them. Screenplays that do this brilliantly are examined in Chapter 2.

Chapter 3 looks at how you might decide which medium to write for—the cinema, festival audiences, television, or multi media—and the question of whether screen size matters.

Planning and writing advertising commercials and corporates—in other words, any 'movies that sell'—can present unique challenges, yet still leave plenty of room for originality. In Chapter 4, short informational and marketing films are explored in detail.

Forms and styles of documentary program-making, along with a guide to markets and audiences, are examined in Chapter 5.

In Chapter 6, a chapter for all storytellers, the many styles and markets for shorter-form dramas (shorts, soaps and sitcoms) are detailed, with plenty of examples and ideas.

For writers who really want to write comedy, humour is the focus of Chapter 7, featuring current and classic examples from television and film scripts.

'The Pitch' is the essential chapter for any screenwriter. From concept documents through to the face-to-face pitch, persuading producers and backers that you have a winner is the most critical part of getting your words to the screen.

Chapter 9 is a complete short manual on how to steal, devise, borrow, and construct characters, from basic principles to detailed biographies. Again, lots of script extracts are provided.

Strategies for plot development are investigated in Chapter 10. Theories of narrative, starting with Aristotle and extending right through to William Goldman, are brought to life with examples from current films and series.

The hottest market of all is featured in Chapter 11: series television. Series such as *SeaChange*, *Wildside* and *Medivac* are examined, giving vital insights into the major world market for all screenwriters.

Chapter 12, looking at feature films and television movies, is a big chapter, full of current film examples and covering most popular genres along with a few more . . . unusual films as well.

A survey of the field of children's film and television, along with an examination of guidelines, regulations and all the most successful genres, is the focus of Chapter 13.

From experimental shorts to series that are yet to go to air, Chapter 14 looks at the role of writers in creating animated films.

The final chapter, 'Scripting Multimedia', is a state-of-the-art survey of the future for most screenwriters, featuring multimedia scripts and pitch documents for interactive projects from *The Last Express* to CD-ROM projects still on the drawing board.

Good luck, and have fun. You've joined one of the most challenging industries of them all.

Jonathan Dawson
February 2000

Acknowledgments

The following people and institutions kindly agreed to give permission to reproduce artwork and other textural materials, and I gratefully acknowledge their assistance and cooperation: scripts for The Wayne Manifesto have been supplied courtesy of Artist Services P/L, The Australian Film Finance Corporation P/L and Film Queensland. Permission to reproduce their original work has been given by Max Bannah, Carlos Alperin and Dennis Tupicoff.

Every effort has been made to trace the original source of all material reproduced in this book. Where the attempt has been unsuccessful, the authors and publisher would be pleased to hear from the copyright holder concerned to rectify any omission.

Introduction
Starting Out

The truth is out there. We are not alone.

—*The X-Files*, the T-shirt

Whatever form of script you are writing, you're always working for someone else. Whether the job is the sprint of a radio advertisement or the long haul of a feature film or miniseries, your first challenge is to catch and hold your audience. Whatever that audience is called—a target demographic, an age group, the masses, or your own idea of the ideal audience—your script must have them clearly in focus.

As screenwriter William Goldman said, *nobody knows anything*.

If anybody *did* then there would be a magic formula on the market and all scripts would be produced by computer program by now. But the simple fact is that computer programs, along with those high-priced screenwriting courses, keep on selling. For a money-saving assessment of all these gimmicks, please read Joe Queenan's (1997) withering descriptions in *The Unkindest Cut*.

Of course, some writer-directors reveal consistent ability to succeed within familiar genres. James Cameron's *Titanic* (1997) is really a deeply conventional love story overlaid by fabulous special effects. Steven Spielberg's early blockbusters, including *Jaws* (1975) and the Indiana Jones series, right up to and beyond *Jurassic Park* (1993) reveal an almost obsessive desire to work within the safety of genre. All such films and the next week's hit TV series after *LA Law* or *Blue Heelers* show that old formulae can work occasionally, but that there are indeed no rules and a huge amount of luck required in all mass media writing. No wonder many writers stay happily within the confines of an ongoing TV soap or series, where the storylines are often provided and the skills of the writer (no less than those of an 'original' writer) are devoted to maintaining the integrity in action and dialogue of the established characters. There is at least some certainty in that.

Remember too, that audiences shift and change. What worked this week (*Twister*, Jan de Bont, 1996) may bomb the next year (*Dante's Peak*, Roger Donaldson, 1997), so 'proven' hit formulae should be as carefully watched and circumspectly observed as are surefire screenwriting primers. One year harsh realism hits (in France, anyway), as in *La Haine* (Mathieu Kassowitz, 1995); the next it's well-crafted sentimentality under a veneer of realism as in *The Full Monty* (Peter Cataneo, 1996). Which way should the new writer jump? The answer is don't jump, just keep writing—but do watch out for the audience, because they can never be under-estimated. Sometimes their ability to spot a forgery or a calculated follow-up seems like the height of critical sharpness: audiences stunned producers and writers by going to see the quirky and small (*Shine*, Scott Hicks, 1996, or *The Full Monty* again) in spite of the massive ad campaigns for *Sphere* (Barry Levinson, 1997), *Mimic* (Guillermo del Toro, 1997) and *Outbreak* (Wolfgang Petersen, 1995). All followed a formula, all had big stars—and all bombed.

In storytelling, it seems, there is no Golden Rule. This book is designed to give you a full picture of what's out there in the industry so you're fully prepared. And you'll meet plenty of successful shows and writers. But no one makes it every time, let alone the first time. Look at writers like Shane Black with *Lethal Weapon* (Richard Donner, 1987). Look at Joe Esterhasz with *Basic Instinct* (Paul Verhoeven, 1992). Great successes. But that guarantees nothing next time around. Visit the same writers, five years on—though their scripts still get auctioned as if they were guaranteed box office gold, the Midas touch has often moved on.

Know your audience

But of course, though the audience must always be at the back of your mind, there is one set of greater powers that stand between you and the public: the producers.

Every form of writing is done to a lesser or greater degree as a commissioned work. 'No man but a blockhead ever wrote except for money', as Dr Johnson put it. And, however pure your craft and your art, sooner rather than later the next step is to get your project up. These agents of change have many names, but most commonly they are called producers, directors or The Client. Australia is a country with many funding bodies, where states and the federal government all have development schemes. The new united Europe also has many funds available for writers and producers to develop projects (for example the Media scheme) and the search for these money pots has become a full-time preoccupation.

Add to these alluring sources of development money another complex equation. Film, television, media, multimedia, and journalism schools are still all in a major international growth phase, expanding both in popularity and in status (though this is a claim hotly contested by some in more traditional disciplines like History or Languages and Literature). Who would ever have foreseen that communications programs would compete with law and medical faculties for top students? But they do—and will continue to do so as the increasing convergence of forms of communication guarantees that we really are now in a global village, and that we have no need of global village idiots. The danger for a writer in all of this is that the number of gatekeepers—the quasi-producers, script assessors, script editors, film funding bodies—is also growing at an equal pace. Many of these groups or individuals have very different agendas from those of writers and directors, not to mention the specialist or mass audience out there waiting, breathless, for *your* words.

Media rules, media money

All media, quite simply, are becoming regulated and bureaucratised at the same time as new technologies constantly alter the playing field. Global megalopolies like Rupert Murdoch's News Corporation, Germany's Bertelsmans Conglomerate (dealing in everything from interactive CDs, TV series and films right down to jigsaw puzzles), Time Warner, Sony, and Europe's other big players such as Ravensberger, Canal+, Berlusconi—the list is endless and always changing—all have rafts of executives ('suits'), advisors and experts who will be available to second-guess your work, whether it's a 10-second TV spot or a children's animated series.

Be afraid—be very afraid—but also be aware that these folks know as little as you do about what the next Big Thing will be!

Remember: in addition to the script editors, producers and advisors, anyone in a position of authority in a company—or sometimes even passing by in the corridor of the production office—has a right to read, comment on and suggest changes to your work at any time. The media are democracies where the maximum number get to exercise power, in spite of all those conspiracy theories to the contrary. This is something you'll just have to get used to. It won't change unless, like the Coen brothers (*Miller's Crossing*, 1990), you can soar above all the hierarchies and little voting groups so that you and you alone control and protect your own originality. But the odds against this—along with the way things work—suggest that you should prepare yourself for a working life of being second-guessed. Worse things could happen.

There is absolutely no point in being wilfully naive or hoping that the game playing that goes on around media writing and production is none of your business. Unfortunately it is. So get to know the players: TV channels, studios, producers, ad agencies (hot and not so hot), funding bodies and their house styles and yes, always, your audience.

When it comes to explaining your own work to others (see Chapter 8: The Pitch), remember to keep it simple—as simple as the lines of your own script. When *Reservoir Dogs* (Quentin Tarantino, 1992) is reorganised by restoring a normal time frame, it plays like a classic three-act play. So do many apparently stunningly innovative stories. There is still virtue—and sales—in simplicity.

After the success of *The Castle* (1996 and still winning international audiences years later—all on a budget of around A$1 million) —writer/director Rob Sitch noted:

> I still think there is courage in simplicity. You always look
> good when you do something complex and fail. If you do
> something simple and fail, you look like an idiot.

But the fact remains: nobody knows anything!

This book sets out to help you learn as much as you can about the business and the key players around the world.

If you're still convinced that you already know what to do and whom to talk to, then go straight to Chapter 8.

But you still have to come up with that story idea all by yourself, though there are some short cuts. Just make sure you are fully prepared before you stick your head (and your beloved script) in to the lion's mouth.

That's what Chapter 1 is all about.

Good luck for the rest of your writing life. All you need is information—and talent. We'll provide the first of those . . .

Chapter 1
Getting Ideas

Although some producers—particularly, say, a Steve Bochko scoring goals bigtime with *Hill Street Blues* and *LA Law*—seem to have a firm grip on the beating pulse of the public, such serial success is very rare and often a matter of timing—and luck. After all, Bochko really wanted to get up a series called *Hotel* when he was asked to produce an outline for a cop show that became *Hill Street Blues*. Luck, timing, and a good pitch will win you a slot more often than pure talent alone.

Nevertheless, there are several key elements that have good sale value in the market, and whose lack in a script idea will normally (there are no absolutes) mean the project will crash earlier than otherwise.

Hooking the punters

The first thing you need to know about scripting is the need for a 'hook'. You've probably heard the Carol Bayer Sager song 'I'm Moving Out Today' about a loser songwriter whose songs 'have no hooks'. Basically, a hook is the germ of the script or ad—or indeed, any storytelling structure that marks it out as being different, or at least interesting beyond a first glance. The famous scenes at the beginning of Robert Altman's *The Player* (1992) show a number of screenwriters making hopeless attempts to pitch their film ideas in as few words as possible. Several of the writers shown are the genuine article, like award-winning writer-director Buck Henry. There is little exaggeration in these scenes. Believe me, you don't appear in a scene like that unless you believe it has a deadly truth at its black and satirical heart!

Jurassic Park (Steven Spielberg, 1993), *The Lost World* (Steven Spielberg, 1997) and countless recent imitators have a wonderfully strong hook: *What if the dinosaurs came back?* The Australian international success *Shine* (Scott Hicks, 1996) asked: *Can a mentally disturbed man overcome his terrors and dazzle the world with his piano playing?* Every great play has its unique hook—just check out the ideas behind Shakespeare's plays, particularly the comedies. All have the teasing *What if . . . ?* before the premise, which is why Shakespeare's works are so often recast and remade. *Romeo and Juliet* becomes *West Side Story* becomes, finally, *William Shakespeare's Romeo + Juliet* (Baz Luhrman, 1996).

The hook is what makes every successful commercial work, every dramatic work flow and every documentary or corporate/industrial film *work*. Without a hook, the work will be pedestrian. Even if it's avant-garde work that is your interest, there must be a central informing idea behind the story you want to tell. Hooks are not just gimmicks.

It is the hook that links the narrative impulses of every story-telling form, and it is the hook for, say, a feature film that will make the advertising campaign for that film so much more effective. Animation films, of course, contain their own visual hooks in the form of their visual 'look' as well as the characters created. An established series like *The Simpsons* or *South Park* is its own hook. More eccentric low-budget movies like *Love Serenade* (Shirley Barrett, 1996) or *Zero Effect* (Jake Kasdan, 1998) gain their audiences more by projecting a certain unique world view than they ever would through a good advertising campaign. Such unusual, non-mainstream movies tend to reveal a narrative that is irreducible to a crude or over-simple formula. But they still have to tell a story—and this often turns out to be surprisingly simple.

Titanic (James Cameron, 1997), by feeding on pre-existing myths, disasters, tragedies, or legends, needed only its title to sell itself. An earlier and excellent version of the same story, the more documentary *A Night to Remember* (Walter Lord, 1957) would doubtless have done better box office with the simpler title. A survey by *Premiere* magazine in 1998 showed that most winners of the Oscar for Best Picture in the 1990s had titles with three or fewer words!

Titles as hooks

A good title is the ultimate hook. The danger is that someone else will like what you like, if you get things too right: the Australian feature film *Final Cut* (Ross Dimsey, 1980) has had its title used for four other films (Canadian, Australian, American, English) right up to 1998, despite running regularly on American and European cable television from its launch to the present (Suissimages, 2000).

Your movie or series is about a group of university students always in trouble and sharing a house near campus. Think of a two-word title, then a three-word title, then a one-word title, like House. Then using your original ideas as starters, see if you can come up with ten similar titles. Hard to stop, isn't it?

Though the title that 'says it all' (like the re-make of *King Kong*, John Guillermin, 1976) is the ultimate hook, it can be overused, or just die of atrophy after too many sequels and recyclings. Another obvious simple hook is the name of the character: Wyatt Earp, Robin Hood, Jane Eyre, (Jane Austen's) Emma, Shaft, and so on. All carry a particular metaphorical, historical, figurative or literary charge with them that should work to your advantage and has the added bonus that it will focus your writing as much as will creating an advertisement for, say, a single product leader like a Rolls Royce, Coke, or a Mars Bar will. Nevertheless, cinema history suggests that a recycled mythical figure might well work, which is why two Robin Hood films came out in a single year (1991), a recurring phenomenon. A recent example of this was two films around a single set of events involving the real Sir Arthur Conan Doyle: *Photographing Fairies* (Nick Willing, 1998) and *Fairytale: A True Story* (Charles Sturridge, 1997), which collided with a shower of fairy dust in 1997–98. As a result the marketing people could do little, and audiences tended to stay away from both, which was a pity.

Make your heroes work for you

If the fictional character is already well established, as with Ian Fleming's James Bond series, or in an earlier age, Raymond Chandler's private eye Philip Marlowe (now and forever identified cinematically with the actor Humphrey Bogart), or Tom Clancy's post-Cold War warrior Jack Ryan (once Alec Baldwin had been replaced by the more identifiably heroic Harrison Ford), then there will be a guaranteed interest in this character by the general public. But heaven help you if you confound popular expectations or play around with the character, as happened with the Bond spoof *Casino Royale* (John Huston, 1967). This movie utterly confused and then lost a host of Bond lovers by offering not one but a slew of actors (including the mutually exclusive though equally iconic David Niven and Woody Allen) playing the archetypal spy within the same movie). Then again—why not? It might just work.

Equally successful from time to time are the equivalent of what is called in marketing slang the 'category-killer', in this case a title that simply pre-empts existing and potentially competing products. And make no mistake, movies, TV series, all media artefacts *are* products. In the late 1990s a series of disaster movies that did not necessarily improve, except in special effects, on the great tradition of French entertainer and cinema pioneer Georges Melies' fantastical entertainments at the turn of the twentieth century, used simple hook titles such as *Twister* (Jan de Bont, 1996) and *Volcano* (Mick Jackson, 1997) to sell movies with the thinnest of storylines pinned onto elaborate and horrific spectacles. It didn't always work.

Sam Goldwyn once claimed that 'no one ever went broke under-estimating the taste of the public', though he still needed writers to do this underestimating for him. He also said that if he didn't hear the busy sound of typewriters busily clattering from the writers' rooms on the lot he got nervous (Goldman, 1983: 21).

Stories that break the rules

Of course, studios and script gurus notwithstanding, movies can get made and will succeed without a recognisable hook. *Love Serenade* (Shirley Barrett, 1996) would hardly have sold off the page as the story of two repressed sisters in a fading country town, infatuated by a smooth-talking deejay—and that's about it, apart from a mysterious giant fish that may have nothing to do with anything. Its very oddity was, in the end, what won viewers.

Love Serenade had no hook, not even a hat rack (see next page) for audiences, let alone producers, to hang their own desires and prejudices on. But the sheer whimsy that drove the project—much like the earlier films of Hal Hartley (*The Unbelievable Truth*, 1990; *Simple Men*, 1992)—did attract backers interested in a fresh take on the American dream, and the film found a more specialised audience. So, once again, there are no absolute rules to guide us, except that a key factor in Barrett's and Hartley's success was their own unstoppable determination to tell stories their own way, outside the straitjackets of mainstream cinema. It happens—a lot. Eccentricity and the bizarre have never been a bar to getting your story told, but you have to find the right entrepreneurs to buy your vision. Hal Hartley's recent films (*Amateur*, 1995) and Jim Jarmusch's extraordinary rewriting of the western genre, *Dead Man* (1996), were financed by individuals outside the familiar production loops. In fact, much of the money for Jarmusch's wonderfully idiosyncratic cinema has come from a Japanese backer.

But a good hook—or even your brave assertion that there *is* one—will work most of the time as a starter motor for your ideas. Apart from 'one idea' or 'High Concept' movies, or those based on pre-existing literary, mythic, or dramatic forms, there are those based on familiar situations. These are the 'hat rack' plots in which audiences recognise what they believe to be totally original plot motors, but which are carefully constructed to look idiosyncratic while actually using predetermined and well-known genre techniques and structures. TV series, particularly, rely on this recycling of well-worn motives and obsessions and in the flow of television programming, the not-so-original can often seem brand new—provided the characters act surprised at the plot turns! The cinema is less forgiving because you only get one shot at the audience, and then it's straight to video. As with a target demographic for a particular product being advertised, you give the identified audience what they want. Obviously this approach works for Kung Fu movies, or the Chop Socky melodramas (Chuck Norris, Jean Claude Van Damme) of the 1970s and 1980s, which appear likely to have their following well into the next millennium.

Later discussions of genre in all forms of storytelling will go into genre plots and audience expectations in detail, but certainly particular sorts of storyline seem to enjoy unlimited success provided the writer can find a new twist on the simple revenge motif. Consider, for example, the vigilante vengeance of the *Death Wish* series (Michael Winner), the Mad Max post-apocalyptic take on the revenge melodrama, and the many sequels to *Lethal Weapon*, *Die Hard*, *Rambo*, *Robocop*, et al. Such series, which tap into some audiences' need on a very basic level (let's not get too psychologistic about it), are known as 'franchise movies': they create a loyal mass audience who will come back for more until the series self-destructs (like *Rambo III*, Peter Macdonald, 1988) or the audience just grows out of it.

Big titles for big pictures
In this sense *Titanic* was just another version of the older form of big disaster movies—and this includes variants on the war movie, set on planes: *Airport* (Mark Seaton/Henry Hathaway, 1970), on ships: *The Poseidon Adventure* (Ronald Neame, 1972), *Das Boot* (Wolfgang Petersen, 1981), or in the 'small community'—the setting for all manner of disasters, from *The Cars that Ate Paris* (Peter Weir, 1972) (bizarre) to any number of natural disaster movies of which few even bother to ring any changes on the standard 'Hero leading the flock out of the Wilderness' plot machine. An outstanding exception is *Tremors* (Ron Underwood, 1990).

Hat racks: Little hooks that work
A hat rack is really just a popular preconception or idea that you hope audiences will recognise and find believable. Hat racks provide audiences with issues and ideas to which they can readily relate—just like tossing their hats onto a familiar hook. You'll find them most often in social issue movies. This explains the presence on 'Movie of the Week' of an endless parade of *Diaries of a Cocaine Housewife* (see any New World movie catalogue), *The Burning Bed* (Robert Greenwald, 1984) and other issue-based plots. Occasionally a breakout feature film traps the popular imagination such as *Kramer vs. Kramer* (Robert Benton, 1979), which relied on intelligent casting (Dustin Hoffman, Meryl Streep) as well as a very literate adaptation by writer/director Benton; but it was basically a big budget 'issues' movie all along.

Much darker or more jaundiced takes on the domestic seldom work, though the box office success *The War of the Roses* (Danny de Vito, 1989) was again due in no small part to the casting against type of Michael Douglas and Kathleen Turner. This success indicates that there is a market for a less mawkish view of the daily disasters that beset us all. It also suggests that dramas based on social issues will be most successful, often despite the script, if the leads are stars rather than actors! That a story is topical or timely may well help you pitch your idea, but good intentions or a social agenda are no necessary guarantors of success.

Amazing tales

On the other hand, bearing in mind that many different readers will be looking at your work, recognisable social problems are more likely to engage interest at the early stage of a story's development than the weird or esoteric. Of course this general rule of thumb must always except such auteurs of the edgy as David Cronenberg (*Dead Ringers*, 1991; *Crash*, 1997) and Gus Van Sant (*My Own Private Idaho*, 1991)—writer-directors whose trademark or unique selling proposition is precisely their ability to sidestep the obvious while making the truly strange or genuinely awful into relatively popular films, as well as genuine critical successes. Don't imagine that Cronenberg would even have attempted to make a film from William Burroughs' ('unfilmable') novel *The Naked Lunch* (1995) unless backers felt that his sensibility matched that of the novel's author in a saleable form of weirdness. To achieve that sort of reputation can take a lifetime's oeuvre—or at the very least a year's long first film shoot like David Lynch's *Eraserhead* (1977).

Sometimes a good title can suggest the whole movie or series to follow. Try to come up with a great title (not *Eraserhead* this time! although a compound word can work brilliantly on the imagination). Now write a one-line pitch for the show. If you've got a good hook in the title, the story will often follow automatically.

A new take on the familiar, a different angle on the well-known—these are not betrayals of what is often called 'originality'. Indeed, the very notion of the 'original' denies the fact that audiences and consumers will always want to recognise at least a part of their own world and identify with at least a key story element even if the 'hero' is, well, less than heroic.

Heroes versus anti-heroes

The concept of the anti-hero or anti-heroine who becomes so *in spite of him- or herself* is a hook that almost always works in the right hands. Both *The Marathon Man* (John Schlesinger, 1977) and *Three Days of the Condor* (Sydney Pollack, 1975) worked well because the hero seemed so outgunned from the very beginning (as well as bookish, in spite of the casting of Hoffman and Redford), and passive. But in fact both screenplays use what we'll call here the Telephone Booth plot device: that key moment in so many genre hits, from *High Noon* by Fred Zinnemann (1952) through to the archetype of them all, Clark Kent transforming into Superman in the telephone booth. All hesitation aside, the hero now turns into an unrelenting force for action as if the earlier 'weak' self had never existed. It's one of the most useful plot devices of them all and for audiences, if well carried off, the most deeply satisfying. *Enemy of the State* (Tony Scott, 1998) was merely the slickest and latest of a long line of paranoid movies. You can't go wrong with the paranoid plot that pits the innocent but resourceful hero against any set of larger forces.

Odds against the hero will always seem the greater if the hero, just as in the psychological westerns of the 1950s, like Delmer Daves' *3.10 to Yuma* (1957) or even recent intense dramas like *The Shawshank Redemption* (Frank Darabont, 1994), seems to suffer from as many human frailties as possible, including terminal indecisiveness, before ducking into the telephone booth. The beauty of the device is that it can always be made to seem fresh by keeping your hero topically and typically of your time.

Originality? Nothing to do with the business of retelling great stories.

What worked once will always work again if you cheerfully and unashamedly bring your own viewpoint to bear on it. Tell stories you want to tell, not what other people tell you to.

Chapter 2
How to Begin Your Script

Beyond the hook: First moments of your script

If your hook is the one big idea that marks off your work from all others, even those in the same genre or with the same kinds of characters, the story is ready to run. Beginnings are where you have to grab your audience—and before them the producers, investors and all the rest of the folks your script will meet along the way. We'll look at appropriate and effective beginnings in every form of media writing as we go. Just as we can consider a hook to be an overall informing principle underlying your entire work, so it is still essential to begin your narrative as effectively, seductively, and powerfully as possible, pulling the audience into your world as you do so.

The first moments of any work for any medium are vital. If they work, then the audience will enter into a bargain with you that they will enjoy and believe in the experience you're about to give them. They're on for the ride, if you like, and so 'suspend disbelief'. Yes, the Coleridgean maxim about poetry (willing suspension of disbelief) works with scripts, which in their resistance to pure prose effects are indeed a highly schematised form of poetry. Words that are engaged in the basic business of giving information are the substance of your descriptive passages, but not of your dramatic ones. Hook your audience early and they will stay with you all the longer.

Ernest Hemingway liked to tell readers that he would go back at the end of a story—even the shortest—and arbitrarily cut the first five hundred words. Well, maybe, but it's amazing how often the early scenes or moments of a script can be cut, and how in so doing you realise that the first drafts were just a way of easing into the business of writing and need not be fiercely maintained against the editor's ignorant scissors. Be prepared to cut to the core up front, the better to fire the script with energy later on.

Who's going to read your script next?

There is another reason for this emphasis on a punchy or engaging start to a story and it is not a happy one. The script will be read by readers not necessarily sympathetic to your ideas, particularly if they are new ideas.

That doesn't mean that there must be a dramatic explosion from Moment One, though that's certainly often a mechanical necessity in writing television drama. But whatever you are writing, the beginning must contain all the seeds necessary to set up your personal vision and make it transmit beyond the page.

What is a subtext?

Personal vision brings us to 'subtext'. By now this concept is so well known that characters in *Seinfeld* and Woody Allen movies can be found endlessly discussing it. What is it and who needs it? Well, it's the reason you are writing—often unspoken, though not necessarily or always. Even in a 10-second commercial there can be a subtext, as in the award winning McDonald's ads featuring a James Dean look-alike waltzing through a classic New Yorkish urban landscape. What's really being said here is something about lifestyles, about 'authentic' values—but also something about the unsayable things that everyone yearns after and no one gets except in dreams and at the movies. But it's never stated; it's simply *there*, to be discovered and read to a greater or lesser degree—or even missed totally without necessarily affecting the desired outcome, which in this case is to make Big Macs seem classier and more part of the weft and warp of our city dreams than they already are. But put it into words and it seems absurd.

Take the opening of *Reservoir Dogs* (Quentin Tarantino, 1992). A group of men dressed in black suits are sitting in Uncle Bob's Pancake House ranting about things that seem to have no importance in the great scheme of anything, like the meaning of the lyrics of Madonna's 'Like a Virgin'.

Tarantino claims never to have studied screenwriting, although plenty of scriptwriting teachers claim him as their student, notably Dov S-S Simens! In fact, Tarantino had studied as an actor and so is happy to let the individualities of the characters establish themselves immediately, as he also does later in the notorious Cheese Royale hamburger discussion in *Pulp Fiction*. These scenes, which seem improvised by the actors, play wonderfully well as ensemble pieces, but also drop us straight into the world of the men in the suits, while reminding us of the sorts of things that such men might talk about and how they would talk if their profession was crime, thus making the scene hum with unresolved tensions and potential violence. When Mr Pink (Steve Buscemi) starts his schtick about tips:

MR PINK

> Look, I ordered coffee. Now I've been here a long fuckin'
> time and she's only filled my cup three times. When I
> order coffee, I want it filled six times.

we are listening to an obsessive-compulsive character who, like
Shakespeare's rash anti-hero Harry Hotspur (*Henry IV Part One*),
will 'cavil at the ninth part of a hair' (that is, argue the toss at the
drop of a hat and undoubtedly go off like a faulty time bomb before
long).

What should never have worked as an opening scene in a movie
is riveting, not least because of the matters that are not spelled out,
but left to smoulder with a slow-burning fuse. The central subtext
(a heist) is what is not spelled out, but is recognised by the audience almost subconsciously. In this case it's a mood: part fear, part
bravado, all deadly.

Conflict: Without it there's no drama

Most stories are about a character who wants something and about
the forces or people getting in the way of that. In a commercial, of
course, the audience are often the 'implied' central character. Many
successful commercials will offer the mass audience an easily iden-
tifiable surrogate for themselves, though nowadays the image of
the Tired Housewife in search of the perfect Cleaning Stuff is a bit
passé—so passé, in fact, that it has a certain postmodern charm.

Whatever you are creating, whether a commercial or a feature
film, your basic idea and the ways in which you develop it must be
checked out periodically, as the script progresses, against certain
criteria. Though many screenwriting manuals will go on about
quests and plot and character arcs, ignore this stuff and look at
what will affect the success or failure of your script in a less hypo-
thetical world. Thus:

- Does the concept have a strong hook? Pitch the idea in a few
  sentences if you're not sure. This is something you'll need to
  do when considering script development and layouts in
  Chapter 3.
- Is there a strong central line of argument (or plot)?
- If the idea seems familiar, is this something that you can turn
  into a plus (carry it out better than so-and-so in such-and-
  such film?) or is it a sticking point that will allow a
  second-guesser to claim you've strayed onto someone else's
  territory?
- Remember: familiarity may mean that you have struck on a
  universally fascinating theme and have every chance of turning that sense of the familiar into delighted recognition on the
  part of your audiences (and, first of all, your producer).

- If the idea *is* familiar, for whatever reason, can you give it a new angle? *Peggy Sue Got Married* (Francis Ford Coppola, 1986) and *Back to the Future* (Robert Zemeckis, 1985, 1987, 1990) are vastly different takes on the notion of suburban time travel, after all? Or are they?

> Write a one-paragraph pitch for a suburban time travel story.
>
> - What is the basic theme, the point of the story? Easy with a product sell, not so easy with characters. But if the central character(s) have a strong focus, and they want something enough, that's a story everyone should want to see.
>
> - What are the forces opposing the characters? Or are they internal (illness, love of a Good Man or Woman, family and so on)? Even indecision, as in *High Noon* (Fred Zinnemann, 1952) or most Woody Allen comedies, can be as frustrating an obstacle as a screaming tribe of Gremlins, no? And is there a clear resolution to the story, or if not, at least a tragic or comic finish that makes dramatic sense?

The death of Jack in *Titanic* destroyed the happiness of a generation of young romantics, but most audiences left the cinema satisfied that, well, life is like that, isn't it? In the end it was the love story rather than the CGIs (computer-generated images) of Cameron's movie that hit the mark with the audience demographic, 'Females aged 15–25', so effectively. Always visualise your script and convey that vision strongly in your work. Whatever the strength of the script and story, do you have a clear idea of what it might look like on the screen? Even if that amounts to no more than 'I'd like it to look and move like *Starship Troopers*' (Paul Verhoeven, 1997), this will help, particularly in describing those wordless moments. As Dylan Thomas said of poetry, to find your own style, first imitate someone whose work you like; just make sure it's good work.

A final tip: show, don't tell. This should be self-explanatory but is so central that we'll return to it again and again!

The wrap

None of the pointers listed above will guarantee saleability or even save you the trouble of analysing your market, but they are far more essential than matters such as, for example, the need to avoid the use of offensive stereotypes or characters that offend your audience. These are more often than not political rather than structural matters—and where would a good villain be without a certain offensiveness, if not pure and deadly charm?

Finally, never let anyone tell you, as many writing guides and classes insist, that coincidence and accident have no place in a story. They do in life, and chance is often a vital element of a thriller. Any scriptwriter who rules out the aleatory or the dream-like won't have much fun. Such rules are the invention of script editors of the sort who would reduce (or elevate) all drama to an episode of *Neighbours*.

High Concept versus dumbing down

> *What the phrase really means is that the concept is so low that it can be summarised and sold on the basis of a single sentence.*
>
> (Richard Schickel, 1984: 82)

When you look at it from every angle, the whole notion of High Concept is actually a simplification of the idea of a unique selling proposition that every successful advertisement must possess, even if it is only creating an atmosphere about a product and telling you nothing specific. See, for example, the Spike Lee Nike spots with Michael Jordan ('I wanna be like Mike'), a sort of über-athletic Nike World, peopled by those superior beings who possess Nikes.

But High Concept is now a tag that a writer will ignore at the risk of ending up out of it. And any residual snobbishness about the notion should be weighed up against the fact that individualist film-makers such as the Coen brothers operate on the principle of a *single* informing notion: let's make a Chandleresque movie become, by increments, an episodic and (in plot terms) gloriously absurd comedy, as with *The Big Lebowski* (1997).

Nevertheless, the term is frequently used in critical broadsides against mainstream cinema, along with the term 'dumbing down'. 'Dumbing down' refers to a general and observable tendency to produce movies aiming at the lowest common denominator, which also happens to be the desired demographic for maximal broad box office reach.

To take a recent Australian example of High Concept. A close and informed analysis of the plot of *Idiot Box* (David Caesar, 1997) reveals the reworking of a plot line familiar from the 1970s Aust-ralian TV icon, *Homicide*: what if two dumb young outer-suburban jerks decide to pull an (inevitably clumsy) heist? Not very original, right? But critics loved the story, perhaps forgetting the TV series, or else half-remembering it and perceiving that a deep chord had been struck. Of course, overlaid on the simplistic plot was a lot of 'attitude', style, and familiar social issue stuff. Audiences didn't buy it, but the film is still mentioned as somehow ground-breaking. This suggests that critics and reviewers in the main have very short memories.

How much shorter, then, are the memories of funding body assessors and producers? And how likely, therefore, that a very familiar plot line or character arc can be gussied up in such a way as to activate the popular memory of readers and help the story along the road to production? No wonder, then, that so many movies today are remakes, retreads of TV series and European (especially French) hits, or even (shudder) based on video game 'characters' (*Mortal Kombat*, Paul Anderson, 1995; *Super Mario Brothers*, Rocky Morton/Annabel Jankel, 1993), producing a third order of unoriginality by pirating forms which themselves are pirated from old TV series and B movies! Roger Corman (New World Pictures) must be wishing he had tighter patents on B movie shock horror formulae!

But how original is High Concept stuff?

So, in the absence of real originality, High Concept can often refer to the (re)use of the familiar. It's another form of recycling, but more financially rewarding if you're really good at it. Of course, what 'originality' really means in media terms is moot and will come up for more detailed discussion in the chapters on character and plot (Chapters 9 and 10).

The term 'High Concept' is often shorthand for the combining of previously successful series or movie plot lines. This is by no means a bad thing—the Dylan Thomas principle of using what you like in the work of other writers as a plotting model or story matrix works for such diverse talents as Steven Spielberg and the Coen brothers, though in vastly different ways. The *LA Times*, for instance, recently offered readers a High Concept Match Game in which *RoboCop* (Paul Verhoeven, 1987) was explained as *Terminator* (James Cameron, 1984) meets *Dirty Harry* (Don Siegel, 1971), and William Dear's fairly typical family/animal fantasy *Harry and the Hendersons* (1987) as *Gentle Giant* (James Neilson, 1967)—meets *ET* (Steven Spielberg, 1982). Spielberg's name also reminds us that some film-makers have built entire careers on populist stories, to the extent that deviation from the set model too early can lead to critical and box office backlash—as with Spielberg's *1941* (1979), a shot at surreal and screwball comedy, and *The Color Purple* (1985), an early attempt to turn a 'great' book into a great movie.

This last example leads us directly into the three components of successful High Concept as mainstream Hollywood sees it. In the words of film analyst Justin Wyatt in his book *High Concept* (1994: 20), the key indicators of High Concept as a working principle for writing scripts and developing projects are:

- The Look
- The Hook
- The Book

By this Wyatt means a combination of production styles (the Look), a very marketable and easily grasped narrative base (the Hook) and a highly reductive plot (the Book).

He lists a number of recent movies that fit this matrix, most notably: *Jaws* (Spielberg, 1975), *Superman* (Richard Donner, 1978), *Gremlins* (Joe Dante, 1984) (possibly remade as *Small Soldiers* by Joe Dante, 1998), *Mad Max Beyond Thunderdome* (George Ogilvie, 1985), *Top Gun* (Tony Scott, 1986), *Twins* (Ivan Reitman, 1988), *Days of Thunder* (Tony Scott, 1990), *Robin Hood Prince of Thieves* (Kevin Reynolds, 1991), *Wayne's World* (Penelope Spheeris, 1992) and to which one would have to add *Titanic* and, locally, *Paws* (Karl Zwicky, 1997).

The use of the term 'the Book', of course, also reminds us that the film and television industries are incurably addicted to the book adaptation as a way of cashing in on a pre-existing market, or even acquiring some dignity and class by association with, say, Jane Austen or Henry James. This can be seen recently in *Wings of a Dove* (Iain Softley, 1997) and *Oscar and Lucinda* (Gillian Armstrong, 1997), which fail precisely because of overly faithful adherence to non-filmic plot and character developments, the egregiously 'tragic' ending of *Oscar and Lucinda* pointing up a particular lesson for all adaptations that is sure to be ignored.

Of course the works of more populist authors, such as John Grisham's *The Firm* (Sydney Pollack, 1993), Tom Clancy's *The Hunt for Red October* (Philip Noyce, 1992), et al.—books that are optioned before publication—are guaranteed to reach at least major script development, and generally production. Can three million readers be wrong? Think what a million cinema tickets sold on the basis of a successful book means for the box office! And just think what it means if almost none of the readers like the movie. It happens.

Nobody knows anything. Recite this as a mantra every day.

With the background sketched out above in mind, it is now time to turn to the markets for screenwriting in detail, noting their peculiarities and some of the myths that swarm and cluster around both individual media and types of storytelling.

Chapter 3
Behind the Screens

The simplest distinction made by the media industry is based on (screen) size, which we all know is not all that important. Or is it? Crudely, the big screen industry is devoted to the manufacture and release of theatrical motion pictures and nowadays, IMAX Special Event movies. The little screen industry embraces all television forms, though does not exclude (as almost all screenwriting manuals seem to have it) corporate videos, animation, short film subjects, experimental and avant garde and, increasingly importantly, multimedia.

Along with this distinction goes another, and quite dangerous and misleading, assumption: that work originated on film (that is, real celluloid, 'just like in the movies') is somehow inherently better, more 'artistic' and certainly more authentically 'cinematic'. This last term is one that has been of great use to movie critics and theorists over the years, but need not detain you from concentrating on the more pressing business of writing a story that actually works.

Does (screen) size matter?
The big/little distinction simply does not hold up as a universal rule or distinction any longer. Recent years have seen the release of cinema features originated on video, such as the documentary *Video Fool for Love* (Robert Gibson, 1996), as well as features where most of the creative work is assigned to computer-generated effects houses like George Lucas' Industrial Light and Magic. Films like *Stargate* (Roland Emmerich, 1996) and *Titanic* (1997) have often more than half the 'budget allocated to the CGIs, though Roland Emmerich on *Stargate* ended up sending for a team of German multimedia and animation students to keep the costs down! If only this could happen more often.

Film or video?
The last years of the 1990s have also seen the recognition of video (tape-originated material) in some categories of film awards at

annual industry bashes. The implications of this partial recognition of video work are enormous and may help remove the artificial gap between big screen and little screen, and 'real' film and videotape and digital tape and disc recording mediums. (Feature films remain a category of work still defined by a technical medium: celluloid film stock.) Of course this process will be much slower to take hold in the United States and Europe, where the interests of 'the Old Industry' (Eastman Kodak, for example) are more formally entrenched than in smaller markets such as Australia.

From the point of view of the screenwriter, however, there are significant industrial differences in work and rewards systems for working in different areas of the industry. Directors of Photography (DOPs) and their guilds such as the American Society of Cinematographers (ASC) have long recognised this, as well as the fact that most film work, whether on features or commercials, operates on many of the same principles and involves the same degrees of craft, art and skill.

TV is cheaper than the movies. So what?

Many of the asserted creative differences between feature length dramatic films and other media forms are defined by budget rather than by art. Simply put, a feature normally costs millions of dollars to make, while television is a quicker and cheaper process. A TV hour in Australia in 2000 costs around A$500,000. Apart from that, the real focus of the writer must be on the ultimate consumer of the finished work. It is the audience, not the budget, that determines the type of writing, the particular skill required and the method of script production. After all, many commercials are shot on 35mm film stock and cost millions, just like feature films, but the audiences are essentially the same.

Let's look at the available writing manuals (up to 1998) on this topic. The differences between a cinema feature and a television show are reduced to the following:

Budget facts

- Feature films cost a lot more money and take longer to finance, shoot and post-produce.
- Films, in first release at least, are viewed in cinemas in the dark. This doesn't prevent most of the audience from behaving as if they were at home watching TV. But more and more, many movies go straight to video—the result of an excess of product released to an industry increasingly focused on the bottom line.
- Films can be shot on a variety of wide screen formats and use millions of dollars worth of computer-generated images. Television has a smaller picture.

- Films (it is asserted) have a stronger and more linear narrative structure while TV series (especially) are episodic and contain 'artificial' commercial breaks disguised as plot climaxes every seven minutes or so. But cable TV has meant that increasingly, these rules formulated in the early days of TV (the 1940s, for goodness sake!) are now superfluous.

So, really, it's still all up to you, the writer.

Starting off very small: The commercial spot

Since many writers generally remain in this field for most of their working lives (with the odd year off for the obligatory novel or two), this is a field that is exciting and challenging despite the limitations of the formats. Like the sonnet form in poetry, it can be said of commercials that the limitations of the form offer all the greater a spur to invention and to adventurous and rule-breaking thinking.

A quick message from your radio

Though we will not be dealing specifically with radio forms, it's important not to forget that television, film and radio often work together (along with print media) as key information and advertising channels. Most of the structural strategies of narrative and documentary writing remain true of radio. The real difference is that spoken words, along with complexity of sound and silence, must do *all* the storytelling in radio.

Radio commercials commonly run in 10- and 30-second spots. The standard 'read' by the station announcer is the entry-level commercial form, but still offers the chance for innovation, especially when there is a hint of willingness to try something new rather than the drearily familiar:

ANN

Yes, Jason's Teabags are clearly the best tasting teas in town. You can feel confident, knowing that the best [. . . etc. for decades to come].

Other forms use music, as in the famous and award winning Levi's Jeans commercials:

MUSIC

Slow back beat continues under

GOSPEL VOICE

In the beginning was the word, and the word was Levi's.

(Ending with)

MUSIC

Reaches full blues finale

VOICE (on ECHO)

All God's chillun got cords!

which ran along the edges of offence to religious orders, but worked perfectly with the target audience.

And perhaps the most challenging for writers is the use of dramatic techniques of one sort or another with last place in audience tolerance going to the obvious:

SFX

Party sounds, champagne corks popping. Yells, whoops.

GIRL ONE (breathless)

Wow, what a party. And what a great drink. What is it?

GIRL TWO (bell-like)

Where have you been, Jackie? Tibet? It's Tiger's Breath—the new rum-based cocktail . . .

(and so on . . .)

As you can see, the real danger with radio writing is the temptation to fall into 'tried and proven' forms, with the result that listeners just tune you out. As Marshall McLuhan remarked of radio, it is a medium that involves the imagination to the fullest extent, since it offers information to the ears alone. A hot medium. That's why silence—the planned use of a pause in radio—is so effective. Yet the very idea of silence terrifies most contemporary producers, especially in commercial radio.

It's a great challenge, as is all advertising work. The trick is to make it look and sound easy!

Television and cinema ads

With the rise of cable television, the more familiar and long-standing forms of the 10-, 20-, 30- and 60-second commercial spots will be changing in the next few years as audiences filter out into more specialised groups, and the image of the family all clustered around the friendly old family TV set is replaced by a clearer picture of the listening habits of individuals and target groups.

Television and cinema ads, with their obvious debt to propaganda films going back to the turn of the twentieth century, offer the greatest range for expression of almost any writerly medium—as well as a chance for the directors and technical effects teams to take over the whole show if your ideas are not clear and detailed in presentation.

There was a time when the simple dramatic address to camera was the standard form of presentation:

TV HOST (gesturing at The Shining Fridge)

> Yes, folks, Kelvinator is not only the best-designed and best-looking family cooler; it's been voted the most effective by nine out of ten dentists . . . [ho hum, ad infinitum].

Actually, this form, in thin disguise and tizzied up with special effects, is still with us as the 'product demonstration'. They are especially common, for some reason, in selling exercise equipment and slimming products. Of course, the hard-sell 'infomercial' which is the curse of daytime television is hardly likely to go away with the proliferation of cable shopping channels. But television and film, now with the full panoply of digital effects that ads normally try out before feature films get around to them, can be as confronting as the hottest new TV series, as surreal as a video clip or as poetic as an arts program. It is also the proving ground for new animation styles and ideas.

It's up to you—and the courage of your client and agency.

Short animated stories

Remember, you don't have to be a trained animation artist to write animated films, but you do need to know what the possibilities, and amazing freedoms of the medium, are.

Animation, relying as it does—or rather, did before computers—on the stop frame camera and the persistence of vision to create an illusion of movement without human actors or documentary footage, is one of the oldest types of film technique (or trick). Animation is also one of the most innovative and broad of media forms in its ability to tackle any subject matter from explicit instruction (the *Grolier CD-ROM Encyclopaedia* makes great use of simple animation to explain complex processes such as human blood circulation) to the avant garde and the digital domain.

Increasingly, animation is produced on computers, even where original and traditional hand-drawn art is the originating medium. Films now even use live actors interacting with claymation (animated clay/plasticine) figures. *The Secret Adventures of Tom Thumb* (Dave Borthwick, UK, 1993) does this and is one of the oddest and most intriguing feature films of all time. The ability of animation to use all and any elements of the world, from carrots to news footage, and to create mythical and magical other worlds by the imaginative use of materials (Jan Svankmajer of Czechoslovakia used anything from clay to kitchen tools, old cardboard boxes, twigs and bird feathers!) means that the form offers inexhaustible possibilities for creativity.

It seems that in spite of the lure of pre-packaged computer animation kits, there will always be a market for animation. The relative flood of big-budget animation features in the late 1990s, such as *The Prince of Egypt* (Sky, 1998) and the digitally produced *Antz* (Disney, 1998), shows that the field is expanding far beyond the 'young adult' market and is looking to reach as broad an audience as possible. It's not just a 'family' medium anymore.

One of the major markets for animators is commercials, which can use anything from animated vegetables to fully developed characters. Animators are also drawn upon in the post-production stage of commercials, to add a 'magical' quality to the work, and in the production of CGIs in feature films. Many more animators toil as colour inkers and as 'in-betweeners', linking key actions by filling in the 'in between' stages, as, say, a character enters a room and walks to a specific point.

Although there are some institutions offering undergraduate courses for animators around the world (The National Film and Television School in Beaconsfield, UK is one; UCLA another), there are also courses at art colleges such as Queensland (a full undergraduate course) and the Victorian College of the Arts in Melbourne, where traditional animation and multimedia are taught at the postgraduate level.

What is harder to teach is how to tell a story. In the chapter on contemporary narrative animation (Chapter 14), the works of international award-winning animators such as Dennis Tupicoff (*The Darra Dogs*, 1994) and Max Bannah (*One Man's Instrument*, 1992), who use the medium to tell their own stories, will be examined in detail.

Obvious recent successes in the animation field include Matt Groening's *The Simpsons*, which has broken through into prime-time slots normally reserved for live action dramas, as has *South Park*, suggesting a long future for this type of program. In the international children's market there is also a constant need for new series and new characters.

Mass audiences and the festival circuit

Although the main and continuing markets are in children's television and computer animations, there will always be a specialist market for original short works. Apart from occasional breakthrough animation features like *Fritz the Cat* (Ralph Bashki, 1972), the field is largely dominated by the regular and enormously lucrative Disneyfication of old myths. *Aladdin* (1992) won technical Oscars normally reserved for live action films. Today the market for short original subjects ranges from the X-rated—Spike and Mike's annual collections screen around the world in art house cinemas—to more traditional animation festivals such as those in Prague and London. There is also an increasing number of special conferences like the Queensland Animators International Festival, held in 1996 and 1998 and part of the international circuit from 2000.

Most works for the festival circuit are financed by bodies such as state film units or the Australian Film Commission (AFC) and rely greatly on the animators' ability to pitch a good story, with the use of storyboards, to assessors who may not be conversant with current developments and therefore may not realise the potential of the medium to break with conventional narrative forms and structures.

In the end, this chance to change the rules is the greatest challenge and the most alluring attraction of animation. There is no more exciting medium—and perhaps no more precarious existence—if creating original art works is your aim. But the rewards are that you can create a perfect, personal world for the whole world to enter.

The next chapter looks at the world of the short film, whose length can be anywhere from a second to half an hour: the world of commercials, corporates and infotainment.

Chapter 4
Commercials, Corporates and Infotainment

The short informational film appears to exist in total contradistinction to the freedom of, say, animation. This can be misleading, for the opportunities for creating new ways of getting across information are as limitless as your ability to convince your clients that such risk-taking is necessary!

Short informational films are distinguished from other forms in that their scripts are commissioned and hence the audience and the message are precisely predetermined. This can still leave enormous room for originality—and often quite a bit for humour as well.

The origin of the informational and corporate film lies in the origins of film itself. From the beginning, film has been used to convey quite complex ideas, belief systems, and of course products and services. Some of the earliest forms of these films were screened with feature films in cinemas more than seventy years ago, including Empire Marketing Board short films about wine, butter and all the produce of Empire. Many short documentary subjects were never intended to be works of art and were, in fact, little more than propaganda for the sponsoring corporation, but had a great effect on audiences worldwide.

Alas, distributors and exhibitors phased out short subjects in the mid-1980s.

What is a corporate?
Corporate videos and films can be about anything from in-house training to more general exposition or trade show usage, though increasingly this work is being done by (authored) CD-ROMs. The enormous success of John Cleese's work in training and corporate videos produced since the 1970s in England has meant that the Cleese style of absurdist humour and informal structure has become almost a norm. Certainly writers responding to a client

brief can expect to get positive feedback for scripts using humour and wit instead of flow charts.

These works have a specialised market and they are seldom broadcast. However, this is not a hard and fast matter, and recently there has been increasing use of free to air time (on SBS and the ABC, notably) for instructional shows and open learning programs. Indeed, a recent open learning series called *Images of Australia* has broadcast on the ABC from 1992 and won critical plaudits as a program series in its own right, as well as reaching screenings in Europe and a Japan Prize to boot. Scott Hicks' *(Shine*, 1996) informational documentary on *Submarines: Sharks of Steel* recently won a number of international documentary awards in spite of its origins as a military commission.

A good corporate program can end up moving far beyond its humble origins as the workhorse of film, and for this reason, as well as the billion dollar annual production slate, this genre should never be ignored by writers.

Other forms of the corporate film can take the place of in-house programming on free to air and cable television alike. Recent out-sourcing by the ABC has led to some embarrassing re-examinations of broadcast materials that ended up looking and sounding more like advertising for outside sponsors than a public broadcasting program!

Teleconferencing, too, has partly displaced corporates, although it by no means replaces them, given the inexpensive potential of video as a recording format and the old adage that corporates are either made to 'save money or to make money'. They are now intrinsically part of any corporation's marketing or staff training structure. Today, many corporates are made as a simple reaction to government or public initiatives in areas such as work practice or management policy. You'll often need a high tolerance for self-righteousness to survive writing too many of these.

Although the term 'corporate video' always seems to refer to private sector business operations, in fact a vast number of programs are now being made for or by almost every conceivable government department, university, college or pressure group. Subjects for the year 2000 and beyond include AIDS and drugs, economic debates, and a whole slew of community group and social issue programs in both dramatic and documentary form.

The old idea of a corporate as just a cheap way of getting across prosaic information has disappeared, and the competition from CD-ROM, the Internet and other digital systems means that today's corporate must be very effective and inventive to hope to hold an audience.

Challenge

Your client wants to boost his business by selling more seaside retirement homes to the aged. Write a short video script that does not insult the intelligence and vitality of the older viewer!

Don't forget to include some dramatisation and a clear idea of what music will be required.

The advertising campaign: Part of a big picture

In the world of commercials and advertising, the development of the script is synonymous with the development of the campaign concept, which in most cases is developed by an agency. Clients encourage agencies to pitch aggressively for major campaigns, and the competition is fierce.

Often three or four agencies will pitch for a particular campaign and all the resources of the agency will be harnessed to win the assignment. The creative forces used to create a campaign will include the client, the copy or scriptwriter, the agency creative director, the director of the commercials, and other support staff. The campaign itself may utilise various media—print, television, radio, and billboard—and the core of the campaign must be focused on promoting demand for a product. The goal is to sell more of an already popular product, either by getting clients to change brands or by increasing consumption of an established brand.

Most successful commercials are themselves little dramas, economical and succinct. The cost of television advertising time, which is many times more than the production costs, encourages brief statements. While preparing for filming *Full Metal Jacket* (1987) in England, Stanley Kubrick began watching football games mailed to him on tape from the United States, and became entranced by the crisp, elegant directness of the short stories told in commercials.

The essence of the 'story' commercial is engagement. Half a second wasted is too much—the audience have already switched off—and the visuals always have more power then the spoken word. Often advertising agencies, or more often the client, can get nervous about being too adventurous. Too often a good concept is developed, then filmed, and then destroyed by the addition of a pedestrian voice-over.

Strong visuals and willingness to try the unusual are absolutely essential to successful advertising. Advertising must also aim to develop a positive aura around the product: the 'unique selling proposition' that makes one product stand out from its competitors. And if the campaign succeeds, then this often leads to more creative licence for the next campaign.

Keeping the customers honest

Commercials are created by developing the visuals along with the script, using storyboards or panels worked out by a visual artist and virtually establishing composition and content. These are timed to the length of the shot and fit with the voice-over or music. At this level of conception there is no real difference between TV commercials and feature films. Many movie directors (like Alex Proyas of *Dark City* fame) also make the most exciting commercials. Detailed storyboards can save a production money, as they define the visual aims of the exercise. They are also essential on any production using extended CGIs or video effects.

Commercials production in Australia is under constant threat due to increasing deregulation. Commercials sourced from overseas often replace home-grown productions. But with new products arriving all the time, and a new consumer market with each new generation, there is no indication that commercials will ever go out of fashion as a favoured method of mass persuasion.

High concept commercials

For simple retail work, the straightforward pitch works best. Things become more difficult when the product is more nebulous and hard to pin down: a radio station, say, or a corporate image for a bank or other big institution. Here there are no obvious product advantages or those Unique Selling Propositions so beloved of marketing courses! Here you must devise a totally new way to sell the advantages of an institution. Such advertising challenges require a response from the writer closer to poetry than to prose. You have to make a lateral leap of mindset to find a way to make the client's company or service fresh and different from anything that has gone before.

And the only way to do that is with visual style and direct appeal to emotion—and in this case, the ambition and imagination of the viewers, your target market:

THE UNIVERSITY

VIDEO

OPEN on a car travelling along a
dirt road.

VIDEO (cont.)

COMPUTER ANIMATED GRAPHICS of road maps appear over the image. The destinations are marked not as main cities but university DEGREES. Roads lead from these to other, smaller cities which are marked as different occupations or careers.	MVO: If you could see yourself in any career, what would it be?
A FLASHING DOT travelling these roads represents the car, which carries two main characters: a YOUNG GUY and a YOUNG GIRL.	
As the car travels along the map we INTERCUT to the couple in various live situations. These maps continually appear drifting over the various scenarios.	
INTERCUT to our couple dressed as LAWYERS. They walk down the steps of the Law Building.	MVO: Equality and justice. Congratulations, counseller.
She stops and looks at herself.	
REVERSE CUT to our GIRL looking back at herself as a LAWYER.	MVO: All rise.
CUT to our GUY dressed as a 'cool' Information Technology person. He is surrounded by other IT types working on laptops.	MVO: Technology is your network to the world.
REVERSE CUT to our GUY seeing himself.	
CUT to a foreign war zone. Our GIRL is a HEALTH CARE WORKER arguing with a colleague.	FVO: Everything is going to be just fine.
CUT to a CRYING CHILD in the mud. Our GIRL picks up the CHILD and comforts her.	

CUT to GIRL in the car. The book she's reading floats in front of her.

MVO: Just imagine it and make it real.

CUT to our GUY by the car. The lights and the wind from a UFO dazzle him. Suddenly our GUY is on a CAMERA and CRANE and drops into the shot. The two SELVES look at each other.

CUT to our GIRL as she runs into shot with a clapper board.

CUT to the COUPLE in the car as it drives along.

VO: One university offers degrees flexible enough to give you the freedom and choice you need to take on any career challenge.

CUT to a closer shot of our GIRL, then our GUY, driving the car.

CUT TO UNIVERSITY LOGO

LOGO (FULL FRAME)

Northern University

SUPER [UNI NAME]

The Way
Fade music

A film frame blow-up from the commercial 'The Way'. Courtesy Leo Burnett and Griffith University 1999

When finally filmed, this cinema commercial was as fast-paced and imaginative as a Hollywood movie.

The more you analyse that TVC the more ways you can also see to film it and add special effects.

Scripts like this are a great challenge to film-makers and generally bring out the best in your film crew. Give them plenty of imaginative freedom and most times the results will sell, as well as enthral. You might even win an award, too! From the TVC and the corporate video (which is really an extended advertisement) to the TV magazine program is a very short step indeed.

Magazine and 'infotainment' series

One of the biggest and most open markets for younger writers to enter is that of the magazine style program, now generally known as 'infotainment' in the industry (critics use the term through gritted teeth). Even the ABC and SBS have increasingly turned to the style as a relatively inexpensive way of filling air time and grabbing and holding an audience.

The series *Beyond 2000*, for example, began as an ABC TV science show. Its great popularity in the field of popular science (for a century a major player in the international print magazine world) meant that the team were able to transfer to a commercial network, for vastly better fees, and the company formed (Beyond) is now a major player in the production and distribution of series and even feature films as well. *Beyond 2000* was the small beginning on which this successful company was founded, much as the Grundy empire of international game show and series production was founded on the ability of its founder, Reg Grundy, to dream up or borrow successful game show formats.

The magazine style program is now everywhere, with the key sectors being travel, house improvement and fishing. All need writers, although some use writer-presenters. They also are a great way into the industry.

We've started out small. Now let's look at longer script forms, specifically the documentary.

Chapter 5
The Documentary

The simplest type of documentary program looks very like a standard corporate and often differs from that form in little other than length.

Documentaries at their simplest are straightforward records of an event, not unlike a news story but more structured. Such programs are normally, if not writer-originated, given to writers after post-production to create a direct voice-over narration, or to provide a script that gives the impression that the presenter—a network 'star'—is somehow wholly responsible for the footage (for example, *Frank Warwick's World*, *John Laws' World*, etc.). Programs bought cheap on the international television trade circuit can thus be recycled endlessly as a network initiative.

High concept, low budget

Another form of shorter documentary has lately captivated international audiences. Originating in Canada, the 'beginner's' program uses unskilled younger program makers, typically clutching a digital camera and a handful of economy airline tickets, sending back documentary postcards from round the world. These low-budget programs have achieved enormous popularity. Series like *Race Around the World* and *Race Around the Corner* give the impression that film-making success lies just around the corner for us all, and younger audiences, especially, have fallen for their amateur, rule-breaking charm. Not always noticed is their highly structured and institutionalised presentation.

These programs also highlight the chance for low-budget programs to make it into the once jealously guarded airspace of the public channels. In the past, expensive film stock and quad (two-inch) videotape were the industry standard and anything less was considered to 'fail to reach acceptable broadcast standards'. But new video formats and especially digital camera have made potential auteurs of us all. The revolution has just begun.

Historical and mixed form documentary

With the advent of cable television, international documentary forms have been effectively relaunched upon the world after a period of considerable decline.

The simplest form of historical documentary takes a theme—pirates, archaeological digs, murder cases—and makes a series or a one-off, usually a one-hour 'special', on that theme.

Commonly, documentaries dealing with historical materials will either use an authoritative voice-over (noted British actor Robert Powell for *Great Mysteries and Myths of the Twentieth Century* and its equally grisly companion *Great Crimes and Trials*) or a professorial type with a beard and a deep voice (Indiana Jones-style hints of an action man beneath) to add credibility.

More often than not, as a sop to the greater audiences hoped for, these popularisations of otherwise academic materials will throw in some gratuitous re-creations of action scenes such as ghostly visitations, pirate attacks, jolly 'Shakespearian' pub scenes and so on, normally without dialogue. So common are these dramatisations that they have become as expected a cliché as the old narration opener 'Since the dawn of mankind . . . '

But there is a large and increasing market for these hybrid documentaries, which differ from magazine-style formats only in length and adherence to a single subject or theme.

Docudramas

More traditional documentaries, generally more fully researched, will also make use of actors in fully dramatised sequences interwoven with actuality footage, archival material and interviews.

Although there has been a reaction against this hybrid form recently by some broadcasters, the form can be highly successful if the casting and the selection of scenes are done with care.

Recent films using this technique include *Eternity* (Lawrence Johnston, 1996), about an eccentric and silent character who wandered around Sydney for decades, chalking, in a perfect calligraphic style, the word 'Eternity' on pavements. *Eternity* used feature film techniques and lighting effects in an attempt to achieve 'high art', with a large budget but mixed success. *The Legend of Fred Paterson* (ABC TV, Jonathan Dawson, 1996) interwove interviews and dramatic re-creations of the life of the only communist ever elected to an Australian parliament. The film combined disparate stylistic elements effectively, to highlight a long-forgotten part of the history of politics in Australia. (The pitch for and the script structure of this last film will be discussed in 'The Pitch'.)

The following section of a quite complex, semi-dramatised documentary biography shows two different forms of narration. The first is easily recognisable as the traditional simple informational link read by an actor or the film-maker. In this case the choice of actor would be critical and the director (advised by the writer) would be looking for a vernacular, relaxed sort of read.

But note that by Scene 3 the authoritative (voice of God) narrator is replaced for dramatic purposes by actual readings (archival material) by Xavier Herbert (the subject of the film).

THE STIRRER

PRETITLE SEQUENCE

1. EXT. BULLDUST ROAD, SOMEWHERE WEST OF THE ALICE, 1984

A Land Rover, incredibly dusty, barrels along, dust-clouded. We crane up as the little cloud disappears into a glowing sunset.

VOICE-OVER (ABC Archive News)

The death was announced today of acclaimed novelist and bushman Xavier Herbert. Herbert, who won the Miles Franklin Award in 1975 for his massive novel *Poor Fellow My Country*, had been living rough in the outback near Alice Springs, since the death of his wife Sadie . . . (fades under)

2. EXT. OUTBACK NIGHT DESERT SKY/HERBERT'S 'TIN HOUSE'

We tilt from the canopy of hot dark sky and, as the sun rises, creep in on Herbert's corrugated tin home (Redlynch near Cairns).

3. INT. SHED (RE-CREATION)

VOICE-OVER

This is where Herbert wrote *Poor Fellow My Country*.

NARRATOR

He could never write a book like that in a big city . . . he hated cities and even in *Soldiers' Women* seemed to be writing about some fire-haunted Other Australia: savage, beautiful and very, very deadly. It was a place that threatened his sense of himself—and a place where all the Big Lies came from . . .

PAN the Interior as we pick up diaries, letters, manuscripts, books, the camp stretcher—and the ancient Remington typewriter.

IN ON HERBERT's empty chair.
SNEAK IN 1930s country music (old phono scratch).
Clatter of the Remington cross-fades.

> XAVIER (VO, reading from *Poor Fellow My Country*)

> There was a goodly crowd dancing . . . mostly
> cross-bred girls dancing with white men of the Ringer
> type with shirt-tails out . . . there wasn't a truly black
> person within the walls . . .

INTERCUT *Lovers and Luggers* (film), the shore drunk
scene.

In general, this approach has been confined to historical documentaries with a certain inherent element of showbiz (about
colourful characters like Xavier Herbert, say, or circus life in the
1930s), or dramatic colour; less often to create bizarre and sometimes clashing or inappropriate effects. This last occurred with the
Korean prisoner of war documentary *Convictions* (ABC/Robert
Reynolds, 1998), in which, according to the critics, visual humour
was used to create an 'ironic, postmodern distance' (the term covers
almost any non-conventional narrative strategy) from the very
moving and authentic interviews with Australian ex-prisoners of
war from the Korean conflict. The same problems occurred with
a recent documentary about the amazing survival under an over-
turned ocean yacht of round-the-world yachtsman Tony Bullimore.
The choice to use Bullimore himself in the inevitable documentary celebration *Miracle at Sea* (ABC/Dick Dennison, 1998)
proved too much for the film-makers, with curious results.
Introducing inappropriate 'witty bits' is a temptation to be
avoided unless you are very certain about what irony, let alone
postmodernism, really is!

When we come to look at multimedia forms, we can begin to see
what these terms might really mean—as well as how big the
changes are that digital media forms and the Internet might bring
to the third millennium.

Flies on the wall

The French call it *cinéma vérité*; the Americans, Direct Cinema. In
practical terms it means a style of film-making where the camera is
present for the maximum possible time in the lives of the subjects
until it becomes unobtrusive and the subjects' behaviour as 'natural' as possible. Of course, the presence of camera and crew can and
does affect people in all kinds of ways, but the results are often
behaviour onscreen that is amazingly open and frank—and almost
always entertaining. The principle of virtually unlimited access by

the recording media has produced such popular successes as the BBC's *Sylvania Waters* (1994) and similar 'family shows'.

The most recent international success using the policy of 'film everything and see what we end up with!' was *The War Room* (D. A. Pennebaker, 1996). This remarkable documentary followed the Clinton campaign in 1992. Just about everything that went on the back rooms of the campaign trail was exposed to audiences in cinemas and on TV and single-handedly relaunched the *verité* doco, as seems to happen every few years. *The War Room* also made stars of Clinton advisors George Stephanopoulos and James Carville and led (indirectly) to providing the staging and characterisations for many of the scenes for the movie-à-clef, *Primary Colors* (Mike Nichols, 1998). Such films depend on a high shooting ratio—that means using a lot of film, or, increasingly, digital stock—but also on the skills of a good writer and editor to structure the story after the shoot.

The recent, feature-length Australian fly-on-the-wall docos, *Rats in the Ranks* (Bob Connolly and Robin Anderson, 1996) and *Year of the Dogs* (Michael Cordell, 1997), are both edited in a chronological fashion but reveal wildly escalating conflict between the subjects. The result is that *Rats in the Ranks*, an unusual take on local politics, becomes something of a black comedy of the highest order; *Year of the Dogs*, a highly emotional tale of an apparently doomed local football club, echoes classic tragedy. The ability to depict complex human problems and the people who have them, usually under extreme stress, is the special quality of fly-on-the-wall films: in their unwinking focus on individuals under stress they can be more affecting and rewarding than almost any form of film-making.

For the writer-director this can be the most exciting form of all—if you have the time and the money. Many classics of documentary like *Grey Gardens* (Maysles Brothers, 1976) capture a part of the world that only the film-makers have access to, and make it real forever.

With the recent public success of local and international *verité* films and 'reality' TV it looks as if they will be around and a popular subgenre for as long as movies are made. But you will need the sort of patience given to few.

Documentary series and miniseries
For the same reasons that general educational films and cable television channels like Discovery and the Learning Channel are generating increasing interest, documentary series are very popular with producers and programmers alike.

A recent series like *Secrets of Lost Empires* (BBC Worldwide, various, 1996) relies on a big hook and an equally large budget.

Each episode deals with some fabulous architectural or engineering achievement from antiquity, such as pyramids or Incan bridges. This achievement is then reconstructed 'on site' using materials available at the original place and time. Thus, each program has historical elements as well as a built-in dramatic 'trigger' for each show.

Apply the same principles to create your own series—*Great Shark Stories*, say, or *Great Failed Explorers*—and you have your show, provided you haven't been beaten to the punch by another writer in another country (nothing gets around quicker than a saleable idea, or is harder to prove copyright on).

Earlier series have covered territory in a pre-emptive way. *The World at War*, for example, was pretty definitive, as was *Civilisation* (BBC, 1968), and Robert Hughes' *The Shock of the New* (BBC, 1982). All were series which had very high budgets to match their aims. The two latter series also indicate another form of the historical documentary: the thematic.

Docos with a theme

Here we are right in cable television territory. Thematic series can take the viewpoint of an individual presenter—*Peach's Australia* and *Geoffrey Blainey's Australia*, Peter Luck's more whimsical *This Fabulous Century*, or a broader category of human activity. Murder, for example, would do nicely. Such series can be made at any time, and re-made or repeated with updates to keep the meter ticking over nicely.

Generally, every producer wants a show that can run beyond a mere thirteen episodes. The broader the theme (*Great Crimes and Trials*, *Pirates*), the more endless and profitable the series. Cable television and specialist channels like Discovery have enormously increased the market for such series.

Finally, series can be unified by a general title that covers almost anything the broadcasters want it to imply through publicity. ABC television's weekly series *True Stories* can contain almost any form of documentary, from whimsical takes on eccentric but perhaps slight stories (*Eternity*, *Men and Their Sheds*) or serious and high-minded contemporary social history. All of Bob Connolly's and Robin Anderson's work, from *Joe Leahy's Neighbours* through to *Rats in the Ranks*, are examples of the sort of work that can only run as a TV special, or, equally neatly, fit into a portmanteau series as a sort of work in progress.

As channels proliferate and the cost of drama series rises inexorably, the relative attractions of high-concept, comparatively inexpensive documentary series can only grow and grow.

Documentary programs are always a hard sell. Simply, they're not as 'sexy' as drama, comedy, or animation to producers and networks alike. But let your enthusiasm and belief in the project shine through the treatment—as did the writers of *The Liners*—and the rewards will be great! The series was virtually sold from the moment the writer-producers decided to feature a classic image of the great days of ocean liners on their short concept document.

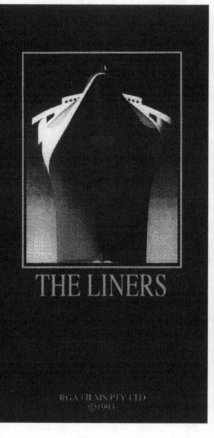

A simple, striking image can sell a series. Two is better!

(*The Liners*, written by Rob McAuley and Peter Butt.)

And if the subject matter is a little out of the mainstream and, well . . . different, then why not let the style of the concept documents reflect the unusual nature and energy of the proposal itself?

no one can find little girls anymore
Kathy Acker and Generation Z in Australia
a film proposal by Paul Faust ©1998

THE SLUGLINE

Kathy Acker in Australia: the punk superstar and former Warhol inspiration meets her fans and turns over some rocks in the night streets.

WHO IS KATHY ACKER?

Kathy Acker is the punk superstar novelist and performer whose shows—and books, of course—have been selling like crazy since she first started out as a street-smart poet in the 1960s art scene in New York.

As well as capturing Acker's whole performance at Brisbane's hot/cool venue Van Gogh's Earlobe, we feature two major interviews with her.

THE STYLE

This is to be a film about the Acker generation of 1990s kids—and how they got there. Acker is filmed moving in this milieu.

So, this is no polite TV Sunday Show. And the soundtrack is by the still-edgy Mekons, who collaborated with Kathy on the CD project *Pussy and the Pirates*.

Acker agreed to get close up and personal with the people who know her as a writer and performer, but also with the more, er, well, straight arts bureaucrats who love to be seen with a brightly burning nova. And she's lived up to her word. She talks with scorching honesty and generosity to Jo Chichester (JJJ; Radio National) and, above all, to Olivia: poet, performer and tattoo designer.

This is a guerrilla documentary with a savage bite, a story of innocence lost, maybe, as Acker puts it, elegiacally:

'no one can find little girls anymore . . .'

There's a sad footnote to this documentary proposal: Kathy Acker died during the making of this film, which was shown in a very different version on SBS TV in 1995 as well as being released around the world for screening during the memorial wakes for Kathy.

And that's the final problem with documentary-making: your beloved subjects are either absent or all too humanly present!

Chapter 6
Shorts, Soaps and Sitcoms

So you've decided to write drama but you're not sure how or where to begin, or what sort of production it will be. The move from an idea for a short film or video to soaps and sitcoms can seem a short one—after all, the forms share limited sets, characters and action. All finish in just around twenty or so minutes. Easy!

Short films: Everything starts small

Most writers start off with the shorter form of the dramatic film, anything from ten minutes to half an hour or so, but normally less. There is an increasing market through festivals like Tropfest and the various State New and Young Film-makers awards systems.

But the sort of story you want to tell or the kind of career you really want in the industry will partly determine what you write and who you write for. You are most likely to begin with the short film because they cost the least, but nowadays it can be almost as hard to get the short movie up as a feature film. It's certainly worth it, as the short can be your calling card. *Young Einstein* (Yahoo Serious, 1989) was one of many feature films that started life as a short.

Film schools and film and TV courses also offer the chance to try out simpler narrative, and the general guidelines for screen-writing apply in terms of layout, plot and characterisation—all tailored to the shorter time span.

Short films in general are made for the Film Festival market. This is not because television audiences are less bright, but because going to a movie, to a film festival or even to a night of shorts at the local film school involves a conscious decision and probably means the audience will bring a more critical mind to the screening.

One thing is certain: a short film idea does not mean that you must never dream of expanding that idea into a feature film or a TV series. But the same differences apply as to sprint runners and marathon runners. A feature film is a long haul for makers and audience alike. The important thing is to stick to what you wanted to say in the first place, whatever the film form.

Unless you are very lucky, you as a writer are now teetering on the edge of the first big relationship that will shape the career of your brave little script idea: the relationship with a producer, the film teacher, broadcaster or film funding body who will choose your film for production. This is a complex relationship, and it is a good idea to know all about the folks who are looking at your script for production, as early as possible. As well, you should be very sure about exactly what you hope to achieve and therefore what you are prepared to fight for. Many details in a script are probably there for quite arbitrary reasons and are not worth having tantrums about later on. Let them go.

Make sure that you know what you want before you begin writing.

Inspiration—or just luck?

No writer starts a story in the same way as another, so here, at least, there are truly no rules. But if you have decided to tell a short story in a short film, don't imagine that the best way is to write a short (literary) story or adapt one. For a start, even a short story, whether literary or popular, can have too much material for a film. Think in terms of what you want to see up on the screen and this will shape your plotting ideas.

Story ideas can start with a single image (indeed, that is all some offer in the end). Alternatively, they can start with a great and complex concept, but get it onto the screen by finding a metaphor for that concept—what is called, in literary criticism, an objective correlative. Whether you decide to deal with AIDS or the horrors of high density-living on the edge of big cities, you will need to narrow down the focus to the journey of a single character. If this is a short film the journey can be as short or as long as you like—though even feature films like *Wild Bill* (Walter Hill, 1996) or *Chaplin* (Richard Attenborough, 1992) failed because the film form could not sensibly contain too many events over a long period of real time. As a rule of thumb, think of significant and telling moments that define a life in a shorter time frame. If, like David Lean and Richard Attenborough, you are hopelessly devoted to the epic form, you might get away with a longer one, but it limits your career options, as well as launching your budgets into the stratosphere.

And where do all stories come from, anyway? Simply from something you want to say about the world.

All stories begin in response to the question 'What if?'. If you know about Chaos Theory that certainly helps. This theory, which has obvious applications to storytelling, takes one single event and then imagines the possible outcomes—one or many—that it can lead to. The classic example is known as the Butterfly Effect. A butterfly in Rio flutters its wings, creating a little warm draft, which triggers a zephyr . . . and so on, eventually causing a violent storm in the Atlantic.

When you are developing a story, a binary choice is offered to you from the moment you write the words:

> Scene 1. Deserted edge of city street. Late at night.

In fact, you've already made a number of conscious and unconscious artistic choices. Why a deserted city street? Probably because you want to tell an urban story. Why at night—a particular urban mood, or danger? And so on. Each choice involves a potential for action. In Chapter 10 we'll examine the implications of this binary model for plot development in detail.

Above all, keep it simple.

You may decide to stay with short film-making forever. However, most writers, having taken that first step, find the attractions of the greater industry too obsessively beautiful to ignore. They move on . . .

Short cuts to prime time

So, after that first short film you decide it's time to get serious. Now is when knowledge of the various areas of the television and film industry is essential.

Assuming you have any choice in the matter, and don't need to make a living just yet, the following considerations may determine what sort of script you are going to write—and thus who you will want to see it next.

For example, is the story you want to tell essentially made up of many short scenes—little stories or episodes in themselves? This may well be the sign that you are a natural for serial drama or soapies, or that your interest lies in exploring many facets of your character's life and goals. Maybe you're a born biographer, or a documentarist—but don't let that stop you extrapolating, from this desire to 'tell it all', the key scenes that will make your story flow.

Or is the story a small one, contained perhaps within a few rooms? Is the story real—a biography of a public figure or of someone you know or have heard of? Remember this: just because something is 'true' (it actually happened) does not mean that it will work on the screen. In fact, the worst alibi for muddled writing is often the cry, 'This is true'—as if that makes it all right. It doesn't.

Plot, character and the big screen

Is the plot more important than the characters? It doesn't need to be a science fiction epic for this to be the case. Many recent thrillers, notably *Fallen* (Greg Hoblit, 1998), fit into more than one genre, mixing naturalism and the supernatural.

The final big question must be: do this story and the characters who inhabit it demand big-screen images, panoramas, staged action set pieces, a stadium full of extras, lots of locations? Does it *really* need these? Or isn't this just a little bit of an ego trip? If you won't budge from that, then this is definitely going to be a big-screen movie—unless you want to become an animator at once. Then your imagination is only limited by your ideas.

With the arrival of digital high-definition TV and home theatre systems, the differences are fast shrinking in number. And even as multiplexes swarm and multiply, so do their screens and theatres shrink in size. You can even make your own popcorn at home. So let's look at the widening television universe.

From soaps to sitcoms

The serial drama or soap is the direct descendant of popular theatrical forms like the melodrama and its 1950s successor, the radio soap opera (*Blue Hills, Portia Faces Life, Doctor Mac, D24*). As the simplest form of storytelling and the most addictive internationally, this despised and perversely beloved form of program is the bread and butter of most screenwriters in the developed world.

Soap storylines are most often by a script editor or storyliner who provides the writer with each episode's plotting in detail. However, soaps also offer greater opportunities for the writer, especially at the beginning of a career, than these pre-written storylines would suggest.

In fact, soaps, echoing as they do the daily rhythms of living, have a great deal to offer.

And don't imagine, just because of the success of *Neighbours* and *Home and Away*, that all soaps have to be about family interaction. The families can be of a very non-standard sort and some of the best soaps—or at least the most intriguing and brave of them—have even tackled the genre itself as a target for satire. Sitcoms like *Frontline* (Working Dog, 1995+) and *Drop the Dead Donkey* (UK, 1994+) seem natural successors to soaps like *Mary Hartman, Mary Hartman* (Norman Lear, 1976), which turned a savage satiric eye on its own genre but somehow left the world of soaps none the weaker.

Soaps, apparently, will always be with us. Writers can ignore them, but the craft and skill required to keep such a rocking boat afloat is as great a challenge as media writing offers.

Challenge

Watch a soap for a number of epsiodes and then write a story (broken up into scenes for the series). Write one (only) dialogue scene.

Great! That's how 9 out of 10 soap writers got their start!

Sitcoms and comedy companies

You don't have to know that English comic Tony Hancock wasn't the only mass media comedian to die lonely and miserable in a Sydney motel room to know that laughter has its price.

Sitcoms now run on cable (the Comedy Channel) as well as on free to air, and the success in the mid- to late 1990s of *The Seinfeld Show* suggests that audiences are more than happy to welcome shows that mix and match styles and narrative modes. *Dawson's Creek* (Warner Bros/TVN, 1998+) even seemed to signal a return to the teen comedies of the 1950s—but with the sexual stakes considerably higher.

Certainly early sitcoms of the 1950s were largely family-based, deriving their humour from familiar situations and a fairly conservative attitude. The box office returns for films revisiting programs like *I Love Lucy* and *The Brady Bunch* indicate that viewers can be aroused from the dead by having their media memories refreshed on a regular basis. These successes also suggest that nowadays a sitcom that doesn't contain a subversive element or two may not work. Certainly traditional soaps about families that are other than dysfunctional are unlikely to attract a wide audience. Such families are addictive viewing for sitcom fans (*All in the Family*, *Kingswood Country*, *Married with Children*, *Bullpitt*).

The regular recycling by American networks of overseas series (notably *Till Death Do Us Part* becoming *All in the Family*, *Steptoe and Son*, *Sanford and Son*, *Not the 9 O'Clock News*, and arguably *Saturday Night Live*) also indicates that network producers often feel that humour will not 'translate'. (However, the continued cult success of *Monty Python's Flying Circus* over thirty years on suggests that this attitude stems from underestimation of the audience.)

On analysis, even apparently deviant shows like *Seinfeld* are still using a fairly classic form of dramatic structure with the usual set-up (the beginning) and the usual closure (the ending, with or without a resolution). And comedy no longer has to fulfil the requirement that it should be the polar opposite of tragedy—at least structurally, for the hero need not survive. Look at the weekly fate of poor Kenny in *South Park* (Comedy Central).

So, really, no structural model is too outrageous or silly for comedy nowadays and some forms simply invert, satirise or subvert existing form, notably the ubiquitous Home Shows (magazine shows such as *Better Homes and Gardens*)—a surefire comic source every time it is used as fodder, as it regularly is, especially on cable.

General rules do exist, however. Sitcoms are (almost always) thirty minutes long (minus commercial breaks, make that twenty-two minutes) and sit on TV schedules between 6.30 p.m. and 8.30 p.m. (the 'family hours'). The dangerous challenges to so-called 'normal' behaviour made by a classic show like *Fawlty Towers* (BBC, 1974–76) meant that when it was first released, sensible programming kept it back until later. But many years later social changes and increased audience sophistication (maybe) means that a thicker-skinned, more '*with it*' audience can cope with the show much earlier—both in the program schedule and in life!

Take a step back from most comedy series, for example *Suddenly Susan* (1998+) or *Friends* (1996+), and you can see that the model of the dysfunctional family is frequently utilised (we'll play with that same idea in the next chapter). The concept is simple. Develop a group of characters in a relatively confined space (office, home, shipboard) and this ensures a comic conflict over almost any basic complication to the routine of their lives. Then you can make the setting a dysfunctional one by nature. *Fawlty Towers* set the standard for comic interaction with its guesthouse, used as a revolving door for eccentrics. Your characters can be added to the brew of any social pressure cooker you like: an advertising agency, a hospital, whatever you fancy.

None of this guarantees anything about the quality of the sitcom. Comedy is notoriously difficult to pull off well and is almost totally reliant on the strength and inherent interest of the characters created as the solidity of your dramatic structure.

Finally, you should understand a little about how comedy works. That's the focus of the next chapter.

Chapter 7
A Short Course in Comedy

The 'What if?'

A key element of developing TV comedy—of forming a concept that will make full use of screen comedy potential—is to ask the question 'What if . . . ?'. For example, what if we could show what actually goes on behind the scenes in a television station and it was funny? This was the premise for the very funny—and near-libelous soap *The Box* (10 Network/Crawford Productions, 1974).

The 'what if . . . ?' is the idea that defines the essence of the show. In *Seinfeld* the 'what if' is 'What if we put four neurotic, self-obsessed contemporary characters together, who all know each other intimately, and watch them cope with their daily problems in New York?'. The next step for anyone intending to be the writer of a successful sitcom is to sit down and immediately try to write thirteen half-hour episode outlines.

Now things get tougher.

> **Try this basic exercise.**
>
> • Think of a comic scene for Mr Bean—or any other well-known character you like.
> • Describe the scene—maybe it's a visit by the Prime Minister, along with assorted pompous politicians and security. All will provide opportunities for gags.
> • Now write the first gag—and it must be visual.
> • Now another gag. The jokes will get more and more absurd as Bean tries harder to escape with each disaster!
>
> As you are discovering (if you're really trying this) all you need is a character with unusual behaviour patterns (or no patterns at all) and a location. For example, maybe it's a building site, a church service, the kitchen of a five-star restaurant . . .
>
> Now go for it.

Remember: no dialogue. You're writing classic gag comedy.
   Notice what a serious business it is?

The running gag
The endless permutations of successful screen comedy (usually running to many sequels), television sitcoms, and even theatre, rely on two simple principles: make 'em laugh, and make 'em laugh even harder. This often relies on a technique called the running gag. Simply, this means creating an onscreen joke—then doing it again, and building up the stakes for the audience at every stage.
   A joke is set up, returns expanded and develops. In Jacques Tati's *Playtime* (1967), Tati goes to a large impersonal building for an appointment. The running gag in this case is that he will never get to meet the person with whom he has an appointment. In running this gag Tati uses every possible delay and complication:
* Tati becomes obsessed by the sound made by vinyl seats while he is waiting,
* He gets trapped in a lift just as he is about to make his appointment.
* The man he wanted to meet has left.
* Tati caps the gag by having another character, already upset by the missed appointment, go up to someone in the street thinking he is Tati. Wrong!

Comedy in Oz
The medium in which comedy is to work has a major effect on the type of humour employed, as does the national context and preference for different types of humour. David Williamson, in his theatre plays, uses snappy one-liners to advance the story and the interest in his characters. The story of *Emerald City* (Michael Jenkins, 1988) is situated in the backbiting world of the Australian film industry, and the overall reek of government patronage in search of the politically correct investment vehicle provides a backstory for Colin Rogers' character's struggle to find meaning in his work. When the play was adapted for cinema, as Williamson's plays often are, the large stage gestures had to be toned down and the dialogue abbreviated, given the intimacy of film, where the camera is literally on the actor's shoulder.
   The Castle (Rob Sitch, 1996) marks another development in Australian screen comedy: it's a highly character-centred comedy drama based on the lives of a typical suburban family. Its theme of a working-class family banding together to ward off a threatened takeover of their home by an airport developer struck a common chord in the midst of a depression. A decision was even made to take over an actual working-class house and shoot there in the

interests of authenticity. *The Castle* was shot in a record seven days by the experienced *Frontline* comedy team and became a national hit in the cinema, on video, and in print (Penguin, 1995). Rapid writing techniques, a sharing of roles, and spontaneous shooting techniques are part of the *Frontline* team's working practice, and the element of control by the writers themselves proved essential.

Sketch comedy

The cornerstone of sketch comedy is the monologue or routine that can be done on stage in a limited time. In fact, this comic form engages its audience by its familiarity.

The comic monologue is a mainstay of sketch comedy shows like the long-running *Full Frontal* (Artist Services, 1989). The well-written monologue with an undercurrent of human anguish can be very effective. *Full Frontal* uses a variety of turns performed by leading comic actors who later spun off into their own separate shows. The character in the monologue can be so effective that he or she creates a whole new genre of local humour.

The inventiveness of Mary-Anne Fahey's Kylie Mole character opened a new, tougher vein of female humour. Kylie Mole went through endless variations on the theme of a young woman telling what has happened in the daily routine of her life. It's the unconscious self-reflection, without insight, and the apparent continuous flow of unconnected thought that makes it funny. And of course a story is being told. The comedy lies in Fahey's ability to stick exactly to the character she has created:

BACK TO SCHOOL

KYLIE

Oh um hi my name's Kylie, and guess what? Adam failed bubs. Again! So good. Bein' back at school is so foul, we have already had to do a essay on What I did on my holidays, and guess what, I got F. So unfair. It's not my fault if I had a spac holiday. And then guess what, Mum, in front of everyone, kisses me and that's not the worst bit, she gets out her hankie and goes (pfff) and rubs her spit all over my face. Fairdinkum I was gonna punch her. I am just too mature to be treated like that now cause I am a 32 B now, 34 if I go like this! So good. Well that one's 34, and that one's 32 and I am sooo mature now, I am just bustin' out of my uniform, and mum wouldn't get me a new one, so I got my cousin's, but this is the good bit, Adam got mine. And I got my cousin's dictionary, so good, saves me work, cos all the rude bits are already underlined, like masticate. So good. But mum is such a scunge, like I rooly wanted good stationery this year, and mum buys me Embassy, I wanted a INXS pencil case, and I got Burke's Back Yard, and I wanted Kylie Minogue school bag, I got Wombat, and I wanted Pee Wee Herman drink container and guess what I got, Rita the Eta eater, spewin'! cos Amanda got a pencil with a rubber on it, don't know why, she never makes mistakes, and it's got a digital alarm and her name engraved on it, I get a pencil with a bandaid wif my name writ on it. So unfair . . .

Mary-Anne Fahey's character work is as good as it gets, as you'll see when you try performing this yourself. This sort of comedy, like classic stand-up comedy (*Saturday Night Live, Full Frontal*), relies on a performer writing for his or her own voice. Fahey also used her ability to catch a tone of voice as well as write to her strengths as an actor, notably a kind of breathless quality that makes the next sketch work so well:

CENTREFOLD

Hi! I'm your Playboy centrefold for this evening!

(laugh)

My name is Candy Stewart! And I'm from Wisconsin. And I'm sixteen and that's also my IQ.

(laugh)

My measurements are 36-24-36 and my star sign is Virgo, and my rising star is Uranus! My goals in life are to gain an understanding of the entire universe, to win the Nobel Peace Prize . . . to single-handedly save the environment, and maybe to go on a date with Mel Gibson! My turn-ons include flowers and warm summer nights on a desert island with really sensitive intelligent guys . . . plural, and Mozart and poetry really makes me hot. Oh, and my turn-offs include plastic people! Yuk!

And my desires are to be taken seriously as an actress and a quantum physicist! Here is my pictorial. It is called 'A day in the life of a centrefold'.

Ooh! Here I am in my garden. It is raining. Wait a minute! Silly me! Under my plastic raincoat, I've got no clothes on!

(flash, laugh)

How did that happen? I better run inside before somebody sees me.

Oh, look at me now!

(walk walk walk)

I am doing the housework in a little white lace-up corset! And a pair of crotchless underpants! Very prac-

KYLIE MOLE

The writer as character

tical, you can never tell when you might want to do wee-wees or something!

Oh my gosh! Ooh, I dropped my feather duster! I might just have to bend down and pick that up! Oh whoops-a-daisy! I just fell over on this big huge white polar bear rug! Hmm. Maybe I'll just roll around on her for a little while. Oh that feels good! I might just arch my back!

(poses with finger, puts it in her eye)

Gosh! I feel so vulnerable today! Oh, what's this? I've got a breast! I wonder how that got there! Oh, it's attached! Oh, I've got two! That's lucky.

(laugh)

Ooh and they are very very large and very very pert! No wonder they keep falling out all the time! Oh, and what's that? A little funny bit that sticks out! Oh, what's that? Oh! A yucky staple! Ouch!

(pulls it out)

(with thanks to Mary-Anne Fahey)

- Notice how the character's tone of voice is kept, perfectly, to the very end.
- Action is set up by the words—and repeated for that extra laugh.
- A good character sketch can go on forever; make sure the punchline (here, the inevitable staple) is what the audience were (unconsciously) expecting all along.
- Keep ahead of the audience, but treat them as intelligent. They may not 'get' all the gags, but they'll be pleased with themselves.
- Meeting—and surprising—audience expectation is always part of any good comedy script.

The comedian as punching bag

Australia's classic TV comedy character of the 1970s, Norman Gunston, uses audience knowledge of the straight television interview to create comedy. Gunston (Gary McDonald) pursues his own agendas while his subjects (or victims) try to remain normal, as happens in most interview situations. Thus the comic character is always pushing himself or herself and others to the edge. Gunston is a carefully worked invention. This interview set up with Mick

Jagger (written by Morris Gleitzman) shows just how much prepa-ration goes into these routines.

Gunston, worried about rumours of Jagger using drugs, hands him a syringe filled with a soft-drink called GI. Note the escape map ('*if Jagger walks out at any stage*') left for McDonald.

JAGGER

(NORMAN hands JAGGER a plastic syringe full of GI)

NORMAN

Get him to switch to GI. You can't get arrested for it and it's got less calories than heroin.

You can't sing 'I Can't Get No Satisfaction' much any-more. Have you found a teabag you like? Do you know any other songs? See if you can keep up with me.

(plays a bit of a Stones song on harmonica)

Come on, sing along. I'll give you the tape for your next album.

(if he won't)

Well, just mime and I'll get Aunty Pat to dub it in later. OK, you play and I'll sing. Oh I see, you need the atmos-phere of a gig. You sing and I'll scream and faint.

(if JAGGER walks out at any stage)

Oh no wait, don't go. These big stars are so impetuous. If you cross your legs you can hold it for hours. He probably heard a groupie licking her lips outside. I hope I didn't offend him. You know, not screaming and faint-ing when I walked in. I should have stuck to the script.

(With thanks to Morris Gleitzman)

In the case of Richard Nixon, Gunston didn't even get the main gate to open, so the interview was conducted with a security guard over an intercom. It was still very funny.

Television sitcoms: Invading your home nightly at seven

Situation comedies are the biggest guns of commercial television in the ratings war and a hit sitcom like *Seinfeld*, *Sex and the City* or *Friends* can dominate evening schedules season after season. Television is the most competitive of all media, as potentially it car-ries the greatest possible rewards for advertisers, with audience viewing figures of half the population being possible for a successful program. Sitcoms have been in steady development since the 1950s, from *I Love Lucy* to the *Simpsons*, and now the ultimate anarchic sitcom: the rough-edged minimal graphics of *South Park*. Of all television forms, the sitcom is the one most justified in claiming to be adaptive to the demands of the TV medium.

Working Dog Productions' *Frontline* series, produced in association with the Australian Broadcasting Corporation in 1994–95, achieves a synthesis of formal television styles, further amplified by the use of home video-style footage interspersed with normal studio scenes.

The writer–producer–director team of Santo Cilauro, Jane Kennedy, Rob Sitch, and Tom Gleisner shared roles throughout the production period. *Frontline* parodies the venerable current affairs *60 Minutes* format, and gives a behind-the-scenes view of prime-time television. *Frontline* challenges the nature of television itself, exposing the foibles of that two-dimensional medium with its reliance on known personalities. Bob Donoghue, ABC Executive Producer for the series, said, 'The public who chose to watch *Frontline* cannot be duped anymore . . .'

Setting and backstory

In *Frontline* the setting is a television current affairs program where 'real' characters are mixed in with the fictional staff members, and the result is an on-the-edge element of real risk. The lines are further blurred by mixing amateur-gauge footage with broadcast quality. *Frontline* pushed the limits of television subject matter to peel away the pretensions, making the show the most popular comedy show in Australia for two seasons.

The scripts of *Frontline* show a high standard of development, further helped by strict script editing and pacing. Collaborative script development includes input by the acting team, and the writers are in fact the players of their own line. The following short scenes from 'The Souffle Rises' act as both perfect character pieces for Mike (Scene 19) and Brooke (Scene 23), but also indicate the 'behind the scenes' insider jokes set up by Scene 22 and the use of 'real' showbiz or political figures—those who are prepared to be satirised, that is. Writing comedy, you'll be amazed at how many people prefer the slight sting of satire over being ignored altogether. Ugly Dave Gray's courage in Scene 23 is exemplary!

SCENE 19: MIKE'S OFFICE

MIKE is being interviewed by two Greek journalists. One asks the questions and then translates MIKE's answers to her (presumably monolingual) colleague.

MIKE

Well, I know a bit about Greece. I mean, I once spent two weeks on the island of Corfu. Absolutely beautiful.

GREEK NUMBER 1

But you have never formally studied the history of Greece?

MIKE

Well, how accurate were those epic theatres?

MIKE's joke is met with silence.

Not formally, no. At school we studied the Pantheon. No, what's it called? Partheon. I mean, I'm obviously a bit scratchy now. Pythagoras, we did one of his plays.

GREEK NUMBER 1 translates this answer to her colleague, who writes it down. The translation takes a little longer than MIKE's answer would seem to have warranted.

GREEK NUMBER 1

Are you aware there is a world of difference between the cultures of Greece and those of the northern Slavic Macedonians?

MIKE

Who makes the dips!

(more silence)

Seriously, of course, I think there's two sides to every issue.

GREEK NUMBER 1 translates for her colleague. GREEK NUMBER 2 responds in Greek. Aggressively.

MIKE

(over the top of GREEK NUMBER 2's reply)

I mean, obviously it's a complex issue. I feel very strongly about that. What exactly are you writing . . . ?

SCENE 22: THE EDIT SUITE

BRIAN, KATE and HUGH are viewing archival footage of UGLY DAVE GRAY. It is accompanied by a voice-over.

VOICE-OVER

Tonight on *Frontline*, we meet one of this country's last living legends.

HUGH stops the tape.

BRIAN

Actually, can you make that black and white?

HUGH adjusts monitor to black and white.

Great. It makes him look like more of a legend.

SCENE 23: UGLY DAVE'S HOUSE (OUTDOORS, BY THE POOL)

BROOKE walks into shot and talks.

BROOKE

For almost fifty years now he's been a shining light of the Australian entertainment industry. The wise-crackin', cigar-smokin' funnyman we know simply as 'Ugly Dave'. But is there a sad face behind the happy clown?

BROOKE's final position brings her next to UGLY, who is seated. He reaches out and gives her bum a slap.

UGLY

Speaking of behinds . . .

BROOKE

Dave!

UGLY gets up to chase her.

UGLY

Come on darlin'. Make this sad face happy . . . (wheezes)

BROOKE restrains herself. STU speaks from behind the camera.

STU

Are you all right, Dave?

UGLY sits.

UGLY

Just the old ticker.

BROOKE

Maybe you should cut down on the smoking.

UGLY

I have. I've taken up drinking.

(*Frontline*, Penguin Books, 1995)

Great sitcom ideas don't happen by accident. Vast amounts of time and money are spent on the development and production of a thirteen-week series. *Frontline* was developed from the premise that what happened behind the scenes in TV would be an interesting backstory for a comedy series. Sitch, Cilauro and the other partners started as revue comics before moving on to sketch comedy in *The D Generation*.

Comedy like *Frontline* or *Seinfeld* relies on the writer setting up a situation which produces new—but expected—reactions from the characters. Write a short scene breakdown for a new *Frontline* episode.

First: What is the set-up? This is the Big Plot Point: It should be something (real or made up) that is topical—and that Mike will get wrong (which is the key to the comedy, and its engine, every week).

Now, all you need do is lay out the running gag:

- Brooke's ambition to get a better job at another station?
- Martin's tampering with the truth?
- Remember—it must all end in disaster!

Talking funny

Comic dialogue is essentially a matter of exploiting plot situations with highly charged short-term responses. Verbal humour is created from a standard set of models: the double take, the explosion of vanity, the response to a failed enterprise. The language patterns of comedy are based on an exaggerated speech that still corresponds to natural forms and responses. The inability of the characters to escape from their familiar settings is in itself funny. Twin elements of surprise and incongruity can be developed into full-fledged belly laughs. Such laughter is the result of disbelief: can this really be happening in front of us?

Writers of sitcoms use a set number of key characters who have a relationship which is in itself funny. In *The Larry Sanders Show* (HBO, 1995) the central character is a TV host who is continually undermined by the toughness of his profession and the constant challenges to his status by his offsiders. Such struggles for personal survival are the heart of comedy.

Remember comic dialogue exists:

- to get a laugh;
- to advance the storyline, which is very basic—a set-up as in *Frontline*—that is, a problem with which the characters will deal in expected but funny ways.

Dialogue is the heart of television comedy: endlessly refined, tested, and modified to perfect the classic routine and the most effective punchline. Good dialogue writers are worth their weight in television ratings; the development of dialogue skills and the timing behind them requires careful observation and tough reworking of material.

> Try to write a one-paragraph (200-word) speech for Kylie Mole or a character of your own invention. Remember that the laughs will come out of exaggerations of the basic character's foibles and obsessions.

A final tip: comedy writers usually hunt in packs, and often in a full team with reserves. It just seems to be a law of human creativity, as well as a necessary reality check, that comic writers work best in pairs at least. Teamwork, however, may not be enough to guarantee sanity. A notorious documentary called *Feeding the Monster* (BBC, Nadia Haggar, 1992) showed the full horrors of working as part of a hassled and strung-out team for a demanding and capricious star (in this case Roseanne Barr). The decision to write comedy may be the bravest thing you ever do!

But maybe not as brave as that most vital of jobs that you as a writer or producer must always face: they call it The Pitch.

Chapter 8
The Pitch

What, me pitch?

Sometimes nothing appears more offensive to one's dream of becoming the heroic and fearlessly individualistic writer than this worrisome and grubby business of having to pitch your ideas. But whether you are writing an advertising campaign, working on a TV series, or convincing a funding body to back your feature film idea, you will sooner or later have to make a pitch.

Depending on your market, there are several stages in the writing of a script, only the very last of which is the draft script itself. First you must toss your beloved brainchild into the shark pool of ideas. In practical terms this means using several different formats to sell your ideas off the page. Each form of presentation depends on what stage you have reached in your writing.

During the early years of Australian television, production houses like Crawfords (*Homicide, Division Four*, et al.) and Cash-Harmon (*No. 96*) employed their own in-house writing teams who worked in offices not dissimilar to the writer's rooms in *Barton Fink*. The cautionary tale of the writer 'in chains' is a staple theme of novels and stories about the writer on the skids in Hollywood. This stereotype is based on some true horror stories, like that of F. Scott Fitzgerald (read Fitzgerald's Pat Hobby stories for the full horror). Such tales date from well before the time of William Faulkner, who was the model for the drunken novelist Mayhew in *Barton Fink*. In fact, though, such security was welcomed by many writers.

Unless you are lucky enough to be employed as an in-house writer on a soap like *Neighbours*, the salaried screenwriter is a thing of the distant past. The days of being actually housed by the studio are also over, partly as a result of a famous writers' insurrection in 1969 when Crawfords' writers, led by John Dingwall (later a leading feature film writer. Look him up!), demanded the right to work from home! Generally, however, episodic television series are sold as concepts in pitching sessions, especially when as with *Medivac* (Liberty and Beyond, 1996+) basing the production in Queensland led to the hiring of some local writers for several episodes—something series producers almost never do when shooting away from their home base. That's why most series writers end up in Sydney, Melbourne, Hollywood, New York. If you have to pitch, pitch, and pitch again you have to be there, *live,* at the centre of the action. Writers hired for the children's series *Round the Twist* (ACTF, series three, 1998–99) were Melbourne-based and had a long association with the Australian Children's Film and Television Foundation. So your pitch can also be a geographical matter! The pitch has literally become the producer's turf.

Clean up your act!

The first thing you must do is make absolutely sure that you are clear about, and can make clear to others, what the fundamental premise of your concept is. Whether it is a unique selling proposition for a product (Nike: Just do it!) or a High Concept movie (*Speed: Die Hard on a Bus*), you must be able to convey it simply.

In Chapter 10: The Plot Thickens, we see how a simple three-part story formed the basis of a successful television commercial (TVC) for a radio station. The central plot premise carries us with a harried young woman through to her change, through the world of music, into a powerful heroine. The premise of this story is that music makes the young woman's world function, and become magical. This is the 'what if?' of the story. Let's expand that into a series or a feature film premise. Remember that at this point you should drop any mention of acts; that's the hidden part of your structure, and it doesn't need to be spelt out in any didactic way. From now on you're writing scripts, not stage plays.

What if a young woman, finding that the pace of the city is crippling her life, opts for a different way of life in, say, the bush? All stories proceed from a premise, and without it there is no 'point' to the drama. The point can be put in terms of morality (the values of the bush are more authentic than those of the city) or just practicality: only escaping the city gives person a chance for a fulfilling life. Beware of making that premise sound too moralistic, though. Not everyone will agree with you if you sound at all preachy.

The paradigm is the model of how your action will proceed. For the TV commercial it is a simple narrative in three parts, focusing on the world of musicians rather than some other equally sexy group of characters. So the world is seen filtered through the paradigm of what you can tell us about musicians' lives, and the plot points will all have something of the flavour of that world in them.

Dreams of escape: *SeaChange*

A television series like *SeaChange* (Artist Services, ABC, 1998+) uses the same premise of a woman trapped in a sterile corporate life in the city. In this case the central character, Laura, is a company lawyer who has forgotten how to be a mum in the heat of office politics. Only when her husband is arrested for fraud and also confesses to an affair with her sister ('I didn't think you'd notice . . .') does Laura pull up roots to head with her bewildered children for the little fishing town of Pearl Bay, which she and her family had visited years before on an idyllic holiday. There she will try to become a real mother in 'the last place we were a family'. Laura's adventures in Pearl Bay as magistrate will reinforce the disjunction between city life (inauthentic, destructive, thoughtless, careerist) and the country (rustic, innocent, capable of corruption but solid enough to survive it, etc.).

Here's how the producers set up the pitch to the Drama Department of the ABC:

SeaChange
Synopsis

A 'sea change' is what begins to happen to Laura Gibson as she approaches her fortieth year.

For almost two decades she attempted to juggle a marriage, a family, and a career as a high-powered corporate lawyer. It was an act she relished and pulled off with some panache. In fact, she was so captivated by her own display of overachievement that she failed to notice she'd dropped a couple of balls along the way—ones labelled 'Husband' and 'Children'. Jack would have complained more if he wasn't busy having his own mid-life crisis as a spectacularly incapable businessman. Miranda, 16, and Rupert, 12, gave up trying to attract her attention years ago.

With her husband in gaol, a career in shreds and the cat almost dead because she was too busy to avoid treading on it, Laura is totally derailed by the painful revelation that her life has no meaning. The fancy footwork of corporate law has kept her charged, but no amount of adrenaline compensates for the fact that she no longer knows her own kids—or the man who fathered them. Instinct tells her to seek cover, to retreat to take what's left of her family back to a time and place before it all went wrong. It was ten years ago when the Gibsons had the happiest holiday of their lives, in a town called Pearl Bay.

But Pearl Bay isn't exactly the idyllic coastal town Laura remembers. The beaches are still beautiful, but what happened to the endless summer of ten years back? And what about the bridge connecting Pearl Bay with the booming tourist industry on the other side of the river? Where is the rolling scrub and bushland surrounding the quaint cottage they once stayed in? And who on earth is this laconic ferryman she finds herself inappropriately but inevitably attracted to? Despite the unexpected changes and all the dictates of common sense, Laura accepts the job as Pearl Bay magistrate and struggles to make amends to Rupert and Miranda for her years of neglect.

Laura, Miranda and Rupert all come to realise that Pearl Bay is much more than a pretty but fading town. Through the sad, funny, petty and sometimes extraordinary cases Laura presides over, she discovers an idiosyncratic town of divided loyalties, old secrets and bizarre machinations. All three of them gradually change, through unexpected friendships and love, until they become part of the weave of this strange place and are able to connect once more with life.

(from *SeaChange*, Artist Services, ABC, 1998)

The hook is now baited: after all, we all want to drop out, don't we, or at least think we do?

By pitching the story in this way the writers have hit upon the same formula that has worked for *Heartbeat* (ABC/Thames, 1985–88: where Constable Nick Rowan turns his back on swinging 1960s London and heads for the little Yorkshire village of Aidensfield); *Ballykissangel* (ABC/RTE, 1987: where Priest Peter Clifford escapes to Ballykissangel in the heart of rural Ireland, and finds real friendships, love and rivalries); and *Northern Exposure* (10: A New York doctor spends four years as a GP in Nicely, Alaska). For more on this nostalgic formula, see Chapter 11.

Once the premise and the paradigm are decided upon you can begin to write the first stage of your script: the outline.

The outline: Starting small

You may want to write down the premise in a paragraph or so as a teaser. This part is called the *concept*, with a *synopsis* running to about three pages of basic plot and character information. But the *outline* is what should 'sell' your idea off the page.

The outline is the brief narrative summary of the story premise and basic plot of your script (to be) and can be anything from three to fifteen pages long, double spaced. As this is really a pitch for your idea over others sure to be competing in the same territory— good ideas never exist in a vacuum—you will naturally take the trouble to point out why your premise is superior to any others!

Here's the concept for a series called *Rags* as it recently went out to production houses:

Rags
© Dada Films 2001
The Background

Internationally, the late 1990s. It's the time of tariff wars and child labour in clothing factories.

In Australia the struggling retail clothing industry has just been given a ten-year reprieve by government, but from now on it will be scary down there in the trenches. It will also be triumphant from time to time, and never less than exciting—even on the shop floor.

Rags offers us the rich world of a small design and clothing label, and boardroom politics. Remember the brilliant and successful English documentary series *The Factory* (1996), about Robertson-Willey, an old and venerable firm in the cyber age having to come up to speed rather too fast?

Well, *Rags* is about a middle-aged company (set up in the late 1960s as a hippy dippy alternative House), now ossifying as the petals fall off the blooms.

Rags is all about survival and new energies in a wired, young, ready-to-wear fashion world, from design studio to the cutting rooms where the clothing prototypes are readied.

The sentences are short, the premise clearly spelled out: this is about international, social, and economic matters seen writ small in a battling little fashion shop and factory floor somewhere in a Pacific backwater!

The original concept pitch for the durable series *Blue Heelers* was even more to the point:

> In Outback Queensland, Blue Heeler means cattle dog.
> They're quick, courageous, smart and loyal. They chase cars and they bite strangers and they never let go.
> In Outback NSW, Blue Heeler means cop.

It's sometimes hard to know which species they're talking about.

(Southern Star, 1993)

And that's it!

The laconic, wisecracking style is just right to set the tone for a very contemporary series that can stretch to encompass any type of story.

Selling your series

Police shows come and go—and they always come back. Less often, but often enough, so do private eye shows.

As always, though, if you're working in a genre that your readers (producers, money people) might think is a bit passé, then you have to mount an argument in the outline. For a series like our example, called *Streets and Rivers*, the argument should be as upfront as possible, while also heading off any potential objections.

This is how the writers tackled the problem of revitalising a genre:

Why another PI series?

As a genre the private detective series has always had appeal. And right now it looks as if audiences are looking for something other than *Police Rescue*, *Water Rats*, and maybe *Wildside*.

Historically, Australian audiences have always enjoyed thrillers of one sort or another, but it's time to look again beyond the boys and girls in blue. In the year 2000 and beyond, a private eye series should reflect its time and have a different flavour, seasoned with cyberspace while retaining enough traditional thriller values to keep the audience coming back for more.

Today's stories have to be more hard-edged . . . like the 1990s street-horror stories of Andrew Vacchs, [they need to] have a heroin edge to them and cutting-edge visual style—like *Wildside* in its time.

(based on a concept by Dawson with Stocks ©1993)

Concept documents: The whole package

Your pitch should actually contain all the elements so far discussed: outline, synopsis and a treatment, or scene breakdown. By the way, some scriptwriters and producers use the terms 'concept' and 'outline' interchangeably; just stick to one of them! The important thing is to make it flow, as well as to look and sound as if you really care about the characters and the story.

The pitch documents for *Streets and Rivers* also had plenty of visuals (character and cast mug shots, great locations) to keep the message alive. Not that that guarantees you anything. But however good and original your concept, it still needs to be supported by everything you can bring to the aid of the premise to sell. You need to be able to anticipate and head off any challenges with arguments well before they come, and that means knowing your genres!

But you can even make a virtue of the business of plot itself, as did the British romantic comedy, *Sliding Doors* (Peter Howitt, 1998). Clearly aware of the existence of our binary plot machine, Peter Howitt creates a double story based on the premise 'What if . . . ?' by showing two stories in parallel.

When a young PR woman, Helen (Gwyneth Paltrow), is about to take a tube train home after being sacked, the carriage doors close in her face and she misses the train.

But what if she hadn't? We follow the two alternative plots until they converge in a single conclusion—the equivalent of a 'psychological' western always ending in a classic shoot out. For no matter how you play around with plot elements, there comes a moment when everything must return to normal, whatever that is. It would be interesting to try the *Sliding Doors* model by yourself and see if any satisfactory wrap-up of your movie can be achieved by never having the two plots intersect at all.

For something very like this last idea you should watch Krzysztof Kieslowski's *The Double Life of Veronique* (1991), as a master of narrative twists takes the double plot elements almost all the way! Kieslowski was never afraid of fooling around with probabilities and neither should you be. Try it—the exercise will tell you a great deal about plot premises.

Of course such playfulness is pretty much denied you in series television, except for comedy. *Seinfeld*, towards the end of the series, offered plots that ran backwards, weird time lines and plots that hit the wall of probability just for fun. Series television usually relies on solid and traditional plotting. That's why the scene breakdown is a key element in presenting your episode proposal.

Treatments and scene breakdowns

Although the treatment consisting of thirty or so pages of prose with some dialogue is currently in vogue, there is absolutely no good reason for not proceeding straight to a scene breakdown of all the scenes and sequences you expect to find in the episode.

Here's a good working definition of a treatment:

- A treatment consists of a written condensation of the proposed film or TV dramatic production. It covers the basic ideas and issues of the production. Main characters, locations and story angles are included.

- In part, its purpose is to sell the proposal to financial backers and to major stars. Treatments should be attention-getting and interesting to read. They are written in the present tense and often read like a short story.
- Treatments cover the story sequence and sometimes contain key dialogue examples. No specific length will normally be specified; just whatever covers the story. Too long and it will probably get boring; too short and it will leave many unanswered questions.

In television production a program proposal plays a similar role.

Overall, treatments seem to be an awkward halfway house between concept and script, neither short story nor full plot. Every writer would do well to use scene breakdowns to spot time and plotting problems early.

Maybe they are so popular with funding bodies because they actually *look* more like prose and less like those confusing machine documents, scripts.

Certainly once you feel confident that the idea is 'sold', the scene breakdown is next—a sure way to check the mechanism of the plot.

Here, with rough timings and the commercial breaks plotted in, is the beginning of a cast introduction and scene breakdown for a planned for early episode, *Streets and Rivers*:

HARRY STREETS

He comes from a working-class background and joined the Navy because he didn't see why all those rich bastards should hog all the good-looking boats! After ten years' service he'd made Petty Officer in the Special Boating Service: those blokes who do their work with brains, speed, and fast firing weapons.

Harry's work included stints in the jungles north of Australia and some he doesn't ever talk about in South America—maybe it was Nicaragua. He won't tell and he's not happy with what he had to do. But his work among the bungling and the bad faith made (in mercenary circles) a name . . . and some dangerous enemies. For a few years he dropped out and worked for a range of profitable little earners. Above all, Harry took on jobs that involved boats.

He's fast on his feet, but street-smart and sea-smart. Harry prefers to work out his problems, and he doesn't like guns any more. Wherever he finds

them. Whatever his hangups, he can act decisively
and hard when he has to.

DETECTIVE SERGEANT LOU STRYKER

Running Vice for the city area, he's a fascinating mix-
ture: tough, but with the perspective of the New
Policeman. He's got a degree in sociology and his wife
MAYA is a law lecturer. Because he's often constrained
in his work by what he can't do, he's developed a
working relationship (tempered by cynicism) with
Harry.

LISA ROWE

A brilliant photographer, trained in art photography,
but now a well known photorealist with edge. She's
half in love with HARRY, half equally desperate to be
independent so she wavers between her Doc
Martens-shod, tough, streetwise routine (Stars and
Bars) and a desire to curl up with HARRY and say to
hell with being an ageing party girl. After all, at thirty-
five, maybe she's . . . no. Not Lisa. Not yet.

STUDS (ALEX TERKEL)

The perfect foil for HARRY, he's a drop-out police
cadet (sacked)—a fact you'd never guess from his
postmodern appearance and stud earrings. He's been
everything from roadie with a failed band on the run
to front singer himself in a post-apocalyptic,
neo-punk band.

Although some story editors and producers have been heard to
declare that they pay no attention to scripts and pitches that begin
with a character breakdown, you can be equally sure that it's better to let your first audience—be they producers or script readers—
know who the cast are, the casting possibilities, and the plot poten-
tials of the characters as quickly and as clearly as you can.

And now for the plotting. If possible, give them more than just a
storyline: let the pitch breathe with a scene breakdown for at least
the first episode, which may well be a telemovie or a miniseries.
Despite some opinions against the obsessive detail and precision of
a scene breakdown, it is precisely because of such detail that a

scene breakdown is the best way to show *exactly* how the plot is going to work. Timings are an optional extra. Check your market— and some producers don't like them!

STREETS AND RIVERS

EPISODE TITLE: 'OLD PALS ACT'
SCENE BREAKDOWN

TEASER
1. EXT./INT. HOUSEBOAT/RESTAURANT. NIGHT.
   HARRY and LISA are dining with BRUNO in the as yet unfinished restaurant; signs of carpentry are everywhere. TERRY arrives late and launches into a blazing row with BRUNO: the classic spoilt daughter carry-on. There are hints that she's seeing a man BRUNO doesn't trust. (1:30)

2. INTERCUTTING INT. AS SCENE 1. EXT. THE RIVER.
   ON: A boat gliding up to the restaurant with THREE HEAVIES, led by BONE. BRUNO is confiding in HARRY; he's having trouble with some southern heavies trying the old protection bit . . . and maybe TERRY knows something about it all. A noise disturbs them. HARRY and BRUNO dash from inside to see a hand coming over the taffrail. HARRY kicks. The HEAVY falls into the river. He's picked up and the boat speeds off. (1:20)

3. EXT. THE RIVER.
   HARRY grabs his boat and takes off after the thugs. (0:25)

4. INTERCUTTING.
   A mad chase develops, tense, but with some near-comic moments as the escaping boat is saturated by the river fountain (ruining BONE's suit). HARRY's boat glances off a pier and swings about, right into the searchlight of a police boat. HARRY curses as the sound of the escaping boat recedes, and looking up, sees LOU STRYKER, grinning at him from beside the searchlight. (1:20)

COMMERCIAL BREAK

PART ONE
5. EXT. POLICE CENTRAL. DAWN.
   HARRY, very bedraggled, is escorted out by LOU STRYKER. STRYKER is laughing at HARRY as LISA waits in her car. HARRY was lucky to get out without a drink-driving

charge. STRYKER pooh-poohs the idea of crims in a boat,
claps HARRY on the back and goes inside. (1:20)

And so it goes. Be careful not to overdo the detail, though.
Producers like matters laid out succinctly.

Pitching the documentary

A pitch for a documentary, especially if it is dramatised in whole or
in part, should look very like a standard drama series or feature
pitch and ideally should also contain a scene breakdown or treatment. A scene breakdown is less likely here because of the degree
to which documentaries can change from concept to final cut.
Nevertheless, it is a highly competitive market with shrinking
funds for developments. The concept documents, therefore, should
contain all the elements of a good pitch for a feature film.

Whatever the subject of your documentary project, it's essential
that you make it sound dramatic! Here's part of the scene breakdown for a successful pitch: the partly dramatised documentary
The Legend of Fred Paterson (ABC, Jonathan Dawson 1996). Because
the film was so reliant on research, the scene breakdown is very close
in form to a final draft script:

1. PRETITLE SEQUENCE. RECREATION (AS SC# 30. IN
    FINAL SCRIPT). EXT. BRISBANE STREETS. DAY.
    (ST PATRICK'S DAY 1948)
    FADE UP SFX of disjointed rallying cries and out-of-step
    marching. The volume increases.
    OPEN ON impressionist high contrast B&W shots of legs
    marching. A baton, seen against the sky, descends. A shout,
    a thud. Impressions of a suited body falling and FRED's
    hat, crumpled, rolls into an empty frame. A tide of red
    colour flows, and the TITLE appears:

RED TIDES

THE LEGEND OF FRED PATERSON

SFX

Percussive piano chords hammer, segue to elegiac
'Fred's Theme' (original music).

2. FALLEN IDOLS.
    INTERCUTTING with the crushed hat: Statues of Lenin,
    Stalin, Khrushchev, Brezhnev—unkempt, vandalised,
    toppled.

SFX A desolate wind blows and Fred's hat slides from the frame.
NEWSPAPER HEADLINE spins out: 'Police and Pickets in Fierce City Fight' (*Brisbane Telegraph*, 17 March 1948)

NARRATOR

On St Patrick's Day 1948, a police baton brought down Australia's only Communist member of parliament.

Fred Paterson was an idealist who fought for a better world. For twenty years, he preached the gospel of Communism in the frontier towns and cities of North Queensland. The Red North.

3. THE EARLY DAYS. STILLS: FRED PATERSON (FROM JOHN PATERSON'S COLLECTION) AND EARLY STILLS OF GLADSTONE.

We hear the voice of Fred Paterson, recorded in 1975.

FRED (VO)

I was born in Gladstone, Central Queensland on the 13th of June 1897. I was one of a family of eleven, two of whom died as babies. (continues)

The advantage of writing in such detail as this at the pitch stage is that all the colour of the final film can be spelt out. The language used must therefore be as riveting and dramatic as you can make it.

Pitching the feature

From shorter forms to the feature film is thus no great distance in terms of the actual concept documents. As with series or dramatised television specials, the elements are still the same: a strong concept or outline and a strong spine for your story, laid out as clearly as possible.

Here's the opening of the concept document for a low-budget thriller, *Brown Sugar* (© 1999 Dada Films):

BROWN SUGAR

A THRILLER

Cane River is a rich country city with a strongly developed sense of place and a society that, while free and easy, is not without its clearly defined hierarchies.

Although violent crime and armed robberies are at a low level, in the last few years the hard drug pushers have moved in, concentrating on the wealthy local kids in their drive to introduce heroin and coke.

Already the police have raided one wild party held at a big home. While the parents were out of town, they've found coke—but nobody's talking. To the kids, drugs (TCP, E and some smack) are around and are a vital part of their high lifestyle. Only a week ago the daughter of a local chain store owner was killed in a high-speed car crash, the autopsy showing that she'd been mainlining heroin for some months and was also stoned at the time of the accident.

Against this backdrop of wealthy young tearaways, the city seems to be business as usual—but beneath are all kinds of volcanic activity due to erupt when the thin crust of society is cracked by violent crime.

MAIN CHARACTERS

PETE TOMLIN

He started out as a local district cricket hero and probationary constable. With the impetus of state selection moved to the big smoke and rose quickly to Detective Inspector, causing plenty of jealousy back home. Now he's back after some nasty business in Sydney went down, and has to win back the respect of the town all over again.

SALLY

PETE's wife, a shy school librarian who loves PETE for his agile mind. Her death will galvanise PETE into cold and unrelenting action.

TAGGART

The Local Police Super, not all that keen on the hard yakka but loves the country and dislikes jumped-up detectives from the smoke—like PETE.

CARL

The local mayor and salesman for everything.

DUFF and LOGAN

Two city crims on their way through.

BROWN SUGAR

INDICATIVE SCENE BREAKDOWN

1. TITLE SEQUENCE.
   Title song 'Brown Sugar' (Rolling Stones) over montage of
   the city, the canefields, sugar storage, etc. Montage builds
   to climax over dusk shots evoking the drama of the area.

2. MOTEL ON EDGE OF CANE RIVER.
   PETE and SALLY drive in, in a dusty car. The MANAGER
   recognises PETE.

3. POLICE STATION.
   TAGGART gets a call about PETE. His face is expressionless.

4. CARL'S OFFICE AT AIRPORT.
   CARL is demonstrating an Executive Jet to JACK TODD
   when STEVE, JACK'S son, arrives. There's clearly no love
   lost between father and son. STEVE says he'll wait.

5. STEVE'S APARTMENT THAT NIGHT.
   STEVE and half a dozen wealthy kids are involved in a
   very unpleasant scene. Drugs are passing hands like choco-
   lates, and one of the girls is freaking out in the bathroom.

POSSIBLE INTERCUT WITH 6
6. LOUNGE BAR MAIN HOTEL.
   PETE and SALLY are having a drink together. TAGGART
   enters and joins them briefly. He makes some slighting
   remark about PETE 'turning his back on us' and walks off.
   PETE explains that he owes the town nothing. It killed his
   dad and it sure as hell isn't going to kill him, but he's
   surprised at TAGGART's attitude.

7. CARL'S HOUSE.
   CARL is joined by DUFF and LOGAN who have just

arrived in town. Their job: to take out the local bank (branch unspecified). At 10 o'clock the following morning there'll be almost half a million dollars in cash.

Note: By setting up this job CARL has let his greed overrule his head. If Hong Kong hears about this he's in trouble.

8. AIR TERMINAL HONG KONG.
LEE TO checks through six boxes of aviation electronic equipment. They are marked for CARL.

9. STEVE'S APARTMENT.
The party is developing into a stoned orgy.

10. STREET NEAR APARTMENT.
PETE and SALLY drive back to the motel. SALLY is drowsy, very much in love. As they pass the block, they can hear loud rock music blaring. Around them the city settles down for the night.

11. VARIOUS STREET LOCATIONS CITY.
DUFF and LOGAN check their watches. Their preparation for the robbery is concise and unruffled.

INTERCUT: SALLY going off shopping alone. She wants to buy PETE some shirts (or something).

The time is five minutes to ten. An armoured truck moves slowly down the street towards the bank, then down a street at the side of the bank. A teller meets the two guards. Two large cash sacks are removed and then suddenly LOGAN reverses his car down the lane. DUFF is out instantly, menacing the guards with an automatic shotgun. The teller tries to dash back through the door but freezes as the gun swings around. DUFF hurls the sacks in the rear of the car and tosses down a smoke grenade. LOGAN guns the car down the lane towards the main street. From the smoke behind them, one of the guard staggers out. Simultaneously, SALLY, clutching her shopping bag, steps off the pavement. A guard is firing now and she freezes in terror. DUFF fires two shots at the guard as LOGAN guns the car into the main street. The guard is hit and topples, still firing. DUFF fires once more but this time it is SALLY who is hit, careering into a plate glass window. LOGAN's car roars away. A sudden terrible silence falls.

12. THE MORGUE.
    A stony-faced PETE identifies SALLY. TAGGART, shocked,
    is with him. There is no trace of the villains.

    Again, this is more than enough detail—and many producers
will still prefer a simple two-page treatment to a full scene breakdown. Check out what your potential backer prefers, if possible!

The final countdown
By now you will have realised that whatever script idea for whatever market you are pitching, there are certain protocols that you
must follow. Here's your checklist of probable essentials:
- The **concept documents** must obviously present the script
  premise clearly. The *Blue Heelers* concept was exemplary—
  short, sharp, colourful.
- The **synopsis** of three to ten pages: Industry feeling is that a
  good 'two-pager' sells the idea quickly and may be all that
  some producers will read—so make every word count.
- The **outline** is really an extended synopsis—some like to fore-
  ground the 'classical' structure by writing it in Acts, but other
  producers dislike the echoes of theatre.
- The **storyline** or **treatment**: ten to sixty pages, although the
  latter length would tire a saint, let alone a script reader with
  eyestrain. If you are asked for a storyline or treatment
  remember that it must stick firmly to the main plot (no
  sub-sub plots, please!) and can include some dialogue scenes
  if you wish. The *Red Tides* presentation included some narration as a guide to the story as well.

But there is always a problem with the longer prosiness of the
outline or treatment: it's very hard to get across all the pathos,
beauty or whatever is the main engine of your plot in what is really a stretch limo version of the short story form. So many writers
feel that the best single way to extend the details and present the
characters is the **scene breakdown**. This presents the skeletal
structure (the spine if you prefer) of the whole first draft to come.
The well-presented breakdown is invaluable for troubleshooting,
or proving that an apparent plot glitch is actually a brilliant and
totally justified storytelling strategy on your part.
    Then if all goes well: the **first draft** (with financial backing)!
From here on in, you're on the payroll.
    There is nothing to prevent a writer from going for broke and
writing a first draft at the very beginning. But since it is that much
harder to convince anyone to read a hundred or more script pages,
you will still have to pitch. That means the script should be accompanied by a concept, characters, outline, and maybe even a short
scene breakdown.

Your movie or series is called *The Back Room*. It's about a group of computer hackers who think they are Robin Hoods.

Write a one-page pitch stressing the dramatic variety of the tale and focus on the big selling point—it's a Now Story about Now Kids! Don't forget to create a semi-permanent opposition (a government agency? crims?) for your team.

Gimmicks

Great presentation and some good artwork (a cover picture, character sketches, for example) can help. Artwork, either photographs or illustrations, emphasises the visual strengths of your script, though many writers feel that relying on this is to become far too market-oriented.

Adaptations are tough to pitch

Unless you have bought the rights to an absolute red-hot bestseller (*Queenie*, *The Horse Whisperer*, *Legends of the Fall*) then the odds are that several or all of the script assessors may not have even *heard* of your source, let alone read it!

In later chapters we'll look at the process of selling adaptations in different forms, and we'll be using the example of Ross Fitzgerald's anti-hero Grafton Everest, who has featured in several books. In this case the writers went to an advertising agency to help in devising a very hard-sell pitch for the story.

This was the start of the pitch document for the feature film version of the novels:

GRAFTON FLYING (BASED ON CHARACTERS CREATED BY ROSS FITZGERALD)

THE STORY

MEET GRAFTON EVEREST

Life for Grafton Everest—novelist, national media hero and the only political forecaster to get it right all the time (a John Pilger for the year 2002) and daring rakehell (well, a bit)—seems harmless enough, apart from several domestic cyclones that are about to descend from the direction of his talented and beautiful wife Janet. All things considered, though, it's the good life in the Sunshine State.

But Grafton's affair with the hypertense and sexy Annie Angel is going to topple him from his complacency into a terrifying new world of plots and hidden schemes that will threaten not only him but his family—and the royal family, as well.

Oh, and civilisation as we know it.

A PLOT?

But somewhere in that tourist paradise in the north of Australia, deadly events are stirring.

Henderson, the ageing, sweetly affable and maniacal ex-premier of the State, is involved in a plot overseen by his former ally in the Police Force: the gross, cunning and brutal Bull Hagan. Their aim is a simple one: to sweep away the new Labor Government by setting up a calamity so dreadful that a backlash will sweep the old rightist Government back into place.

But of course they'll need some scapegoats. And Grafton's name is never far from their lips or their secret plans. From now on Grafton and his family will be swept up as apparent pawns in a game of double jeopardy.

GRAFTON AND THE BIG BANG THEORY

Hagan has cunningly piggybacked his schemes on the lower-order plottings of a group of youngish anarchists led by the almost charismatic Gavin Driver. Driver's crew have a big plan: to blow up the royal visitors soon to open an International Symposium of World Significance.

What Driver doesn't know is that Hagan will help him—and then use the efficient rounding up of the anarchists to trigger a right-wing backlash that will sweep the old order back into power.

What Hagan doesn't know is that Driver and his team are expert ball-fumblers—world land speed record holders in fumbling, in fact.

What Grafton and his family don't know is that, among other complications, their little daughter will be kidnapped—an act that'll galvanise the disaffected Grafton into action.

THE MAGUFFIN

In all good comic thrillers (as in life) there has to be a maguffin: something that everyone wants, but that the hero/anti-hero gets hold of and is thereby forced to become involved in somebody else's drama. In this case, it's quite by mistake that Grafton pockets a floppy disk while visiting Annie.

The disk contains details in code of the Driver master plan—though of course nothing at all about Hagan's sinister string-pullings.

Now the chase is on!

THE BIG PICTURE

What a terrifying dilemma for Grafton, with his family, his loves and maybe a nation at stake. What more can happen in this harrowing chapter in the life of the remarkable Grafton Everest?

Well, there are bombs, villainy of the blackest sort, tropical scenery, betrayals, a new and beautiful mountain retreat for the Everest family. And then there's Annie Angel, the sensual link between the anarchists and Grafton. Will Annie survive her own liberation? Will Greta Scacchi take the role?

Above all, there's Grafton's new novel *Going Out Backwards* and his 'career' as a truly awesome and nationally renowned television intellectual and prophet and anything else that the 1990s can throw in the path of a sensitive artist. What a sprawling canvas!

(© The Consultancy, 1994)

This is pitching at a very high 'noise' level—but it did succeed in attracting script funding. We'll return to Grafton Everest later, but whatever the form of work you choose to adapt, you still have to make it sound like a film or series that people will want to see. If you think some great gimmick will help—a CD-ROM, a storyboard, even a music track—then do it!

Somewhere, deep in cyberspace ...

We cannot finish without another cautionary tale. Out there somewhere on the Web you can hear the sobbing of many frustrated film-makers. One of them, trying to sell his second script, *Spacklebeast* (not the real title), has recorded his long battles to sell this script. He has suffered so that you may be enlightened, so here he is at his first real pitch:

4 NOVEMBER 1996

I ventured out to the offices of the production company and stewed in the waiting room for about ten minutes, occasionally pulling at the Lilliputian bottle of Evian water that the receptionist offered and I accepted.

Eventually the development guy greeted me and showed me into his office. He started out by telling me how much he loved the script, etc.

The whole meeting lasted not quite an hour. By the end, I was certain that the development guy was genuinely enthusiastic about my script, but I would have felt a hell of a lot better if I thought anybody at the company other than him was equally enthused. They weren't.

19 JUNE 1997

Two days ago, I called the company to see if whatserface had read *Spacklebeast* yet, but she wasn't available, and of course she didn't return my call.

Stand back kids, there's an assumption coming round the bend! She hasn't read it yet. Seems feasible to me.

25 JUNE 1997

Amazing. One call from Captain Agent and development gal read it that very night. Don't let it ever be said that writers get any respect in Hollywood, because we just don't.

She passed. I confused her. I can live with that. Apparently, she apologised for letting it 'slip through the cracks'. Cracks, my ass. I'm sure she knew exactly what she was doing.

I think this is the last of *Spacklebeast*. I recently learned that an upcoming film, one that promises to be quite popular, bears numerous disturbing similarities. In case you might be wondering if there's a possibility they ripped me off, I can assure you that's not the case. I'm aware of the project's history (though I only learned of the story recently) and I know it predates me. After that movie comes out, *Spacklebeast* will look like a huge rip-off in comparison, so it's probably dead as Dillinger.

20 JULY 1997

So now not only is there a big movie coming out whose story mirrors that of *Spacklebeast*, but I just read a couple days ago that a different film altogether is going to start shooting soon, and it has the same

title. When I read ' . . . so-and-so will be starring in
Spacklebeast . . .' I just about fell out of my chair. Sigh.

Like you, the author of *Spacklebeast* is undaunted. There's
always another script to be pitched!

But before there will be a script, there must be characters to
care about. And that's the focus of the next chapter.

Chapter 9
Creating Characters

More than any other dramatic form, broadcast and performed media need characters—that is, *human* agents—for the words that are spoken or acted out. Even a totally action-driven movie or a CD-ROM game of interplanetary wars requires characters to carry the narrative forward, and even the most prosaic documentary or instructional film needs a narrative thrust and a sense of human discovery to keep the audience involved. However you try to write down the skeletal outlines of a story plot, the descriptions of place remain just that: a static piece of prose until the first character comes along to inhabit your chosen world.

Any screenwriting class that begins by demanding that the plot structures be fully laid down before character is delineated is literally missing the plot! Novels and short stories, especially this century, can be driven by plot, landscape, social theories, what you will—but must still, in the end, be alive with human interaction.

Literary works can proceed for chapters without advancing the life of a central character. They can even, as with Alain Robbe-Grillet's avant-garde prose works, describe only objects: yet even these objects are connected by the readers to people, even if they are characters the readers themselves construct from their own experiences. One of Robbe-Grillet's most interesting works was his first film as a director, *Trans-Europ-Express* (1966), which sees three film-makers on a train endlessly rehashing a plot for a new thriller film they're to make about a smuggler. Again and again they change their minds—and the plot. We see the character Jonas forced to relive events subtly and whimsically altered. For this film is a meditation on the arbitrary nature of the creative process, among other things! In the end, though, Jonas becomes fascinating to the viewer in spite of the quite artificial plot actions he must perform or endure, and the film has many of the satisfactions of a good thriller. Character had won out again; even Robbe-Grillet had to confess that in the end the 'hero' took over the movie. Even the most highly complicated and esoteric experiments in style (James Joyce's *Finnegan's Wake*, or William Burroughs' *Naked Lunch*, for example) still, in the final analysis, are powered by human interaction.

So, unless you are writing for a Dadaist audience of one, character will come before everything. It is the situation of your characters that is the engine of your story and it is they who carry your message, for character brings life to the most abstract of ideas and remains in the audience memory long after the show is over. *Les Miserables* (Victor Hugo) is unthinkable without the terribly put-upon Jean Valjean, as much as *Star Wars* would collapse without Luke Skywalker (or Princess Leia, if you prefer)—although they are complex in very different ways.

Love your characters

You must be fascinated by your own characters. Even if the plot is light on big moments, or lacking in action by mainstream standards, the strength of your creations can make everything else work and seem natural. How much 'action' is there, really, in a Woody Allen movie? Allen's work is entirely character-driven, apart from his love of bizarre plot twists and coincidence, all of which are papered over by the intriguing and laceratingly honest verbal exchanges. This touches on another matter: give your actors a good part and they will reward you by giving you more back.

Every tyro scriptwriter should be aware that the script is in many ways a selling document. The pages must be lively enough to grab and hold a producer or a client, and give off the glow of involvement on your part, even if it was unbearably hard work. So if the characters don't intrigue, obsess and interest you and hence the readers early on, then there may be real problems with your characters and they will remain forever locked in the printed page. You'll know when your creations are coming alive—they start to talk back to you and take off and do things on their own that you hadn't planned for them. This is a good sign, though it can be a bit of a wild ride! For a wonderful exploration of how even apparently stable characters in famous novels can behave 'out of character', please do read Woody Allen's short story 'The Kugelmass Episode' (1980).

Out of character? Forget it. Unless you want to create one-dimensional figures forever, then please allow your characters to behave oddly at times; it can make for wonderful and unexpected plot turns. Anyway, if you or the character have gone too far, the script editor will ruthlessly excise the offending moment.

Flat or round characters

At Hollywood preview screenings, comments from audiences on films they didn't like are instructive. By far the most common criticisms relate to character:

- 'The Bruce Willis guy was a creep.'
- 'I didn't like Sharon Stone's [character's] morals.'
- 'Why would anyone behave like the guys in *Good Will Hunting* (1997) or *Bad Boy Bubby* (Rolf de Heer, 1994), or . . . ?'
- 'What they all did just didn't ring true; for example . . . [fill in names, events from any genre].'

It all seems to come down to the human element. Let's face it, no one had any trouble believing *Jurassic Park*, filtered as this mega-fantasy was through the eyes of characters who were 'ordinary folks'. Most writing theories have clustered around the notion of the need to create three-dimensional or 'round' (as opposed to 'flat') characters. And certainly a one-dimensional character can be defined as one who is just there in the script for no reason other than to move the plot along.

Think of any villain in a Sergio Leone spaghetti western (one regular favourite was Lee van Cleef) and you remember physical things: a sneer, wrinkled eyes. Nothing they say, no hint of a motive (except money or revenge) ruffles their purity as villains. But as Butch Cassidy said of the Super Posse in *Butch Cassidy and the Sundance Kid* (George Roy Hill, 1969): 'Who are those guys?'

The answer is, they're a plot device—but nobody you should actually care about!

If characters are to spring to life in your story and grab the audience, there must be more to them than just their action. There are exceptions, but they are unusual and well thought through. You can readily see that this is why a documentary series like *The Shock of the New* (BBC, 1982) succeeds where a thousand other Fine Art programs fail: by providing—in this case in the colourful and rugged person of Robert Hughes—a focus and narrator without whom the series is unimaginable.

Your characters should be so essential to the story as to render it unworkable without them.

Think back to any film that has featured a strong central character. Take *Dead Poets Society* (Peter Weir, 1989), *Self Made Hero* (*Un Héros Très Discret*, Jacques Audiard, 1996) or *The Player* (Robert Altman, 1992). You'll find you can recall much more about the characters than whatever appeared up on the screen. You may not remember their names, you will probably remember the actors (Robin Williams, Mathieu Kassovitz, Tim Robbins.) but you will certainly recall what drove them, what they believed in (or significantly failed to believe in enough) and why they behaved as they did.

This is because you are given so much information along the way as well as a very strong and memorable setting: a strict and staid boarding school, a hard-nosed Hollywood Studio, or the period just after the Second World War when France was trying to forget its collaborations with the Nazis and celebrate (or just plain invent) heroes of the Resistance.

For each protagonist there is much at stake, and you sense (rightly) that the writers had much they wanted to say about both the times and the places, through the actions of their central character. Three-dimensional? Really much more like four-dimensional, because time plays an all-important role in the construction of complex and intriguing characters.

We call this element of past time the backstory.

Backstories: The street maps of character

In literary texts the character is often defined initially through physical characteristics, often stereotypical ones:

> JACK is tall and rather weatherbeaten. He looks a bit
> like the Marlboro man in a city suit—as if he spends
> a lot of time outdoors at weekends (and so on).

This would be just fine except for little matters such as what goes on in the character's mind, let alone casting, where the very precision of the description may be a problem or lead to the wrong actor getting the part. It's rare for a writer to have a great deal of input into casting—unless you've written a part exclusively for an actor and know that he or she loves the part and will kill to get it!

What all characters need is what is called 'backstory' but might as well be called a biography. Dialogue and action can give some hints as to a character's full psychological make-up, but much more is generally needed for a producer, director, backer, casting agent and all the other interested parties to get the full picture of your creation. You don't need to write a complete biographical profile, but some consideration must be given to where the character has been and where he or she hopes to go. Some manuals advise using a sort of grid of binary opposites:

- Is the character internally or externally driven?
- Active or passive?
- Physical or cerebral? And so on . . .

But all this can end up looking like a mathematical equation. Though it may be helpful as you begin scripting, it probably will not be useful beyond the early consideration of your character. The simpler and clearer way to achieve a fix on the character is to draw up a background for the character that pays attention at least in part to:

- the look;
- the name (normally you'll have imagined the appearance of the character before considering the right name);
- the speaking style (dialogue);
- behaviour (expected, and occasionally unexpected);
- any personal tics or traits (often called tags or markers).

We'll look at these in detail in a moment. But when planning a long-running show that may have several writers—and may even exclude you as creator of the show if you're unlucky—a much more complex backstory is necessary.

Here's how writer Gordon Williams drew upon a character initially created in a novel co-written with soccer star Terry Venables, writing under the name P. B. Yuill. The character is a private eye called Hazell. The actual character sketch runs to over a thousand words but this is a representative sample:

> HAZELL is in his early or mid-thirties, divorced, slightly old-fashioned, big, good-looking, slightly battered and has an intermittently painful ankle.
>
> He has mass tastes: *Daily Mirror*, slightly old-fashioned pop music, films and paperbacks—yet is aware of being conned by the mass media and makes critical remarks of a common-sense, perhaps simplistic, kind.
>
> London is his only possible environment. Birmingham he would think of as Siberia, Scotland as Zululand. Yet he is painfully conscious of the size and anonymity and unfathomable diversity of the vast sprawl.
>
> He is continually looking for Miss Right, for kids of his own, for a chance to push a pram down High Street on Saturday morning. Naturally he's not going to get these things.

> (Gordon Williams, BFI 1978)

In this extract from a virtual short story about Hazell we find the clues to what makes him tick, how he'll react to certain situations, how he'll talk, what he drinks and where . . . and so on. A complete guidebook, in other words, to a voyage around a character. Also suggested is the sort of place where you might expect to find the character: in the more colourful, rougher parts of London—Soho, Clapton Dog stadium, Battersea Heliport, Shepherds Market and Southbank, perhaps.

Of course it helps in such a series that the writers and executive producer (Verity Lambert for Thames Television) also decided on a voice-over narration, in the tradition of Raymond Chandler and used to great effect in Ridley Scott's *Blade Runner*. The actor's voice can set up a mood in a quite different way from an establishing shot of a warm July evening:

SCENE 1. EXT. STREET. DAY ONE.

HAZELL (VO)

Tracking down the Abrey family was like a trip down memory lane, a warm July evening in the east end of London Town and I was thinking ain't life grand. I was earning at last, I had a new motor, new gear and it was at least a month since I'd stopped trying to drink myself into the happy communism of the graveyard. Nothing could be finer in the state of semolina.

POV HAZELL, we see high-rise blocks.

Herbert Morrison House was your usual barrack block in the sky. You don't have to be poor to live there, but it helps.

(from: First Draft script, 'Hazell Plays Solomon', 1978)

It is very rare to have the luxury of a wise-cracking characterful voice-over like this—but you can see how the writers have poured a great deal of the backstory into these few words and set up the character as a true relation of Philip Marlowe and all the other knights of the Mean Streets. Character voice-over like this is not only rare, it's unfashionable at the moment—but that doesn't mean it won't be back, like *Terminator*, to win the day again, and give a lot of pleasure to screenwriters and audiences alike.

Looks and the unbelievable truth

Looks, as they say, aren't everything, but it's often a help to suggest a personal style or an aura from which the reader can get a sense of 'uniqueness' about the character. As well, you can add in physical traits that may (like Hazell's occasional limp) prove a useful plot element.

One potential problem is that of basing the look (or traits) of a character on someone you know (in a worst case: yourself!). This almost always leads to great arguments in the script editing process about how certain actions or looks (blond hair for example) are essentials, because they are 'true'. Just because something has actually happened in your universe or someone looked a certain way in 'real life' doesn't mean that this will necessarily work in a script. Just the opposite is more often the case.

For you are now, early in the script process, too close to your drama to see the problems that may have arisen.

Never, ever (please) use the actual events in life that might have triggered a particular script or character as a *justification* for the character and his or her onscreen actions. The world of the living and the dead may be the source and inspiration of all drama, but actual events should never take over from the dramatic imagination.

WRITER (reacting to criticism, aggrieved): But—it happened *just* like that.

ANOTHER WRITER (sobbing): But—she . . . she always behaved like that.

Real events, even ones that have deeply touched you or those close to you, are not automatically going to turn into beautifully working and deeply affecting scripts. If it were that simple, a transcript of your friends talking would suffice. And does anyone really have friends like *Friends*?

It is much better to let your mind's eye rework the world into a better—and dramatically more effective—representation, through the imagined appearance and actions of your scripted creations.

> Your movie or series is called *The Back Room*. Remember the pitch for it? It's about a group of computer hackers who think they are Robin Hoods.
>
> Write brief descriptions of your five central continuing characters. Again, don't forget to create a semi-permanent opposition (a government agency? Crims?) for your team.
>
> Now give them all names!

Names

Just because you know of someone called Aloysius in your street doesn't mean that now is a great time to use this otherwise splendid name for your protagonist. It might work—or it could send off all the wrong signals.

Naming characters is something that requires a lot of thought, keen social observation and a good ear. Whether we like it or not, most of us have prejudices when it comes to names. These feelings may be because of events in the family, at school (a bully named Dick) or around the neighbourhood. It may be as simple as an aversion to all of the apostles' names, just on principle. Crawford Productions used to have a long list of names, particularly sur-

names, that were not to be used at all (particularly for criminals)
and this list was compiled with possible legal action in mind.
Certainly you shouldn't name a character for someone you love or
loathe for those reasons alone, though the name may be perfect (at
first sight). You may even find your writing becoming skewed as
emotions leaked by the names seep out!

In general there are many neutral names—Jenny, Julie, Tom,
Bill, Mary—and then there are names that seem to carry a freight
of social meaning. Cedric, Cyril, Hepzibah, Doris, Clarissa? Forget
it. For various and obscure reasons, these names are just saddled
with unfortunate connotations. Of course, this has never stopped
an entire generation from naming their children Seagull, Skychild,
Meadowlark and Chastity. If you want to 'tag' your characters as
from a certain generation you probably need to check out 1960s
and '70s names—and then make sure that your character reveals
that he or she has always loathed the name bestowed by zonked
parents back in the Woodstock Years!

If the character works, the name will probably grow on the audience until it seems the most natural thing in the world: think of
Nice Guy Eddie in *Reservoir Dogs*. What kind of name is that? But
then again, what kind of movie title is *Reservoir Dogs*? Or the John
Duigan film *Lawn Dogs* (1997) for that matter? Perhaps a little
mystery is no bad thing, after all. Just don't get carried away: *Who
Is Harry Kellerman and Why Is He Saying Those Terrible Things
about Me?* (Ulu Grospard, 1971) probably holds the world record
for bad titles!

Overall, you should be wary of cute, bizarre, pretentious, mytho-
logical or classical names. 'Ulysses' and 'Paris', for example, might
be all right for specific characters, but otherwise carry connotations of pretension. It's a good idea to say your names aloud to see
if there is likely to be a chance of mis-hearing (Troy, Roy, for example). It may not matter in the long run, but it can drive some members of your audience up the wall!

In general, any name that carries baggage from earlier uses in
other stories or historical events is awkward and troublesome: for
example, Adolf, Madonna (now, though not so much twenty years
ago, apart from the possible offence to religious sensibilities),
Homer (which might have been okay before *The Simpsons*).
Generally speaking, the wider your reading the more you are likely
to stumble upon names that carry meanings that can set up
blocks to audience understanding of and sympathy (or loathing)
for them.

One popular sport for tyro writers is to use 'funny' names for
their creations. For some reason names like Pansy, Hildegard, and
their floral or operatic fellows are considered amusing by some
writers. The last thing you want to do is draw undue attention to

characters by eccentric naming. Try it yourself—or just try *being* Ethelred for a day. After that, you'll be more cautious.

Pin the tail on the characters

Try to name the characters and pay special attention to the effects names can have on the way they are perceived, especially by other writers or producers. Name all the characters, then expand the character descriptions.

Here's a short character line-up for a projected television series called *Rags*, which we first met in Chapter 8:

KEY CHARACTERS (AS TYPES, NO NAMES YET)

ON THE SHOP FLOOR:

TERRY

She's indomitable and flamboyant, a Greek with wild red hair and a wilder lifestyle (with hangovers to match), and always bubbling. In the small cutting and manufacturing workshop, the workers have made her their natural leader.

THE GANG

There are the six youngish workers (mainly design school grads and then there's the matriarch (well, thirty-something!), who knows it all and used to work at GloWeave before the lights went out.

IN THE DESIGN SHOP:

SALLY

She's the star of the design show, but at fifty she has metamorphosed into a harder-edged 'power' version of her hippy 1960s self. With an almost fanatic zeal to make the company the best, she's finding it hard to come to terms with the fact that maybe they're just too far out of date.

JACK

He's Sally's husband, but the poor fellow often seems stuck in the styles, thinking and gear of the 1960s and 1970s. It's just as well the late 1990s has seen a '60s revival, because suddenly he feels he's *in* again. He's wrong. His misperceptions only encourage him in his truly out-of-sync schemes, which often extend beyond the Threads office into wild speculations in neo-punk bands or low budget movies.

POLLY (THE KID)

All of this parental folly is watched and taken advantage of by this very pragmatic daughter. She's a very sharp kid who dresses cool but runs very hot indeed. Her interests lie more in movies and movie-making; she wants only what she can get out of the company, while still insisting on having her dollar's worth at the boardroom table. She's the social and sexual motor of the series.

Notice the simple, neutral names!

Dark glasses, a sneer and a cane

Each character you create should have some distinctive trait, generally of personality, perhaps even a peculiarity of speech. This can, for smaller roles, be more of a guide to the casting agent. For example:

> BORIS is a short pockmarked figure in a soiled trenchcoat. He chews endlessly on a burnt-out matchstick.

This gives enough detail about a character's appearance, as well as a distinctive feature by which the audience will know him or her.

For Chaplin's *Little Tramp*, we had the bowler and the cane. For Leonardo Di Caprio in *Titanic*, there are the cowlick and the ever-present sketchpad. The traits or attributes serve to define the character and make it memorable.

All human beings have singular personality traits, often several, by which we recall them, but for the mass media the traits should be simplified rather than multiplied. Your job is to invent or use that single significant trait that can do so much of the character work for you. In *Love Serenade*, Dimity's pathetic gift of a balloon featuring the words 'I Wuv You' starts off seeming like a sign of her infantile approach to life, but ends up as a tragi-comic marker of her vulnerability and, in the last scene, of the generally comic nature of an unfathomable Universe.

Sometimes a memorable trait or habit can play a part in the plot. In almost every movie that features a ghost returning to earth (*Heaven Can Wait*, *Ghost*, *Always*, *Sixth Sense*) the memories of the living are always flagged by a verbal or a physical sign that others suddenly recall and recognise: 'It's . . . it's you, isn't it, Jack?'.

A classic example of the imagination providing the surface cues to a character are in Jean Luc Godard's rule-breaking movie, *Breathless* (1959). Jean Paul Belmondo plays the small-time crim who's obsessed with the screen persona of Humphrey Bogart. Godard gives us the clues by salting the movie with cutaways of cinema featuring a 'Bogey' movie, then has Belmondo saunter up and gaze in awe at a one-sheet poster of his cinematic hero, the guy on whose style he's modelling his life. Then Belmondo imitates a trademark Bogey gesture, touching his face in just the way that Bogey had, then uttering the magic word 'Bogey!'. He'll repeat the gesture later and even adopt a pseudonym based on a Bogey role. Movies meet real life—or maybe vice versa. In the very underestimated American 'remake' of *Breathless* (Jim McBride, 1983), Richard Gere as the young hustler also finds himself imitating Elvis and in the last, violent, scene, confronts the guns of the police with a hip shakin' routine.

Tags or traits as clear as this can make a screen character utterly memorable, but they can also act as a reminder of what the character is all about as you're writing the role. And of course, actors love you for it!

As a writer it is important that you do not over-describe your character's physical appearance, or cling to these descriptions as production looms. It's interesting to note how often casting choices have not only changed the advertised appearance of a leading part, but even the sex as well!

That said, backstory becomes all the more important in defining the actual engine room of your drama: the leads.

A word on gender

One terror for writers is that of writing for characters of the opposite (or same!) gender. Gender plays a major role in your character make-up, particularly in this age of equality. Your characters—unless you're making a particular social point about victims—will be aware of the great social changes that feminism has brought, as well as those that it has not.

Equal or not, though, men and women do react to threat and challenges differently. Feminism never meant to eradicate difference completely—just to create a balance and equity.

It can in fact be a fascinating concept to make your character act in an atypical way—not just for the sake of a gag, as with *Mrs Doubtfire* (Chris Columbus, 1994), or *Tootsie* (Sydney Pollack, 1982), where the cross-dressing is the joke. Some of the laughs in these rather heavy-handed movies seem more than a little hollow, based as they are so firmly on older gender stereotypes.

Of course, sometimes a script will benefit from reworking a character as one of the opposite sex—or working the fine line of androgyny as actually happens with the *Alien* series right through to the end. Ripley is first a warrior and only in the largely ignored backstory a mother—until the last *Alien Resurrection* (Marc Jeunet, 1997).

No rules or psychiatric texts can help you here. Only your own observation and an absolute openness to the complexities, assumptions and myths about sexuality will make your writing of characters work.

Tread carefully, for you tread on many dreams.

Finding characters

And if, finally, as you stare at the wall, you see a thousand characters file past but are unable to pin down what drives them, you might try checking off a list of attributes, then refining this down to the character you want.

Basic questions about your character's backstory can run to more than fifty if you follow some advice in recent writing manuals (Dyas, 1990 and Wolff and Cox, 1988). Computer software programs for writers, such as Collaborator, interrogate you like a major market research focus group. Indeed, Collaborator typically provides a complex physiological and psychological questionnaire before you start, to keep you on the approved path. But sanity dictates that you keep it simple. Software like this is for the utterly confident or totally clueless.

Character is the second of Aristotle's key elements of drama. The others are plot, thought, diction, music and spectacle, all of which are still star players in the craft of writing for the media, though under different names. Diction is obviously dialogue, spectacle nowadays can mean everything from scenery to High Concept.

But here are the rock bottom basics you should get down on paper:

- Name (obviously, but let it change if it must, no big deal here).
- Sex (yes).
- Age and looks (approximately—don't get stuck with this; it's not that critical unless it's the plot point itself).
- Family background and education (this may be essential to the dialogue).
- Dialogue (speech): how does the character speak? This will have to be consistent and may be the key to the role. Eliza Doolittle is hardly the only fictional (or real) character utterly defined to others by the way she speaks. So speech can even be the gauge by which other characters judge each other.
- Ties (family, criminal, whatever is relevant).

- Intelligence (as opposed to education—you know they're not the same thing! Don't you?).
- Job and/or aims (often a key to plotting, too).
- Philosophy (could be as brief as 'Life sucks').
- Politics (maybe—for dialogue purposes, or as a key plot point for, particularly, baddies or their outfit (The Church, CIA, KGB, ASIO, etc.).
- How does the character feel about the others and the past? Think of the importance of Riggs (Mel Gibson) grieving for his young wife in the first *Lethal Weapon* (Richard Donner, 1987)—and how the sequels lacked that subtext and were the sillier (though just as lucrative) for it.

These questions should give you all you need to know to start writing. If not, you probably do need that computer software, or a whole new character and plot.

Here's a fairly basic character description from the screen adaptation of the novel *My Love Had a Black Speed Stripe* (Harry Williams, 1974). Meet Ron and Rose:

> RON (central character): Young, good-looking Australian, about 25 to 28. Superficially he's utterly normal; he likes football, girls, beers with his factory mates and his 'old pack'. But under the strain of marriage he has a deep-rooted misanthropy which turns itself into a total obsession with motor cars.
>
> ROSE (his wife): She is from a poor family but she has 'aspirations'. Her outlook is limited by house, washing machine and the romantic bliss peddled by the women's magazines. Her girlish simplicity cannot even begin to combat RON's concealed but very real neurosis.

Now, these are basic descriptions indeed, and in the draft of the full screenplay would be information fed out as and when the characters appear and act. But generally, to write much more than this for public scrutiny is to invite unnecessary criticism.

We'll return to Ron and Rose in Chapter 10 and see what they're up to in more detail.

How to find your character in other writings
But what if even these simple processes fail and all you have left is a list of attributes, a dossier that would do credit to the CIA—and still no character who grabs you? Or you find out (too late!) that you and your cast couldn't care less and have nothing to say about your character?

There's a simple way of finding out what you really might want to say before you start writing: by testing your reactions to some metaphorical triggers.

Think of your favourite poems, or a song. Just a line will do. What are the words really about, and why do they haunt you?

For starters, here is a line from a poem by Thomas Wyatt. Its central image can conjure up a maze of human interactions and relationships:

> They flee from me that one time did me seek
> With naked foot, stalking in my chamber?

It's poetry and it's old (sixteenth century, to be exact). But the image of someone (young, old, rich, poor) abandoned by lovers or friends is as modern as tomorrow.

Challenge:

Try to tease out and sketch a character based on Wyatt's two lines. You'll have to make artistic decisions (based on your own feelings) about whether to set it in the past (Casanova, maybe) or right now (an abandoned and ruined businessman alone in a flat).

The choices are nearly infinite, but the characters you begin to build will also bring with them the plot for your script. You may even decide that the image of loss is so intriguing that you want to find a real-life human interaction and make a documentary. The Maysles Brothers' classic *cinéma vérité* film *Grey Gardens* (1976), about two former society princesses alone in a decaying mansion on Long Island, is as riveting as classic tragedy, a poem to loss.

If old poets don't do it for you, try this line from Stevie Smith's more recent poem: 'not waving but drowning . . .'

It's so evocative that a band swiped it for their name, then reversed the title to be 'not drowning, waving', which sort of loses the point.

But think of the range of characters that can spring from this one image. The middle-class business type who's so superficially upbeat about his or her lifestyle and success has been the subject of so many dramas, and the plot range is infinite—from tragedies like *Falling Down* (Joel Schumacher, 1993) to darker comedies such as *Planes, Trains and Automobiles* (John Hughes, 1987).

Whatever quote, catchphrase, or fragment of a novel, prose, or poetry has stuck in your mind, it's there for a reason! Why?

Try this little exercise and you'll soon find that it is your own fascinations or maybe obsessions that emerge—and suddenly you'll have not just one human interaction but a whole world of them.

And maybe they'll bring your plot along with them. Good characters usually do.

Chapter 10
The Plot Thickens

There are these characters that fascinate you. And maybe a hint of something that's going to happen to them. The rest is blank.

So let's assume that you've decided you do still have something you want to say dramatically, after all. Exactly *how* you tell the story and in what order is the plot. Plots, like jelly beans or poems, come in different forms and flavours.

As we've noted already, episodic television and the miniseries are very different from feature films, not least because the feature film (whatever its length) has no arbitrary breaks or other structural laws imposed by the medium. There's nothing more sobering than watching your show cut from a moment of deep emotion to an ad for Aeroplane Jelly!

Although feature films are free of externally imposed interruptions, they nonetheless must have structure and many will tell you that the structure should be a 'classic' three-act one. Well, maybe. More importantly—and this is not something we owe to structuralist or semiotic theory—any story needs a beginning, a middle, and an end.

Of course it's got to be a little more complex than that. Basically, for a story to work you need:

- a set-up: a scenario where we meet the key characters (or at least hear about them);
- an action or a series of actions that changes the balance discovered in the first part. This is normally the major part of the story;
- a climax! Resolution (maybe). Things are changed! Industry toughs like to call this the payoff—which is a reasonable characterisation given that you're writing for a hungry audience, but doesn't mean much in dramatic terms.

It sounds like a simple formula, but this is precisely where most dramas come unglued.

It's all a plot

Let's start by looking at the most minimal story form: the commercial. Let's say you want to convey the ineffable joys gained by listening to a particular radio station that has an area of musical territory marked out for itself—great rock tracks of the sixties, perhaps. With this sort of 'product', as with commercials that focus on the 'corporate image' of a company, your aim is to create positive feelings about the organisation rather than to hard-sell a product. You're selling 'mood' and that means drama in its simplest form.

What you need is:

- that set up;
- a vision of the joys associated with rock and roll; and
- a resolution that produces a favourable outcome as a result of the musical experience.

Here's how one award-winning campaign did it:

ACT ONE

VIDEO	AUDIO
Montage of shots of a feisty independent-looking girl getting up, snatching a breakfast, leaping in the mini-moke and fighting the peak hour evening traffic to get to work.	Montage of rock tracks about hassles, conformity, how tough it is to make it in a tough, smoggy old world.

That's the set-up.

ACT TWO

VIDEO	AUDIO
The girl arrives at a music recording studio and is greeted by a groovy pack of pro musos—session artists all. We realise she's the lead singer. Montage as they jam, laying down tracks like there's no tomorrow.	Music reflects 'getting together' and harmonies musical and personal.

That's the action part—the transformation—or the middle if you like.

ACT THREE

VIDEO	AUDIO
Dawn. The girl and two session musos emerge, laughing, tired, heading for a burger joint, maybe.	Music to climax: coming together, people and good rock and roll beat the middle class slog any day . . . (heaps of tracks around to do this—we can't afford the copyright, so write it yourself!)

Now, that's your payoff: a complete story in thirty or forty-five seconds, leaving a feeling that the circle has been squared—in other words a complete little plot.

Longer stories need more plot action, but the basic principles remain the same.

The minimal story

In the internationally award-winning short film *Swinger* (1996), Gregor Jordan achieves the same classic three-part structure in one shot and in one continuous time frame.

The camera pans across an untidy bachelor's pad as the answering machine records aloud a series of cruelly comic messages commiserating with the occupant about the loss of his girlfriend, his job—and as we reach the swinging legs of the hanged man—apparently his life.

A room and a life in tatters make up the first two parts of the story—and it would be flat if it ended there (though still comic and bizarre).

But the last messages turn events around—the job, the love affair are still intact. Too late!

Suddenly, shockingly, the legs kick and the hanged man returns to life and prepares to free himself. A life crisis in three parts moves from tragedy, to sudden hopes, to a final, breathless escape from death. *Swinger* is a classic short drama—and deeply satisfying as a story.

The structure is also that of the classic joke, where the expected turns to the wholly absurd and inverts audience expectations.

Now obviously these two minimal narratives use plot structure at its most basic, but they do use it—and audiences responded. The important thing to notice is that the turning point—in the commercial the music session, in the case of *Swinger* the last-minute reprieve (just like *The Perils of Pauline*!)—is what makes the story something more than a sketch. No turning point, no plot.

Why three acts?

Although the Aristotelian notion of the three-act structure as essential leaves out almost all experimental movies, it is still the basic one. It is important to realise, too, that it is that 'classic' structure with which those who come to assess your work are most familiar and comfortable. Therefore, if you have other than arthouse success in mind, it is that structure that will be deemed necessary as you begin building your plot. Plot and three-act structure (the story) are very different. The three-act structure is the hidden motor of your drama. The plot elements are all the little actions that contribute to the whole narrative flow—pace, character, and momentum. They get your audience to the end, and keep them with you on the journey.

If the idea of the three-act structure as the basic building unit of drama seems blindingly obvious to you, keep in mind that plenty of scripts fail because they simply fail to sell the story (convince the audience to go with the flow). The story that the author is struggling so hard to communicate should never be far from the minds of the viewer. The simplest errors of omission are easy to spot and deadly to a plot. For example:

- Digressing from the story. This includes flashback disease, Tarantino anecdotal twitch and other ways of sidetracking the yarn so that the digressions take over the plot. Digressions and sidetracks can be quirky and appealing, but if they end up replacing the original plans you've made, you'll lose the audience—as well as the plot.
- If you don't define what the lead character(s) want so that the audience are caught in the same defined universe as your protagonists, then no amount of drama in the climax will make the whole drama work from soup to nuts.
- Last-minute solutions used to be called the *deus ex machina*—a reference to a very stagey device whereby a God descends from the stage roof to fix things up, regardless of what has occurred in the drama before this arrival.

All of the above, of course, are terrific in moderation and there are plenty of scripts that have worked precisely by using these deviations or short cuts. But using a film like *Reservoir Dogs* as a model (it has the lot!) could be a mistake. Take away the flashbacks and rearrange them and you have a classic and unified drama. What made it seem so fresh was precisely the exceptionally well thought-out breaking of so many conventions—while all the time Tarantino hewed close to the strong central line of plot and character.

Hits and myths

The best way to keep to the line of your script is to have an overview of what the story is all about from the start. Apart from the importance of having a short outline written before writing, you should also have at least some idea of where the story is heading before you begin. Some novelists can start with a flying leap at the word processor, but scripts are above all machine documents: they contain all the instructions and clues necessary for a finished production, as a way of preventing either too much reliance on the technical or, conversely, too much free association in the writing of the script. A relaxed approach to structure is dangerous in any form of scriptwriting. None of this is intended to cramp your creativity, just to remind you that a script has more than one function. When it comes to production, the script, along with a short outline, is perhaps the only document that will sell your ideas to the producers.

That outline has another function. It may be the only material you write that the overworked producer or house script readers get to read. If it isn't clear, then however good your script, it may be forever unread, let alone produced. Remember, we've already looked at this and other hurdles in Chapter 8 'The Pitch'.

For Italian semiotician Umberto Eco, the success of *Casablanca* was not that it had an original plot line, but rather that it simply used a series of historical myths. Eco felt that the characters were all made up of old stories, that is to say, recycled plots, so that Bogart himself embodied at least three familiar types of story: the Ambiguous Adventurer, the Lovelorn Ascetic and the Redeemed Drunkard. The plot he saw as a confection of myths: 'They're Playing Our Song, The Last Day in Paris, The Last Outpost on the Edge of the Desert . . .' and so on. Of course, you can play this game with any plot and it is likely that the more popularly successful the film, the more rewarding the game (*Star Wars* and *Titanic* come to mind). But you still have to find a way of enlivening the familiar. That's where structure comes in.

Act One: Throw the dice

As this may be the last page the script reader looks at, make it good. There are plenty of ways to start a drama, but turgid description is certainly not one of them:

SCENE ONE. DAWN. THE MOUNTAINS. DAY ONE.
The slow light creeps across the ineffable beauty of the Tasmanian hills and slowly the feathered orchestra begins to strike up their dawn performance.

Of course, if you are absolutely determined to show that this is Literature, and if you are adapting a Great Book, then this approach might work. It certainly did for Fred Schepisi, whose released script for *The Chant of Jimmy Blacksmith* (1978) was flowery in the extreme. But the production was by then a done deal so a little poetic licence was in order. This is not a path to be followed too enthusiastically in either general fiction or in scripts.

But every script (yes, even for radio) starts with an evocation of place. It can open slowly, or it can begin abruptly with an in-your-face action sequence: nowadays a wild car chase or a shoot-out is *de rigeur*. *Mercury Rising* (Harold Becker, 1998) begins with an extended shoot-out, with the hero, undercover agent Art Jeffries (Bruce Willis), caught in the middle of a blood bath. The sequence could have been extended to make a film story in itself, but is in fact just another example of what seems to be a house rule for mainstream drama: a longish action set piece that also established a key backstory element for the hero.

Witness (Peter Weir, 1985) starts out quietly enough with scenes of Amish life—a strong visual counterpoint to the quickly intercut scenes of murder that follow.

Both openings are highly visual, and both use dialogue sparingly. They also perform the key action of the first act: they set up the story so that we know who the main characters are, what they do in the world of the script, and even establish right away what sort of drama this is—character drama, genre (thriller), ensemble piece (*As Good as it Gets*, James L Brooks, 1988) or whatever mix you have decided on. Mix and match is fine, as long as you let the audience in on the secret early enough.

All this is accomplished in around ten script pages for a feature film, less for other types of script, but leaving plenty of script 'space' for the all-important middle of your drama—the part where things get done!

From now on, with luck, the audience will go all the way with you.

Act Two: The frying pan and the fire

We've met the key players in the story and we know where they're coming from, and now we want to see where they're going. In a feature film you'll have about sixty or so script pages out of around 100; in an hour drama, thirty or fewer, and so on down the sliding scale of dramatic time.

The middle is where the protagonist falls or jumps or is pushed out of the frying pan into the fire. In a classic chase narrative like *The Fugitive* (Andrew Davis, 1993) or *US Marshals* (Stuart Baird, 1998), the actual set-up takes ten minutes; the serial chases and the attempts of the fugitive to discover the secret (or the treasure, the love, etc.) that will make him free run almost to the last five minutes of a two-hour film. That's a lot of 'middle', but this is what the action fans want.

Everyone in a movie must *want* something, or already possess something they want to keep. The attempt to get it or keep it is often called the Quest or the Journey, but Hitchcock put it best when he called the thing that everyone wants the maguffin (plans, photos, nowadays very often a computer disk).

Certainly, whether it's a chase, a murder investigation, slapstick comedy or a long courtship that we're watching in the second act, this is the hardest and most demanding part of the writing. Each event throws up another possibility—who are the natural allies of the hero? Are some characters hiding their real motives? This is where the whole machinery of your plot must swing into action. Let's stay with Act Two and investigate the very basis of plotting further.

Oh no—the binary plot machine again!

Everything we do in life—and thus, logically, everything in a dramatic plot, which imitates life or presents it in a more linear, understandable form—is the result of binary choices. In the first act, had our hero looked left instead of right he would never have seen the beautiful woman framed in her window, being attacked by a bulky and menacing man just as in *Rear Window* (Alfred Hitchcock, 1954).

Plot is really a series of your choices which must in the end lead to your desired conclusion. However absurd the ending may seem if viewed in isolation, it must be set up by the causal or emotionally satisfying (logic does not always work!) chain leading up to it—and most of this work is done in the middle of the drama. The last scene of *Romancing the Stone* (Robert Zemeckis, 1984) has the heroine (Kathleen Turner) surprised in the street by a truck carting an ocean-going yacht bearing the grinning hero (Michael Douglas). Silly? Not in the world of this film genre or of the characters: romance novelists and adventurers. All the narrative and character choices then combine to make the ending seem charmingly natural. Every film story has its own internal logic. And audiences will go with you and your heroes whatever you decide.

The more choices you make to introduce new plotting points, the faster the action, the greater the momentum of the story. But whether a drama is slow or fast, the relationship between the scenes may be causal, visual, plain arbitrary—but in the end must seem a natural part of the dramatic flow. Audiences will accept improbability even if critics baulk at it, but they will never accept patent and wilful silliness, unless you are Monty Python.

Make sure the stakes are high

The cumulative effect of all these binary plot choices means that the drama will be functioning best if the challenges, obstacles and dramatic confrontations are progressively upping the ante. That there should be more and more at stake as a drama proceeds may seem obvious. But it is very easy—and tempting—to throw your biggest challenge at the protagonist up front. Then you run the risk of leaving your audience stranded on a mountain peak as your characters plod on along the valleys.

It is in this section that your character is heading towards the final battle or confrontation—the Moment of Truth. Earlier we referred to the telephone booth from which Superman emerges for the final battle. Whether your character is a writer with a block, a lover about to lose all, or a superhero doesn't matter. Sooner or later the big moment approaches. You can always be sure that audiences will recognise what's going on. The hero must always reach a low point, when the worst that can happen has—the bleakest moment for him or her. After your protagonist is brought low, the next door is a telephone box, because the worst, as we all know, brings out the best in a hero. How you approach that is dictated by how you have decided to pace your drama, and this is literally a matter of timing.

All in the timing

Pacing in drama means a great deal more than just a hectic or leisurely succession of events which you cut between with appropriate frequency. It's true that a chase scene can be structured in that way, but here we're talking about scenes that may involve a range of emotional registers—and that pacing will be different for every script you write.

European films particularly, for example Eric Rohmer's *Moral Tales*, are sometimes regarded as being about 'nothing much'. But, in fact, the best so-called art house films and plenty of mainstream movies can be as riveting as a thriller and engross the audience without need of pyrotechnics. To do this you need to have the utmost confidence in your characters and the courage to let them talk—and even to be seen 'just thinking'!

Certainly some genres demand speed, but audiences will trust you and go with the pace you set, provided you keep up the human intensity. Sometimes that can be done visually (or aurally) by letting image and sound tell the story, all the while remembering that your work is not destined for the print media. Not many viewers will not stay around for digressions, or beautifully written or 'artistic' passages with no plot purpose.

Pacing is not something that has rules, since any rules are determined by the nature and form of the story you are telling. To paraphrase the samurai character, James Coburn in the *Magnificent Seven* (John Sturges, 1960), you are only 'competing against yourself'.

This also means that the artificial injection of an action sequence into the drama—a pointless car chase, say, or a gratuitous death—still leaves you with the problem you had before you inserted the scenes: why did you feel the need to spice up the action? What was missing anyway? Most often the answer is that you had drifted away from the protagonist's main purpose, and hence potentially also lost the audience along the way.

Back to the real action—the moment of truth is upon you and your drama.

Act Three: The final conflict

Now the whole reason for writing at least an outline of your whole script is clear. In fact, though, by the time you've typed on through the emotion-drenched or hilarious middle of things you may well have changed your mind about what will happen. And that's quite reasonable of you. Nothing should be set in stone unless you're writing to a very tight contract.

The increasingly powerful role of the preview audience focus group in America is no secret any more. When you realise that so many films suffer considerable surgery in the last act as the result of these previews, you might well feel that there is no justice for the honest writer. But, just consider the numbers of producers credited on major mainstream movies. Would you really expect so many cooks not to spoil the broth? Even *Jurassic Park* (Steven Spielberg, 1993) was subject to a reworked ending. At least no one (it is assumed) attempted to alter the end of *Schindler's List* (Spielberg, 1993).

Sliver (Philip Noyce, 1993), which ended with Tom Berenger's character revealed via a video camera as the villain, wasn't going to end that way—until after the previews. Even more mysteriously, though the whole movie is set *inside* the 'Sliver' apartments, a film crew was dispatched to a volcano in Hawaii to shoot a new ending! Sadly, the helicopter crashed, although the crew survived and still won't give away the proposed new climax. Hawaii?

Many dramas play it safe by offering several endings. Indeed, this is expected in genre works, notably horror series like *Halloween* (John Carpenter, 1978) and almost anything from the Hammer Studios, where the last (or even post-credits) scene has to contradict the previous gruesome killing of the monster by hinting at a later return from the grave.

Other obvious examples of the multiple ending include almost all recent action movies, where shoot-out succeeds shoot-out until the whole movie runs out of puff. This sort of ending is not what you'd call a resolution in the classic sense, but in the age of the sequel who wants to write The End too soon?

The end the way you wrote it

All good things come to an end, and in your ending must lie the resolution, if not the solution to the problems set up and lived through in the first two acts. The last scenes are all about closing down plot lines, resolving problems, maybe leaving others for the audience to ponder. But there must be an ending that carries with it a sense of rightness, and satisfaction of a sort. In action movies that's easy: there's a final shoot-out (followed in early James Bond movies by the signature sexy sunset clinch).

In more character-based drama the ending will arise from some realisation on the part of the protagonists that there is a way out of all this. In romantic comedy like *When Harry Met Sally* (Rob Reiner, 1989) and *Sleepless in Seattle* (Nora Ephron, 1993), the two lead characters simultaneously see what has been staring the audience in the face all through the movie: they're mad for each other. Both films succeed by providing a resolution that has been anticipated by the public all along! It's a great trick, simple in effect and hard to pull off without becoming cloyingly sweet.

All genre narratives, therefore, can be said to have a built-in guarantee of an ending that the audience knew was coming all along—in fact they demand it. Did anyone really doubt that Gary Cooper in *High Noon* (Fred Zinnemann, 1952) or Clint Eastwood in *Unforgiven* (Clint Eastwood, 1992) would blow away the opposition in the climactic scene? Only exactly how and when was uncertain. Indeed, the 'psychological' westerns of the 1950s specialised in second acts that are all dither and delay—for moral and ethical reasons, of course—then returned to blood and violence in the climax.

Even though contemporary audiences can handle a lot more ambiguity in their endings than audiences in the past, you still must pay attention to some of the little details—while characters that just 'disappear' in the last reel are common, this is not keeping faith with your audience or your work. Certainly no one minds that at least one murder is never explained in *The Big Sleep* (Howard Hawks, 1946). Style and Bogart win out over logic. This is *not* a good example to follow, in the matter of endings at least.

Looking at the Oscars in 1998, William Goldman wondered why in *LA Confidential* (Curtis Hanson, 1997) the ending just didn't work:

> An ending is for me the most important part of a movie and the hardest to make work. I think the ending of *Butch Cassidy* [George Roy Hill, 1969] is the best of any I've been involved with . . . The worst ending of any great film is *Psycho*'s—seven *minutes* of awful, awful psychobabble. . . Anyway as I sat there a deep chord of phoniness was struck . . . because

Russell Crowe, the cop who was killed in the house, he lived. Cromwell, the most lethal and evil guy in all of LA, missed. Crowe goes off into the sunset to live with [Kim] Basinger who—guess what—is a whore no longer. I'm sorry guys, you can't do that.

Goldman basically says that Hanson is trying to pull off an art film ending (evil exists, we can't win, etc.) *and* a Hollywood glitzy ending where the good guys win out, like Superman, and whores have a heart of pure platinum and everyone lives happily ever after. He ends:

But not in *LA Confidential*, it is dead wrong here, it is phony here and it kills what was and is a wonderful achievement. Just not wonderful enough.

(Goldman, 1998: 85)

The Goldman Test

See if you can spot the following problem in *Saving Private Ryan* (SKG/Spielberg 1998).

Remember that a **flashback** is always set up by a shot of the person involved in the flashback.

A woman staggers, clutches her brow—and we flashback to the past.

Now consider the opening scene of *Saving Private Ryan*. It's *now*. An old man weeps in front of a grave in an American war cemetery near Omaha Beach (the American landing zone featured). We move in and flashback: we are in the middle of the 1944 D-day landing. We seem to be there.

But . . . was the old man whose flashback this supposedly is, actually there on the beach in 1944?

Think about it.

The end

One last point about the three-act structure: of course you can write as many acts as you want, or start in the middle of things just like *Reservoir Dogs*. But analyse the plot and put it back into chronological order, and it still has a beginning, a middle and an end. Of course you may think it doesn't—but look closely. What you thought was another act was really the subplot all along!

Subplots: Chips with everything

Though your plot can be as simple and straightforward as a conversation, or even a wordless real time exploration of two people in
a room (and there are plenty of stage dramas that do with less),
there is still likely to be a subplot lurking somewhere. Subplot is
not the same thing as subtext (which is everything that isn't in the
text), but it can have profound effects on the structure and pacing
of your story.

Subplotting is a fascinating part of your work. It cannot be done
by simply writing a small-sized plot and then integrating it into
your script. It must be essential to the story you have decided to
make your main line of action, but it will carry less of the dramatic
freight.

Whether the subplot is about characters (friends, family) or
things (bureaucracies, big business, computers) it will bring shade
and often humour to your writing, for it is in the non-essential plot
moments that you can often convey enriching information about
the world the characters inhabit—even provide welcome relief
from the plot points that can come to seem endless to you.

Subplots can be as simple as a throwaway line from a character that lights up the drama, or a character hook that suggests
other stories to come: the classic line 'I'll be back' from the
Terminator series is credited to William Goldman. It suggests
much, while saying little. It can be a whole life—another world,
as when, in *Titanic*, Di Caprio takes Kate Winslet down to the
party in steerage, opening up romantic (and false) images of
authentic lives and real, down-to-earth pleasure. Or the subplot
can be a pervasive feeling; in *The Parallax View* (Alan J. Pakula,
1974) it is paranoia itself as the shadowy agents (CIA, NSA? it
doesn't matter) go about their twilight work until subplot and
plot merge in the final shot.

A more recent film, *Twilight* (Robert Benton, 1998) runs a similar
subplot in terms of menace as Paul Newman's ageing ex-cop edges
close to a dangerous affair with his employer's wife (Susan
Sarandon). Often it is a love interest that forms the most powerful
(and distracting) of all possible subplots. For love—with the constant hint of something much more important than whatever else
is going on—is always at the back of the audience's mind. But that's
another plot.

Hitting the wall: When plots fail

There comes a moment in most plots when the improbable meets
the unlikely and you can see no way out.

The answer is to rejig the whole plot—or let a character turn the
implausibility into the very texture of life itself.

Thus:

JACK

(sardonic) Oh, brilliant! Bill's plane landed just in time
for him to run into Marjorie in Customs. That's stretch-
ing it a bit!

MARY

Well, it happened—just like that!

JACK

God, this is getting more and more like a soapie!

It may well be. But at least Jack's speech has defused the rather
too convenient coincidence. After all, life is full of them—it's just
that audiences don't seem to accept chance as readily in drama.

Then there are the absurdities that circumstance and producers'
whims and foreign co-productions bring upon you. In the thriller
The Assignment (Christian Duguay, 1998), for reasons wholly to do
with financing, the CIA/Mossad training of Annibal Ramirez
(Aidan Quinn), who is to assume the fake identity of Carlos The
Jackal, takes place in the snows of Canada—even though the subsequent action will take place in the deserts of Libya.

The screenwriters could see the audience's objections to this
fatuity a mile off. But there wasn't much they could do, except to
have Annibal throw a tantrum at the end of the training, shouting
that it's ridiculous to train in the snow when he's about to be
shipped off to Libya. This ploy might not have worked perfectly—
but it helped.

Sometimes all you can do is tough it out. Annibal's enraged
plot-bashing certainly must have given the actors some minor pleasure, if nothing else.

Don't get it right, get it written (but get the copyrights first)

Of course, it may be that you have decided upon adaptation as the
way to go. You may also be influenced by the fact that the majority
of Oscars for Best Film in the 1990s have gone either to an adaptation from another medium (*Schindler's List* from Thomas
Keneally's book, *Schindler's Ark*) or from actual events—and even
from earlier movies (*Titanic* scores on both counts).

The adaptation of existing work can involve you in much more
work than you will save by borrowing a plot. Copyright and associated permissions and payments can be a nightmare, but if you do
have the rights in full or merely an option for a specific period of
time (cheaper), then this way into screenwriting can be enormously
rewarding.

Let's see what happens with a successful novel. It's one that has almost made it to the screen with three different writer and producer teams, *My Love Had a Black Speed Stripe*. The first problem is that this is a book told from only one point of view, and that view a decidedly restricted one. For the protagonist, Ron, is a man of very limited interests. Remember him from Chapter 9? He's the young, good-looking Australian bloke, utterly normal on the face of it, but with a pathological dislike for people and an obsessive fascination with automobiles.

In the novel, Ron, in short order, gets married, buys his dream car, buys a house, meets some interesting neighbours and decides to kill them and his wife after his car is defaced!

Yes, it's very dark comedy, which may tell us something all too familiar about certain Aussie obsessions. Of course all satire runs the risk that people will fail to get the message and become infuriated. Precisely this reaction greeted misanthropic movies, from the grimly realistic *The Boys* (Rowan Woods, 1998) and the darkly comic *In the Company of Men* (Neil La Bute, 1997). Both stories had a protagonist regarded as pure evil by some critics, but the intent was of course to condemn the sorts of behaviour depicted (vicious, sexist, even murderous male behaviour in *The Boys*), not to endorse it.

There is also very little by way of physical character description in the book—apart from the beauty of cars, that is. This is Ron's take on his wife Rose:

'She always looked good in those days. Never in curlers, hair and eyes shining, cool, sexy, spot on.'

As for cars:

'They talk about love at first sight with sheilas, but with sheilas I don't think it ever lasts like that. A sheila can knock you for six the first time you see her, hair, eyes, chassis, the lot, but it doesn't stay like that if you start seeing her a lot.'

The novel sets up the story very quickly and with far more detail about cars than people. So it was felt by one writing team that a psychological reason for Ron's obsessions might frame the story and give the plot an extra dimension. Another writing team disagreed, but here's how the 'psychological' backstory version begins:

SCENE 1. EXT. FARM CIRCA 1972. NIGHT.
The farm is very run down. A few trees straggle along the edge of the house. MARGE, RON's mother, is down at a dilapidated chicken run. She has just finished feeding the chickens. With a sigh she straightens up and trudges back to the house. Behind her the sun is slowly setting. Overhead,

there is the whoosh of a group of jets receding fast. She looks up at the sky for a moment, then climbs the verandah and goes in. After a moment she emerges onto the steps. She looks around her, searching.

MARGE

(Calling) Ron. Ron.

There is a squawk from the chickens and a small boy runs out from behind the chicken run.

MARGE

Hurry up.

RON runs towards the house. He joins his mother on the steps.

MARGE

Come on then.

She clucks at the mess all over his overalls. She pushes him inside.

SCENE 2. INT. FARM KITCHEN. NEXT DAY.
MARGE is rereading an old letter. The envelope lies by her on the kitchen table, its censor's stamp and Vietnam postmark clearly visible. RON ambles into the kitchen trailing a teddy bear by the arm. The toy is dirty, battered. RON comes up to her chair and points at the letter.

RON

Daddy.

He smiles at her. MARGE smiles back, clutching the letter.

MARGE

That's right. It's Daddy.

SCENE 3. EXT. ROAD NEAR FARM. SAME DAY.
The MAILMAN, a grizzled man of over forty, whistles as he drives the bent ute along the road.

SCENE 4. EXT. DRIVE NEAR FARM. SAME DAY.
The MAILMAN pulls up near the house. MARGE and little RON emerge. RON runs on ahead as the MAILMAN gets out and goes round to the back of the ute.

MAILMAN

'Day, Marge.

He continues to search. Finally he hauls out a large parcel and hands it across to MARGE.

> MAILMAN
>
> For the kid. Got his name on it. Oh, and there's a letter.

He finds the letter on the front seat of the ute. He hands it across. MARGE is ripping open the parcel as RON watches, fascinated. The MAILMAN steps behind them to watch. A beautiful red car is revealed, about a foot long and made of painted wood. RON squeals ecstatically.

> MAILMAN
>
> Jeez. Not bad. Must be payin' 'em OK over in 'Nam.

RON is overjoyed with the car. He gives it a push, delighted. The MAILMAN reaches for MARGE as she straightens. He caresses her breasts.

> MAILMAN
>
> How's it going, Marge?

> MARGE
>
> OK. How you doing?

> MAILMAN
>
> Same as usual. (pause, leers) How about it? I'm ahead this morning.

> MARGE
>
> Come off it, Norm. Not when I've just got a letter from Jack.

> MAILMAN
>
> What's the difference?

> MARGE
>
> I just don't feel like it. Not now.

MAILMAN scratches his head, puzzled. Then he grins and nods.

> MAILMAN
>
> OK. I'll be seeing you. (calls out to RON) Look after yer mum, Ronnie.

RON smiles deliriously. The MAILMAN climbs into his ute and starts it going. He waves and bounces off down the track. MARGE has already opened the letter after a cursory wave. She begins to read it, mouthing the words, as she walks back to the house. RON zooms by her, making car noises.

SCENE 5. INT. FAR—KITCHEN. DAY.
Open on an old radio. MARGE is listening to the news.

RADIO VOICE-OVER

. . . maintained an aggressive role in day and night attacks on Viet Cong-controlled zones. . .

During this, RON comes into the room pushing his some-what battered car. Teddy lies discarded in another corner of the room. MARGE ignores him. Outside, the honk of the MAILMAN's ute is heard. MARGE gets up and goes outside.

ANOTHER ANGLE
Through the window we see the MAILMAN, grim-faced, handing MARGE a telegram. She tears it open and stares, stricken at the contents. The MAILMAN makes as if to comfort her but she tears herself away and runs back to the house. RON is crooning to his car. MARGE enters clutching the telegram and throws herself, weeping, into the chair she had just vacated. RON twigs that something is wrong and looks up. He stares as she begins to keen, on the edge of total hysteria.

RADIO VOICE-OVER

. . . casualties had been extremely light and were less-ening daily as the Viet Cong supported by suspected N.V.A. troops have now been reduced to impotence against the combined American and . . .

MARGE sobs, helpless.

FADE IN OPENING TITLES
Move in slowly on RON, absolutely terrified. He stares wide-eyed at his mother, clutching the car tightly to him.

Now the story moves into the present. But the writers also felt that for Ron just to buy the new car that is going to become his obsession would be to ignore the dizzying media images of car ownership that create people like Ron (assuming they exist!). Thus another plot element comes in to act as motivation and a shorter line of subplot: the marketing of Ron's dream car. This necessitated the creation of an ad agency, a marketing campaign—and The Car:

SCENE 6. INT. ADVERTISING AGENCY. DAY. PRESENT.

It is an agency presentation room with a big screen and a bar, exotically furnished. LOGAN is standing by a chart stand, showing a graph of car sales predictions. The other two men are sitting back in large chairs. LOGAN flicks an intercom by the screen.

LOGAN

OK. Roll it.

He settles back into a nearby chair. The screen brightens.

SCENE 7. EXT. SAND DUNES. DAWN.

The commercial is one continuous shot, extreme telelens aimed at the rising sun. In the extreme distance a tiny car swells and grows, computer enhanced to the point of silliness. It is COUNTDOWN. The Supercar is heading for the camera. The sounds of sea and gulls are at first all that can be heard. As the commercial progresses, the sound of a powerful engine swells gradually, punctuated by the click and whine of super smooth gear changes.

VOICE-OVER

'Countdown'. Maybe you haven't bought your ticket to Mars just yet. Hold off a bit. And buy a ticket to the Outer Limits. 'Countdown'. It's on the way.

The car thunders up to and over the camera. A reverse shows it streaking away. In the corner of the scene a superimposed computer readout runs down from ten to zero. Freeze on the zero.

VOICE-OVER

'Countdown'. This time you'll be pressing all the right buttons.

The screen goes to black.

SCENE 8. INT. ADVERTISING AGENCY AS SC 6.

As the lights go on YES MAN ONE is out of his seat. His face is flushed with the ecstasy of it all.

LOGAN

Well?

YES MAN ONE

It works!

LOGAN

Yeah, well maybe. It's only a demo for the launch. But it's clean.

YES MAN TWO

As a whistle. That'll get them where they live. Why jazz it up when you've got a winner?

LOGAN

(grinning) And who doesn't want to be Arnie? In *Terminator 2*?

YES MAN ONE

Or *Twins*, maybe . . .

He's ignored.

The backstory has been structured as a series of key plot elements that give Ron motivation for his crazier impulses later on—and also provide a satirical commentary on the social context.

Now the plot can move into top gear and follow the novel's more simple and linear structure. Things won't 'just happen' as in the book; there will be a dramatic reason for them to happen, if no real explanation.

The plot has begun to thicken at last. It's time to look at the story business in detail. Series television is every writer's dream of a lifetime job, so let's start there.

Chapter 11
Writing Series TV

Nice work if you can get it

The majority of screenwriters who earn a regular living do so from two forms of screenwriting: corporate work and series drama. Whether these series are weekly soaps, episodic series like *Wildside* or miniseries, this is where most of the continuing work is. This is also the field where associations are most readily formed and writers become known, and hence relied upon to produce quality scripts.

A scan of the trade journals over the past twenty years shows a high degree of continuity among writers, although the production houses are always open to new talent. But they want talent that is well developed and able to handle the exigencies and forms of series television without need for training or special consideration. The old days of ABC traineeships or Hector Crawford's 'master's apprentices' have gone. That said, most production companies have former or experienced writers as creative chiefs; Simpson Le Mesurier, Gannon/Jenkins, for example, are partnerships of writers. Your job is to convince the old firms that they need your skills and freshness.

The more things change . . .

If you take a long view of television series, certain genres seem quite indestructible over the long run. Others evolve out of more recent success. *Wildside*, for example, is structurally very like episodes of *Division Four* or *Homicide*, when the focus is on police work rather than on the work of the legal centre. Indeed, the dialogue, though overlapped and more scatological and 'streetwise', is very similar to most earlier police shows, including *Division Four* (which had its rural counterpart twenty years on, in *Blue Heelers*).

On the other hand, *Wildside* can also be seen as a development of the more sociological concerns of the quality soap opera *Heartbreak High* (based on the feature film: Michael Jenkins,

1992), whose predecessor was *Blackboard Jungle* (Richard Brooks, 1955). *Wildside* comes from the same production team as *Heartbreak High*, and where these two series really differ from earlier successes in the TV series wars is in the technical 'look and feel' of the shows. They use overlapping dialogue (*Wildside* features a 'dramaturge' on the credits), nervy jump cuts and wobblycam (handheld camera) shots to jazz up the visual style. But listen to just the dialogue and you will hear a classically constructed drama piece that but for the 'language' could have been written any time in the last three decades. This simple truth should be more reassuring to writers than it is!

New series, old formulas

Television channels are always on the lookout for new series ideas, but for many it can be a long time between drinks. The Nine Network in Australia, for example, until the success in 1998 of *Good Guys, Bad Guys*, had done little by way of drama beyond the needs of the ABA Quotas and had had no real ratings success since *The Sullivans* (Crawford Productions) in the early 1970s (though that show is still playing in Ireland and other overseas markets).

Good Guys, Bad Guys, like many similar initiatives, went through several changes before it arrived on the screen in its final form. In a world where a single ratings point can be measured in millions of advertising and sponsorship dollars, the channel can end up with a lot of say in the creative outcome.

Good Guys, Bad Guys was originally developed as a telemovie series as a star vehicle for actor Marcus Graham, who had attracted favourable public and network notice in the very first *Halifax fp* telemovie (9/Simpson Le Mesurier, 1996). The initial brief from the network heads was to develop a series for the younger audience demographic (the *Heartbreak High*, *De Grassi High* ABC demographic set). The first pitch was for a character very like that of Harry Streets for *Streets and Rivers* (see Chapter 8)—a former SAS man who was demobbed after the Gulf War and returned, very disillusioned, to Australia to become a troubleshooter for hire. It's the classic private eye background. The channel liked the concept (what's not to like in such proven materials?) and ordered three telemovies.

At this point, as Roger Simpson tells it, the writers decided they didn't like the format of the new series and decided to take some more development time. This move reveals two key elements of the relationship between writers and networks.

First: if you can't argue from a position of power (Simpson Le Mesurier had a successful production company that had delivered the goods before) then you will have to be prepared for change imposed from outside.

Second: writers bargain better when they know their markets and their audiences—and have a 'bankable' star in the package.

The team next came up with an *X-Files* look-alike called *Fake* (featuring a rogue academic who was also clairvoyant), as well as *Spook* (about a pulp fiction publisher with a split personality)—both of which were deemed far too eccentric for the commercial networks at least, though probably, in theory, perfect for the ABC.

Finally *The Maginnis*, the original title of *Good Guys, Bad Guys*, was settled on—but without the original backstory of a former cop from a criminal family who couldn't escape his past (memories here of the Euston Films success from the early 1980s, *Fox*). As Simpson says: 'The world and Australian television has seen enough ex-cop, ex-crim, private detective series and we were determined to be different'.

How 'different' the series actually was is moot, but *Good Guys, Bad Guys* has that key element of a successful series: a clearly defined trajectory for the lead. Elvis Maginnis' aim in life is to avoid getting involved in things that don't concern him. Each episode had to present this crucial dilemma: Maginnis becomes involved in a situation from which the only escape is the problem's solution.

Thus when a new story was proposed for the series, the key question about the plot was: 'Could Maginnis walk away from this scenario at any point? If the answer was anything other than no, we looked for another story'.

Add a bizarre setting—Elvis is a dry cleaner, an offsider with Tourette's Syndrome (why so many at the end of the 1990s?)—and a feisty (is there another sort?) manager, and the series plot and character matrix is set. To this mix was added humour and the key plot point that Maginnis always sorted out the problem without assistance from the police (as in *Minder*, also from Euston Films). The final (in) joke was that a 'maginnis' is a mythical Aussie wrestling hold from which no one was supposed to be able to escape!

The proposal in its final form received both channel blessing and seed funding from the short-lived Commercial Production Fund (set up for 'quality 'commercial series, it disappeared after the 1998 government Budget). *Good Guys, Bad Guys* went on to win critical and ratings success in the late 1990s, but remains a perfect example of how the original idea for a series can be far removed from the final concept and even further from the successful series concept that is finally commissioned.

SeaChange: Banking on nostalgia

It's now apparent that certain genres seem to have a permanent life on network television and in the cinemas. Police procedurals (*roman policiers*), emergency hospital wards, typical suburban streets (the soapies for the 1990s), and typical suburban high schools (*Heartbreak High* was a top-rating drama in the French domestic market in 1999!) have all been endlessly reborn in various countries and in the global television economy, and will sell in nearly every market.

Series based more upon a theme (or a myth) also recur, not least since the phenomenon of corporate downsizing and the collapse of various economies in the last years of the 1990s in countries where this might least have been expected. There are myths such as 'the charm of simple country folk and values' (*Ballykissangel*, RTE/ABC). There's the idea of 'escape into a simpler, more authentic past' (*Happy Days*, Paramount, 1974–84). Prairie and outback and 'family' sagas, from *Lonesome Dove* (Simon Wincer, 1989) to *Everlasting Things* (Colin Grieg, UK/Scotland, 2000), have returned to screens just as the pundits were noting their demise. In times of high stress the theme of 'dropping out' has made dramas of escape from the rat race perennially popular, particularly and significantly as a fin de siècle (or new millennium?) obsession.

In *Heartbeat* (Yorkshire, 1990), Nick Rowan turns his back on Swinging London to head for the little Yorkshire town of Aidensfield. In *Northern Exposure* (CBS TV, 1990), a New York doctor spends four years in Nicely, Alaska. *Hamish Macbeth* (BBC Scotland) will do anything to avoid being transferred from his beloved Scottish village by the Loch. And so on. It is a universal dream to escape the patterns of work and become part of a (largely imaginary) leisurely country lifestyle where the values are more basic and, in the end, more rewarding.

SeaChange (Artist Services, ABC, 1998+) fits absolutely and precisely into this genre of the myth of escape. From the opening titles the city is set up as a place of rush and dishonesty against the quaint but ultimately more real life to be lived in Pearl Bay.

The one-line pitch

A 'sea change' is what begins to happen to Laura Gibson as she approaches her fortieth year and leaves the City for quiet Pearl Bay.

In the series outline (see Chapter 8), the creators are careful to validate the underlying myths of escape as part of their own world view. Any writer who admits to writing a series merely 'for fun' is likely to run the risk of being written off as a mere dilettante. Sincerity is vital, especially where the myths of escape and country values are concerned. Screenwriters and producers, as well as politicians, have ignored this simple fact of presentation to their cost.

Here's how the writers themselves put it:

> *SeaChange* is the latest collaboration between Andrew Knight and Deb Cox. They have worked together on numerous projects over the last twenty years since their happy collision in the tearooms at Crawford Productions. In the last few years, the two have become a formidable team, with such high quality productions as the award-winning mini-series *Simone de Beauvoir's Babies*, the ratings phenomenon *Kangaroo Palace* and the soon to be released feature films, *The Sound of One Hand Clapping* and *Dead Letter Office*.
>
> The two wanted a different series with *SeaChange*. 'We're looking for a series which viewers can almost escape to. Not conventional television but not nauseatingly comfortable either. One which fuses slightly surreal comedy with the real stuff of life,' says Deb. 'We weren't out to make gritty, cutting-edge television; there's probably enough about. We just wanted a build a world people can relate to—not through artifice and elaborate plot but through an exploration of character.'
>
> (ABC TV Press Kit, 1998)

With the concept thus sold, the project went to the ABC Drama Department with a series of short-form storylines, for few series now are likely to be pre-sold on the basis of a script. It's the concept that counts. Have a look again at The Pitch (Chapter 8).

Of course, all this is as close to advertising copy as it is to an accurate storyline and of course that is its job—to 'sell' the story of each and every episode in turn. But after a while it becomes hard to tell whether you are selling stockings or a story idea, so remember exactly who your intended reader is. Producers are not all alike (by any reckoning) but nor are they like PR people—well, not all that often.

The trouble is you can never be certain. Just look at the career paths of those titans of the late 1990s, the Dreamworks SKG team: Spielberg, Katzenberg, Geffen. They all started off very differently, but their ability to sell old ideas (repackaged) should be a model to advertising copywriters the world over.

In this scene from the *SeaChange* episode entitled 'Balls and Friggin' Good Luck' (Episode Nine, Scene 6) we can see the mechanics of a character-based rather than plot-based scene between the laconic Diver Dan and Laura and her children. The characters are by now well established with the audience (for the ABC, a very large audience) and the dialogue has a shorthand quality that gives the actors full scope within the parameters of their characters.

This script, written by series co-creator Andrew Knight with Max Dann (who had collaborated on the film *Spotswood*, Beyond/1992, though the actual screenwriting for the film began in 1988) shows the advantages of clearly established characters and a clean, simple dialogue line, uncluttered by 'fine writing'.

SCENE 6. INT. DIVER DAN'S. DAY 3.
LAURA, RUPERT and MIRANDA share a breakfast. LAURA is growing impatient, MIRANDA couldn't care less—and RUPERT is strangely withdrawn. DIVER appears with some toast and a coffee and juices.

DIVER

One short black—and toast.

LAURA

We ordered scrambled eggs.

DIVER

Too late. The ferry's going in a tick—you wouldn't have had time to eat it.

LAURA

That's why we ordered them 45 minutes ago.

DIVER

Exactly—you've got to give me proper time.

He walks off and addresses three SCHOOLKIDS.

DIVER

All people with surnames beginning with 'A', please assemble on the foredeck.

He exits.

LAURA

To think I used to fantasise about having breakfast in a

cafe by the sea. (She sips her coffee) Still, he makes a good coffee.

LAURA notes RUPERT's glum look.

> LAURA
>
> Are you all right there, Rupe?

> RUPERT
>
> Yep.

> LAURA
>
> You've been a bit quiet lately. Everything all right?

> RUPERT
>
> Yep.

> LAURA
>
> How did you go with that essay?

> RUPERT
>
> Good.

> LAURA
>
> Terrific. What did you get?

> RUPERT
>
> Four.

> LAURA
>
> Out of ten? Rupert, that's not all that good. It's a fail.

> RUPERT
>
> Mrs Marchand said I could write it again.

DIVER enters. Only LAURA and the KIDS are still there.

DIVER

I'm taking all other rows now.

LAURA looks at MIRANDA, trying to determine what is wrong with RUPERT, but MIRANDA only shrugs. The KIDS grab their belongings and move off.

DIVER (to LAURA)

You've got the Hall boy Inquest today, haven't you? He used to do the ferry ropes for me.

LAURA

You know his family?

DIVER

Not really. Good people. Farmers—done it hard (looks at the untouched table contents). I won't charge you for the eggs.

DIVER leaves her. LAURA waits for him to go—then smiles.

(*SeaChange*, Artist Services, ABC, 1998, written by Max Dann and Andrew Knight)

Rough stuff: From *Homicide* to *Wildside*

Though at least twenty-five years separate series like *Homicide* from *Wildside*, the subject matter, themes and format are often surprisingly similar. In spite of beliefs to the contrary (notably those of Philip Adams, finessing film history in his columns in *The Australian*) the 'old' series like *Homicide* and *Division Four* were not simple derivatives of older radio forms such as Crawford's *D24*. They were Big City police series, but they tried to introduce a real edge to the older radio models.

Homicide and *Division Four* dealt routinely with petty crime and murders, but also with teen suicide, STDs, unmarried mothers, pensioner terror, street kids, smack, serial murder, psychopathology, police violence and corruption—and even early forms of punk before it was called punk!

In one episode of *Homicide* in the late 1960s, Spanish writer Luis Bayonas even cast an entire episode in the form of a surreal dream—hardly something that many contemporary writers, let alone producers, are brave enough to attempt, except in comedy shows.

With regard to pacing and construction, by the 1970s, even conventional drama series such as *Division Four* used jump cuts, montage and hand-held camera as well as fast-paced intercutting between scenes that would do *Wildside* proud. In other words—give or take some 'vocabulary'—nothing has changed all that much if you know your television history.

This also means that, as in advertising, what goes around comes around. Yesterday's dead issue can be tomorrow's hot new episode of the coolest new show on the tube.

Here's a scene from the *Division Four* episode, 'The Man in the Savile Row Suit', a conversation between an old 'leftie' (DOUG) and his niece (EMMA) who has got involved with a nasty piece of work in the form of an ex-army officer turned to crime (shades of the stereotyped Vietnam Vet as a key character/plot generator!). The episode, by the way, had more than seventy scenes plus montages crammed into its forty-odd minutes of screen time.

DIVISION FOUR: EPISODE SS5
'THE MAN IN THE SAVILE ROW SUIT'

SCENE 5 FILM: DOUG'S PLACE: DAY ONE: DOUG, EMMA.

They have just finished an alfresco lunch on the back patio. An empty wine bottle stands on a garden table littered with press cuttings, files and a typewriter. However, things are not as relaxed as EMMA had hoped. Right now she's pacing the patio testily as DOUG watches.

203
EMMA

I don't care what you think. I love him.

204
DOUG

After three weeks? I didn't think that sort of thing happened any more.

205
EMMA

Then you're more out of date than I thought. (grins) And you're a prejudiced old man.

206
DOUG

Em . . . little Em. I know his type. There's nothing more cold-blooded than your over-educated soldier. And *he* was a mercenary. He admitted it that night I met him.

207
EMMA

He's not any of those things . . . he's a man. And he's been sick . . .

208
DOUG

(sly smile, probing) In other words, you want to mother him . . . proper little Florence Nightingale.

209
EMMA

(exasperated) Oh Doug . . . I love you but you're absolutely impossible.

He grins suddenly.

210
DOUG

We old lefties can be prejudiced, too, you know.

211
EMMA

Well, this time you're wrong. Oh Doug, let's leave it at that. I'm not going to lose my favourite uncle over Bill— or anyone.

212
DOUG

Then drop him.

213
EMMA

You!

She goes over and kisses him. He smiles at her with real affection.

214
EMMA

'Bye, darling. Thanks for the lunch . . . and the Dorothy Dixers.

215
DOUG

Take care, Emma.

She leaves and he watches her go. His smile fades, sadly.

Though the layout has changed a little and the numbering of each speech shows the effects of the Crawford assembly-line approach to television series, the pacing and the naturalistic, clean dramatic approach are little altered today, as we shall see when we look at *Wildside*. And the highly modular script form was very necessary in 1975 when a production house, as here, produced the quite remarkable number of episodes it did—over forty per year! Overseas producers still wonder at that figure, which would never even be attempted in these more 'professional' times, and with far greater and more complex crewing arrangements it would anyway be impossible.

Wildside: Hot writing for a hot series

Wildside was *the* TV success of the late 1990s: critics called it a totally 'new' television show with a shockingly realistic edge. That key term, 'realism', makes an appearance every decade or so: ten years before in *Blue Murder* (Jenkins/ABC TV); twenty years before in *The Sweeney* (Euston Films, 1982). By the late 1990s the series that was considered the most cutting-edge, and violent indeed, was *Wildside* (Gannon Jenkins/ABC), notable for its visual style and hectic dialogue pacing with overlapping speech (as noted, the production employs a dramaturge to help key actors gather intensity in delivery).

All these production decisions make the show seem very 'in-your-face', 'out there', and contemporary. *Wildside* is the result of decisions made on every facet of the production process, from dialogue writing to camera angles and lenses. For example, view an episode and see how many shots are tracking shots of actors, viewed through semi-transparent surfaces such as wire mesh, fences, and window shutters. Indeed, in one later episode (June 1998), written by Bob Ellis and directed by David Caesar, almost one hundred shots are composed in this way! Now that's what you'd call following a House Style.

In addition, the double structure—setting the show both in a police station centred on Bill McCoy (Tony Martin) and also in an inner city Crisis Centre, where the drama revolves around Dr Maxine Summers (Rachel Blake) and Vince Cellini (Aaron Pedersen)—delivers a strong structural rhythm. This basic plot structure quite classically opposes two different milieus to generate further sensations of pace and tension. For the writer concerned with the question of script presentation, the series requires quite studied scene layout and presentation, and a full attention to characterisation and naturalistic language.

The following scene is from episode 17 written by Tim Pye. (No episodes in *Wildside* have actual program titles.) Three street kids are implicated in the horrific murder of a taxi driver, and the show takes a unique dramatic approach to a standard criminal investigation. The police have the (by now, expected) intense and often shouted interrogation scenes. But when attention is turned to Maxine and Vince at the Crisis Centre, the writer seizes the chance to broaden the approach from simple cops and robbers to a deeper investigation of the surrounding issues.

Here Maxine attempts to get through to the mother of Mandy, a street kid pregnant to the leading suspect, the smart, tough Aboriginal boy, Mitch:

SCENE 43. INT. CRISIS CENTRE/MAXINE'S OFFICE. DAY 2.

MRS LEECE

Pregnant?

MRS LEECE's hand goes to her mouth. MAXINE sits between her and MANDY in her office. MANDY stares at her mother defiantly.

MANDY

I'm going to keep it.

MRS LEECE

Oh Mandy . . . You can't . . .

She reaches out to touch her daughter. MANDY shrinks back.

MANDY

Don't.

MAXINE

I think it's important to respect Mandy's choice in this, Mrs Leece. Even if it's not the choice you'd have her make.

MRS LEECE

She's only fourteen. You're a doctor. Didn't you tell her . . . ?

MANDY (to her mother)

You can't control me.

MRS LEECE

I only want you to have a good life . . . And I've missed you so much. This is all just . . . like a bad dream.

MANDY

Not for me.

MAXINE

Mandy . . . Your mother wants you to come home again . . .

MANDY

Why would I? Listen to her! It's just the same as it always was!

MRS LEECE

I only want what's best for you . . .

MANDY

Shut up, Mum. You don't know what's best for me! You haven't got a clue!

MAXINE has a frayed look. This is not going well.

MAXINE

Mandy . . .

MRS LEECE

Who's the father? Do you at least know that?

MANDY leans in, taking sadistic pleasure in telling her mother what she knows is going to shock her.

MANDY

His name's Mitch and he's fifteen and he's the best guy in the world . . . And he's going to go to gaol 'cause of people like you.

MRS LEECE

My God . . . Do you really hate me that much?

(continues)

This highly verbal scene, running almost two minutes on screen, is not what a new writer might expect from a fast-paced action series, but, in fact, shows like *Wildside* offer rich opportunities to develop screen characters to an extent unusual in action series. Nevertheless, when the action scenes come, the action—as well as the inventiveness and detail—are expected to be relentless.

SCENE 48. INT. MOVING CAR/HORNSBY POL. STN. DAY 2.
Outside Hornsby Police Station, chaos reigns. The media interest in MITCH, GREG, MANDY and the whole case has grown to a fever pitch and the throng being kept back by uniformed police is as large as the extras budget will allow. Television cameramen with their connected sound operators and reporters stand alongside radio reporters toting microphones emblazoned with station logos, all poised for some cheap publicity on the six o'clock news. In amongst them are newspaper people and interested bystanders. They all jostle for a better position and are being kept back by uniformed officers . . . as BILL and CHARLIE race from the police station, each tightly holding onto one of MITCH's arms. For the second time in twenty-four hours, MITCH has his face hidden from the public by an article of clothing which is not his own. BILL and CHARLIE fly for the patrol car waiting at the kerb, almost lifting MITCH and carrying him as the crowd surges forward . . . firing a barrage of questions and remarks . . . 'Has he been charged?!' . . . 'Why did you do it, son?!' . . . 'Kill the little bastard!' . . . 'Show your face!' . . . 'Coward!' . . . 'Where are your parents?!' . . . etc. BILL, CHARLIE and MITCH get to the car. They bundle the boy into the back seat so that he is sitting between them as the media gather around the car. BILL and CHARLIE slam down the door locks.

BILL

Go!

The car takes off, cutting a swathe through the middle of the crowd. Suddenly, MANDY's face appears through the front windscreen as she flings herself across the bonnet of the patrol car.

MANDY

Mitch! Mitch!

Tears are streaming down her face. The car does not stop.

BILL

Keep going!

MANDY

I love you . . . I love you! . . . I love you!

MANDY half falls and is half dragged off the bonnet by her mother. The car speeds off, with some keener members of the media giving chase with their cameras, snapping as they go. In the back seat of the car, CHARLIE turns to look through the back window and sees MANDY in an inconsolable heap on the ground, sobbing into the road, her mother bending to put an arm around her.

(Wildside, ABC TV–Gannon Jenkins, script by Tim Pye)

This very detailed scene times out at a sharp onscreen half minute, yet takes more words than the previous dialogue scene. All series require that the writer, in conjunction with the script editor, spell out every action in detail, for the hectic pace of production allows no time for philosophical debates on the set.

But in the end, *Wildside* succeeded because of its human interaction as much as the explicit and 'realistic' (perhaps naturalistic is a more useful term) action scenes. And indeed many episodes, when first viewed, seem to be almost all action with little dialogue. But even—or *especially*—these episodes required very close attention to characterisation, particularly the differences and similarities between apparently opposing forces and the characters who represent these forces.

This last scene from the same episode was added later in the screenwriting process, as the producers felt that the half-Aboriginal half-Italian Vince should be given (by the writer) a chance to express his particular world view and sympathies to

Mitch—now revealed as an 'accidental' murderer and maybe a human worth saving.

The result is arguably one of the strongest scenes of the series. And, of course, it is the sort of scene that actors thank writers for and delight in.

SCENE 48A. INT. POLICE STATION/BILL'S OFFICE. DAY 2.

BILL has left VINCE a moment of privacy with his client. MITCH stares at VINCE, giving nothing away. As far as he's concerned, VINCE is just another member of the establishment.

VINCE

Can I ask you why you did it?

MITCH

Survival.

VINCE

You cut someone's throat for survival?

MITCH

You don't need to jump on me. It was an accident.

VINCE

You got any family? (MITCH shakes his head) What about the old people?

MITCH

They can't help me.

VINCE

I know how you're feeling but . . .

MITCH

Bullshit.

VINCE

You don't have to put a fence between us.

                              MITCH

Can you feel my pain, can ya? My closest brother gave
me up.

                              VINCE

Your fingerprints gave you up.

                              MITCH

See how it is. There's a fence. I'm on one side, you're on
the other wearing a whitefella suit. You don't care about
me. Maybe one ounce, maybe one ounce you care.

                              VINCE

I care a shitload. Listen, Mitch, you've seen how the
media treated you, it's not gonna be easy in prison
either.

                              MITCH

Don't worry about me. I'm gone. But I want to know my
girl's gonna be okay. You look out for her?

                              VINCE

Sure, I can do that. But it's not me Mandy needs. She
needs you, Bro.

                              MITCH

I've got nothing.

                              VINCE

You've got something, you've got the people before you
who walked the land, who fought for you. You've got
them in here.

    VINCE slaps MITCH's chest.

                              VINCE

You've got their strength in here. You have to face
what's going to happen in prison. You can feel like
you're a worthless piece of shit, you deserve everything
that happens. You can get screwed, take drugs, or you
can use the time to repair yourself. Take control.

VINCE sees that this is sinking in.

VINCE

You do this for yourself and Mandy and the kid. And you do it for the old people.

(*Wildside*, ABC TV–Gannon Jenkins, script by Tim Pye)

It's hard to find a relevant social topic or problem that's not addressed in this highly energetic piece of dialogue.

Action and intensity are not of course merely the province of police shows. But they are the reason why certain genres are perennially popular. In 1998, along with *SeaChange*, *Wildside* became one of the most critically successful ABC series since *Rush* twenty years before. The decision by ABC management not to continue with the new series for 1999–2000 was, ironically enough, the result of the short-term inability of the producers (Gannon/Jenkins) to achieve international sales outside the English-speaking market. National success is no longer enough.

Medivac: The insider writing style

When many series go into production, it is with the expectation that there will be a 'family' of writers aboard. Often the writers are selected for at least the first series (normally thirteen episodes) in advance of production. If there's a series you really want to be a part of, then make sure the producers know—as quickly and personally as you can—that you're a dedicated writer, love the characters and know them intimately and, yes, you're an unashamed fan.

By the time the second series of *Medivac* went into production in Brisbane a number of local writers had already beaten a path to the production office, and some were taken on a trial basis. The new writers were given the *Medivac* 'bible', containing backgrounds of all the characters, their particular personality traits and idioms, as well as a take on the style of the show, sample storylines, and dialogue excerpts, so that they could absorb it all, then go away and start creating.

As a new writer you don't have to pass an exam in the stylistics of the show (not a bad idea though!) but you should arrive with a story or two of your own featuring one or more of the leads as key players, along with sample scenes.

With a show like *Medivac* there is often a production shorthand that develops and you should also be aware of that.

Look at this scene draft for an episode featuring the febrile Dr Wayne (Eugene Gilfedder). The plot twist here is to be an elusive tummy virus that runs through the hospital like wildfire.

It's easy to see that the whole script is written in a very specific, almost telegrammatic form, and that a lexicon of special *Medivac* words (ambo, gurneys, etc.) is necessary equipment for the screenwriter. It's good to feel that you're part of a team of insiders, isn't it!

MEDIVAC

EPISODE 31

SCENE 1. INT. TRIAGE/WAITING AREA. DAY 1.
WAYNE is sour.

> WAYNE
>
> It's worse than I could possibly imagine.

> ARCH
>
> No way. We could have done this over at the restaurant, in front of all these other people. Now that would have been your worst nightmare.

GOSIA and BREE approach from the staff room end with a huge birthday cake, ablaze with candles. JULIA, MACY, MARINA and TOM are with WAYNE and ARCH, all in upbeat party mood except WAYNE.

> GOSIA
>
> We couldn't get a cake big enough to hold all the candles, so these are yours, too . . .
>
> (handing WAYNE a few more candles)
>
> . . . ninety-eight, ninety-nine, a hundred!

Much laughter at WAYNE's expense. OOPY works in the background, envious at being out of the party.

> MACY
>
> Well, aren't you going to blow it out?

> BREE
>
> He's going to wait till they've melted a bit more. Make us eat wax.

> ARCH
>
> Wayne's revenge for reminding him of another year under the bridge.

MACY

Nah, you're just getting too old to blow, aren't you, Wayne?

WAYNE

Very well. But only if you promise not to lead this puerile rabble in a chorus of 'Happy Birthday To You'.

MACY

Close your eyes and make a wish.

With a suffering roll of the eyes, WAYNE bends towards the cake. The doors burst open, and the party is blown apart by a rush of colourful chaos: a heap of minor injuries from the Royal Show. There are kids with showbags and broken dolls on sticks, young people in silly hats, an older couple hobbling, a few blokes in country gear—moleskins, Akubras—real cowboys; a woman on a gurney with bandages and a twisted leg. An AMBO wheels a gurney in with another cowboy flat on his back, his bush hat on his chest. As the party breaks up to deal with the invasion, JULIA flashes a knowing look at OOPY.

OOPY

A runaway bull at the showgrounds. Got into the crowd. Mostly abrasions, contusions. Two suspected fractures.

JULIA

And you didn't think to pass the message on?

OOPY

You seemed too busy.

He goes to help one of the patients.

JULIA

Get back to your duties, you little twerp.

OOPY retreats. JULIA takes in the WOMAN and COWBOY on the gurneys.

JULIA (to the WOMAN)

Big day at the show, huh? Don't worry, we'll soon get you patched up.

> (to WAYNE, indicating the COWBOY) I'll take her in
> Resus Two. You can handle Hopalong here in One.
>
> (indicating the other casualties to ARCH) Arch?
>
> The team springs into action. MACY follows JULIA with
> the WOMAN on the gurney towards Resus Two. GOSIA
> attaches herself to WAYNE and the COWBOY. ARCH takes
> charge of the rest.

(Medivac, Liberty and Beyond, written by Garrett Russell, 1997)

This is exemplary series script layout and presentation—there's no excess verbiage, lots of insider language, and all contributing to a sense of team play that is so often missing from the ego-dominated field of program making. Of course such script layouts and their crisp exclusion of the outside reader also make for a real sense of there being a magic circle which only the charmed can enter. And why not!

Finally, let's return to Grafton Everest, the outrageous creation of writer Ross Fitzgerald. The novels and stories had attracted the attention of writer-directors Denny Lawrence (*Goodbye Paradise*, 1982) and Bob Ellis (*Warm Nights on a Slow Moving Train*, 1989) and in 1998–99, the two had developed the Grafton character into a satirical television comedy series called *Fool's Paradise*, based on Fitzgerald's characters. The two had already collaborated on the dark political comedy set in steamy Queensland, *Goodbye Paradise*, so this seemed a good chance to use the character to develop their satirical intentions further. Grant money and some terrestrial channel interest allowed the full development of the series concept.

It is interesting to compare the following extracts with the feature film treatment of Grafton Everest and his adventures (detailed in the next chapter). The film script development of the stories is more broadly comic, and shows Grafton as more of a bumbling yet sweet anti-hero and less of a politically involved figure. The 'feature film version' of Grafton was, therefore, much more the classic 'innocent abroad' as developed in the script we have looked at. Such a familiar type of character has enormous popular appeal in many genres of writing, and remains the centre of many novels and films. This is not to say that the Candide-like Grafton is not an original creation. But the figure of the 'holy innocent' has a long and honourable history and can be developed in any direction and with any amount of original detail, with the certainty that audiences will always respond to and identify with such a character.

But look at the edgier construction of Grafton Everest by Lawrence and Ellis. This is a considerably different character in thought and expression from the fellow in the book! Note particularly the dialogue style of the 'new' Grafton. He is different here from the book's hero in both his style of speech and his approach to life. In fact, if you know the work of Bob Ellis you will be able to observe (as film critics have opined of Bob Ellis' male characters) that Grafton now sounds lot like . . . well, Bob Ellis himself!

The first scene shows Grafton now established as a TV pundit:

FOOL'S PARADISE

EPISODE ONE 'THE ROAD TO DAMASCUS'
(PART OF SCENE 1 ONLY, PLUS SCENES 2 AND 3)

SCENE 1. INT. EVEREST HOUSE. BEDROOM. DAY.
On a television monitor appears the title Wake Up Australia, accompanied by kookaburra sounds and an old-fashioned boinky melody. This dissolves through in a juddery primitive way to GRAFTON EVEREST, the famous academic pundit, sitting up in bed with a tray of breakfast cereal on his lap. He addresses the camera in a slightly sourpussed yet confident way.

GRAFTON

Wake up Australia, it's later than you think. The sea is rising, the polar icecaps dwindling, Indonesian fundamentalists flooding though cannibal New Guinea, new super-microbes evolving and diving in their thousands glub-glub-glub into our unsuspecting bloodstreams, three new ones every minute . . .

A bored camera crew, scrunched up in the bedroom, are recording him live, and a tall raven-haired female producer, CASSANDRA BATES, is watching him with large-eyed anxiety.

GRAFTON

. . . plague and overpopulation everywhere, *and* God help us we have a new Premier.

He eyeballs the camera with practised menace. The CAMERAMAN yawns.

GRAFTON

Apart from anything else he'll have me to deal with, and the watchful horror of every decent Queenslander, proud of our mosquito-bitten culture and scared for our future. And there's a few of us left. Enjoy the sunshine while it lasts, my children.

He begins theatrically to pour the milk on his Weet-Bix.

> GRAFTON

Obediently yours, Grafton Everest, historian and political commentator.

The character of Janet as revealed in later scenes seems more familiar, if a rather more outspoken and snappy character than in the feature film version:

SCENE 2. INT. EVEREST HOUSE. LIVING ROOM. DAY.
The crew is carrying the big old-fashioned camera through the living room towards the door. It dislodges an expensive-looking vase, which falls and smashes. In the kitchen GRAFTON's wife, JANET, an attractive blonde woman in a kimono, aged about thirty-eight, looks on in horror.

> CAMERAMAN

Ah, sorry.

They go on out the door.

SCENE 3. INT. EVEREST HOUSE. BEDROOM. DAY.
GRAFTON is in his bedroom, putting on a dull grey suit over his red ant pyjamas. JANET comes in and starts clearing the uneaten Weet-Bix breakfast away.

> JANET

They're slowly, daily, wrecking the house.

> GRAFTON

They are beasts. Close relations, when they move in swarms, of the white Siberian buffalo.

> JANET

You could do it in a studio.

> GRAFTON

I need the extra hour in bed. When you don't sleep, you need a lot of rest.

> (*Fool's Paradise*, written by Denny Lawrence and Bob Ellis
> based on the books by Ross Fitzgerald)

In the television series Grafton comments on the state of the nation (and the world); the tone is that of a biblical prophet wheeled out to comment on the End of Civilisation as we know it. He is a much more dramatic and voluble figure than the one in the book, though doubtless familiar enough to devotees of the life and works of Bob Ellis!

It is a splendid thing if you can sufficiently escape the restrictions of producers and script editors and have your *dramatis personae* utter what you yourself have always wanted to say! What could be more satisfying?

The last word: On script editors

Script editors are nowhere more evident than on television series. Partly a product of producers' controlling impulses, partly the result of funding body fantasies about many drafts being better than a few, the script editor is now an essential and often very useful part of the industrial flow of television and film production.

Since your script is going to be edited, and since you may very well become a script editor for at least part of your working life, it pays to become good at spotting redundancy and false notes in scripts. Of course, script editors will often have more mechanical functions and in the 1970s, at Crawford Productions (*Homicide, Division Four, Cop Shop*, et al.) they were also charged with the task of making sure that the regular stars, the detectives or 'Ds', who were on contract, appeared in enough scenes. This was both a dramatic and an economic imperative that still holds true in television series.

British stage and screenwriter Simon Gray (*After Pilkington*, BBC, 1987) provides a balancing note of caution:

> The real curse of the BBC today is all those script editors.
> What are they? A script editor should be a beginner, but now
> they seem to have almost complete power and it's hard to get
> past them. Often, I suspect, they make a decision to absolve a
> producer from the responsibility of having to decide himself.
>
> (in *Talk of Drama*, Sean Day-Lewis, 1998: 201)

Whether you're a script editor, a writer, or both, you'll have to reflect upon the great power that script editors have been given and whether you might wish gently to resist that, from time to time. You are the writer, after all.

Chapter 12
Writing Feature Films and Television Movies

Features—this is what everyone becomes a movie maker for, isn't it? Not necessarily, but certainly writing feature film scripts brings the greatest risk but also maybe the greatest benefits. The degree of difficulty is rewarded by the judges according to a system known as luck.

In earlier chapters you've looked at all the elements that you need to consider. A good but not necessarily a high concept. A working plot, characters that fascinate you as well as any potential audience, and a basic story that is much more than the sum of the plot elements. In the end, plot is just a lot of things that happen! Story is what your movie is all about. There must, in the end, be something you want to say that drives the scenes along.

The source
Though we've mentioned it already, a primary source for your story may well be someone else's writings. We've looked at the laying down of some characters' elements from the novel *My Love Had a Black Speed Stripe*. Then we saw how backstory gave extra drive (maybe too much) to the plot. But what is the interesting thing about any story for you as a writer? You shouldn't just choose any story because you feel it *might* make a good movie. Worse, don't choose a hot new novel just because it is popular. Odds are that you've seen literary merits in what is destined to remain in print and would never make a movie. Sometimes you can try the impossible as David Cronenberg did with William Burroughs' *The Naked Lunch* (1992). The result was a fascinating movie that had little to do with the book—and never found an audience. No problem if you're David Cronenberg, or David Lynch, or Australia's Rolf de Heer (*Bad Boy Bubby*, 1994). But not everyone gets paid to make personal, bizarre, or cultish movies. You have to earn the licence to be personal—or 'quirky'—an adjective that has, like a spider,

trapped far too many writers in its charms, as has the name Quentin Tarantino.

No, you have to feel that something of yourself—some subject or idea that intrigues you—is bound up in the story you choose. Let's assume that in *Speed Stripe* you see a chance to make a satirical black comedy about male obsessions in Australia—or, really, in any developed country where cars are often the public measure of a man's virility. The novel by Henry Williams had achieved this in a fairly basic comedic way, but that was some time ago. Things have moved on. Or have they?

Certainly, since the novel was published in the 1970s, things have changed industrially all over the world. For a start, the late 1990s has seen the amalgamation of major national car manufacturers—even icons like Rolls Royce in the UK and Citröen in France have been swallowed up by local or overseas conglomerates. But that too can be another subtext to the film, and can form an interesting subplot.

So, different times dictate that you take a different approach to the story to keep it fresh and right for the year when it gets made into a film—which will be sometime well into the third millennium if the normal time line for film development is followed! But the basic drives and motives of the characters are probably much the same, however much cars, industries, and whole economies have altered.

So now you begin to write. Assuming that your scene breakdown seems solid, you must begin to write the first draft as if it were the last one. Unlike many forms of writing, you never know at what stage your work will be taken up and go into production—there are no absolute protocols. But since you know that a script editor, a producer, or almost anyone can and will come along and fiddle with things from the very moment your script gets out, you should assume that the first draft is also the last! It won't be—but it just might . . .

All the elements in the right order

The script must contain:
- a title page;
- a character list: this can disappear later as the script moves into production. Some producers prefer that the character descriptions be in the actual script, but don't assume that this will work, because few people read everything;
- all the dialogue; and
- every scene numbered and locations and times indicated (this varies in detail—keep it simple).

The title page and character list should be laid out something like this:

SPEED STRIPE

Screenplay by

Paul Faust

Based on the novel

My Love Had a Black Speed Stripe

by Henry Williams

First Draft

July 2001

Don't forget that all important authorial declaration—right there in the bottom right-hand corner:

© Paul Faust
75 New Street
Blacktown

And make sure you have an option!

On the next page or as soon as you have finished your beautiful title page layout, you should begin a list of characters (or a one-paragraph synopsis, if that's required):

CHARACTER LIST (LEADS ONLY)

ON THE HOUSING ESTATE

RON (central character)

Young, good-looking Australian, about 25 to 28. Superficially he's utterly normal; he likes football, girls, beers with his factory mates and his 'old pack'; but under the strain of marriage he has a deep-rooted misanthropy which turns itself into a total obsession with motor cars.

ROSE (his wife)

She is from a poor family but she has 'aspirations'. Her outlook is limited by house, washing machine and the romantic bliss peddled by the women's magazines. Her girlish simplicity cannot even begin to combat RON's concealed but very real neurosis.

The lights fade and then the movie starts

You already know (from Chapter 10) that the developed story now begins with the formation of the character of young Ron as a bewildered car-obsessed kid who has lost his dad in the Vietnam War and is headed for a pretty lifeless sort of upbringing. Prime fodder for the image makers.

Then we've met the image makers—and that great new car, the Countdown, that they are about to sell to the innocent public on behalf of the (imaginary) multinational car company, Holden-WaiShu. The subplot/subtextual social comment bit has now been introduced and given a name.

Now we meet Ron and Rose, and the film story connects with the simpler plot elements of the novel for the first time.

The layout used here is as complex as you ever need to get with a screenplay. You may wish to add the scene number on the right margin as well. Some producers prefer it, but it's a cosmetic matter.

Action, not camera angles!

Nothing irritates a script reader more—but especially a director—than an excess of technical detail in a script. A script is a machine document in the sense that it, like a blueprint, carries all the character and plot information. However, the use of camera angles and movements are not required or welcomed. Avoid the temptation to show off your knowledge with zooms, tilts and pans, let alone camera angles (LOW ANGLE ON RON, CRANE SHOT OF THE SUBURBAN STREET). The exception is when plot or character is advanced by a specific movement. Thus the following scene contains complex actions but absolutely no camera instructions:

SCENE 19. EXT. FLATS. THE YARD. DAY (SATURDAY).

The yard is the scene of ritual activity. Several men are tinkering with their cars, most of which are identical types, standard models with all manner of GT stripes, mag wheels, etc. We move slowly down the line of cars, ending on RON who has the bonnet of his car up. He is absorbedly checking the ignition systems on his car. He tests the response by tweaking the accelerator line and the car roars powerfully. RON listens critically. He doesn't notice JOCK who has suddenly appeared beside him. JOCK is all dressed up as Boy Racer complete with string gloves and a fireproof jacket.

JOCK

Hey up, Ron. Hard at it?

RON

(straightens up with a groan) Points!

The description of the weekend scenes of car worship is essential for background and plot, but to instruct the director or confuse the actors with CUT TO BIG CLOSEUP OF RON is unnecessary—and will be cut out or ignored until the shooting script is readied anyway. Nowadays everyone knows what a CLOSEUP or a PAN is. That doesn't mean your script has to have all that technical stuff in it. If in doubt—cut it out!

Technical instructions to actors are also often written into scripts. It's a hangover from theatre and generally quite unwanted and often misleading. This is the insertion of what are sometimes called 'Rileys' as in:

RON

(wryly) Points are buggered!

So in the example above, the fact that Ron straightens up with a groan is close to superfluous. Exactly what he does can be left to the cast and the director. Of course if he straightens with a groan because his back is wrenched for some key plot reason—well, that's acceptable. Otherwise, leave it out.

Your focus should instead be on the dialogue. The characters must all sound like real people. However, conversational tics, such as a character using a swear word repeatedly, or with a speech habit such as saying 'you know' every few words, may be 'realistic' in life but irritating beyond endurance in a drama unless there is a really solid reason for it.

Of course becoming too involved with your characters can have curious by-products. As one critic on national radio noted of Bob Ellis' movie *Warm Nights on a Slow Moving Train* (Bob Ellis, 1989), 'all the male characters over thirty began to sound alike—quoting Yeats and worrying about getting old. It was as if the audience were trapped in a party with a room full of Bob Ellises, all talking at once' (ABC Metro Radio, 1990).

Get into the habit of reading your scenes aloud—with a colleague if you can, to test the rhythms and texture of the spoken words. This helps you to time and find the pace of your scenes as well.

But first, get that scene written—and whether you use a computer script system, set up protocols in your writing program or just bang away at the old Smith Corona, the script layout should always look basically like the next scene. Note that it's actually pretty simple and doesn't require a software program—just a few simple indents and CAPITAL LETTERS for SCENE SLUGLINES and CHARACTER NAMES.

SCENE 11. EXT. DRIVE-IN THEATRE. NIGHT.

We move slowly along a row of cars in the ageing drive-in. It is soon clear that no one is watching the movie. All are engaged in threshing sexual activity of one kind or another. Legs and arms protrude, couples struggle and the odd item of clothing is thrown aside.

SCENE 12. EXT. THE SCREEN. NIGHT.
EXCERPT FROM A SAM RAIMI PATENTED MOVIE (SAY *EVIL DEAD II*?).

A GIRL screams in terror. The screen goes red.

SCENE 13. EXT. DRIVE-IN AS IN SC 11.

The camera tracks along until it comes to rest in front of RON's car. ROSE has her legs up on the back of the front seat and they're hard at it. It's clear that they're both in some pain and their faces show few signs of ecstasy. Suddenly the film is heard to end, the music swells and all around them lights come on. ROSE pulls away quickly.

ROSE

No, Ron. They can see!

RON

Just a sec.

ROSE

You'll just have to wait until the second feature.

She adjusts her clothes as RON pulls away. RON composes himself. (scene continues)

In general, the basic script format that is most likely to work—for all genres, not just feature films—is the simplest. However, radio, advertising, and certain forms of documentary do not necessarily conform (nor should they be expected to), and comedy scripts are always a bit idiosyncratic (see the Kylie Mole and Norman Gunston sketches in Chapter 7). If you're a star, you can get away with just about anything!

The almost original screenplay

Adaptations are okay for some but you've decided to go it alone. However, the effort of adaptation is often an effort well spent: there is no quicker way to see the difference between what works as a poem, a short story or a novel than to try adapting it for the screen.

Then there's a middle course between the original screenplay and the straight adaptation: basing a character on a known figure from literature, or, like *The Adventures of Barry MacKenzie* (Bruce Beresford, 1972), on a character from a cartoon strip by Barry Humphries for *Private Eye* magazine. The advantage is a known and loved (or loathed) character—and (we all hope) an enormous potential audience who have been waiting for a great movie about the character all this time!

The danger is that you'll write a new story that nobody thinks fits their conception of what the character would do. The advantage is that you have a licence (if you have both the copyright and the author's blessing) to create a cinematic world that brings that character bounding off the printed page.

> Ross Fitzgerald's *Pushed from the Wings* is a comic master-piece. Massively funny. I can't wait to make the film.
>
> (Rowan Ayers, Film and TV Producer)

When you read that sort of comment on a dust-jacket you can be sure that someone probably already has the film rights. The book is probably being talked about in movie-making circles as the next Hot Property. Many options are taken out by producers (writers less often—they have less to spend) before publication. But let's assume we have been lucky and hold an option for a year. What do we do now?

Ross Fitzgerald's comic anti-hero Grafton Everest is one of the most interesting comic creations of recent Australian writing. In a series of books and short stories he has bumbled his way through apocalyptic events of all sorts, from terrorist plots to Gotterdammerung itself.

The stories are set in and around the semi-tropical wonders of the State of Queensland. Queensland, like Texas or Florida in America, has been a fertile ground for comic, absurd and wild adventures in many films, notably *Goodbye Paradise* (Denny Lawrence, 1982) and more recently a series of big-budget films, many produced and financed in America, that make full use of the bizarre physical aspects of the state. Among these are *Sniper* (Luis Llosa, 1993) and *The Thin Red Line* (Terence Malick, 1999). Australian films set in the tropical north include *Paperback Hero* (1999) and *Dear Claudia* (Chris Cudlipp, 1999).

The writings featuring Grafton Everest, then, seem ideal for adaptation into either a television series or a feature film. The initial problem is twofold. First, Grafton's adventures are often sexually very explicit. This is not necessarily a problem, but it suggests a particular film classification (MA 15, say) for the movie if this aspect of the original work is adhered to.

The second problem is that the novels deploy very familiar and possibly easily recognised figures from Queensland politics and public life, and from the staff of at least one university (called here, Bowen) where Grafton works. How faithful to the satirical intent can the film afford to be?

In this case it may be better, after talking it through with the author, to reduce the elements of direct satire and invent a *totally new* plot revolving around familiar characters. That said, the ability of film director Mike Nicholls in *Primary Colors* (1998) to sail close to the winds of political reality suggests that the writer can be reasonably brave in tackling 'real' events and people—provided they are heavily fictionalised.

The novels *Pushed from the Wings* and *Busy in the Fog* both feature Grafton in some trouble with his marriage as a subplot and caught up in some major terrorist or politically extreme groups in both. Both novels end with major action scenes and much hysteria.

This play between public events and private worries is a very dynamic and useful one for the business of plotting. Let's decide that for the time being we'll write for a feature film. The TV series can come later!

Who then are our key characters?

> GRAFTON: described sparingly, but variously as asthmatic, 'sixteen stone' and, by his wife JANET, as 'fat and loose and heavy jowled. And all your bad features are beginning to show in your face. You need to exercise and lose weight', etc. (*Busy in the Fog*: 103)

Not promising for a hero, perhaps, but fine for an anti-hero. The point is that the appearance of Grafton is less important than the general impression he gives of 'looseness' and of running to fat.

> JANET: 'a willowy 180 centimetres . . . Equitable Janet was never bored, her life filled with projects that actually interested her' (*Pushed from the Wings*: 10)

It sounds as if the audience might find Janet more interesting, and maybe more sympathetic.

> MR HORTON: a retired schoolteacher of GRAFTON's who takes a kindly interest in his former pupil and

acts as a kind of philosophical and moral centre of the stories, through a series of letters to GRAFTON as well as the occasional intervention. 'He didn't look any older than Grafton remembered him at school—thin, erect, thick black glasses, curly hair.'

LEE-ANNE (Let's change that to ELLIE—easier to say and sounds better): GRAFTON's talented daughter. (A baby in one book, nearly ten in *Busy in the Fog*.)

There's real potential here for a bright, articulate kid who can probably outwit her dad on a good day. She could be a vital ingredient rather than just a bit player as she is in the stories.

Other characters include assorted politicians; the Head of the Special Branch; various lunatic plotters including anarchists, radical feminists, right-wing nutters—flat earthers, the lot!

A classic three-act structure might then be:

* Act One: establish Grafton and his family, with attendant problems. It should establish the villains.
* Act Two: the working out of the plot and Grafton's unwilling involvement.
* Act Three: the denouement—explosions and alarms! Resolution.

This model would work as well for a tragedy but here it is the spine of the comedy—the needs of all genres are, structurally at least, the same.

We'll skip the Pitch and the scene breakdown now and dive headfirst into the first draft. So let's set up the story:

GRAFTON FLYING

Screenplay by

Paul Faust

Based on

the novels and short stories of

Ross Fitzgerald

Revised Third Draft

July 2001

SCENE 1. EXT. THE GABBA STADIUM. NIGHT.
The giant floodlights throw the light from the ground high into the rainy city. A howling crowd is enthralled by the gallant Brisbane Lions football team locking horns with that old working-class mainstay, Collingwood.

CLOSE IN ON
GRAFTON and his daughter ELLIE, at first lost in the roaring mass. GRAFTON, plump, freckled and pale, looks like he'd be a good father to a loutish Irish sort of kid, but not to this bright, bubbly and dark eyed girl beside him. Massive closeups of bodies clashing on the muddy plain. Wallop! You can feel their pain and their desperation. They bash and bruise again.

ELLIE

Dad? Aren't they hurting each other?

GRAFTON

It's a game, Ellie . . . a beautiful game. (Rhapsodises) What a kick!

SCENE 2. THE GIANT SCOREBOARD. CONSEC.
A jolly cartoon lion smiles and the encouraging words appear: GO LIONS!

SCENE 3. EXT. STADIUM. NIGHT. CONSEC.
A loping Lion, clutching the football, cops a huge blow. He topples. ELLIE winces and turns to GRAFTON who's smiling, reliving a simpler childhood. Now GRAFTON'S face is turned into television lines as we
CUT TO:

SCENE 4. INT. HONOURED GUEST BOX. NIGHT. CONSEC.
An array of monitors show the match while a separate, sinister matte black bank show selected Special Branch targets. BULL HAGAN'S snoutish face brightens as he spots GRAFTON. He smiles at the mouldering yet princely face of ex-Premier Henderson.

HAGAN

Got him.

So now the story is under way. It contains many of the characters of the novels, but has set sail with a new plot and new villains:
Hagan, the villainous cop, and Henderson, a quavering but ruth-
less ex-premier who wants his power back.

Now we need to establish Grafton at home, for this is what is
really at stake in all the Grafton Everest tales:

**SCENE 8. EXT. ROSS STREET, ROSEVILLE.
DAWN.**
*Roseville is so green and subtropical that you can barely see
the houses. The birds are waking in the glorious dawn light
as the MILKO's van pulls up outside GRAFTON's house. A
magpie starts up in a tree near the small above-ground pool.
The MILKO puts down his bottles, collects an air rifle from
his seat and pots the warbler. It falls with a squawk into the
pool. The MILKO smiles.*

**SCENE 9. INT. BEDROOM OF GRAFTON EVEREST'S
HOME. DAWN.**
*JANET, slim and tanned in her broderie nightdress, gazes
impassively outside, watching the gawky figure of her
nine-year-old daughter ELLIE rush out to rescue the dying
bird. GRAFTON stirs plumply behind her and croaks.*

GRAFTON

Tea? Chamomile?

JANET

Bloody Brisbane! Grafton, we have to get out of the city.
I can't stand the noise and the cruelty any more. I need
air!

GRAFTON

(scratching his floppy thinning hair) Bit of toast?
Darling?

She spins and stalks from the room. GRAFTON rises on an
elbow and spots ELLIE with the now deceased bird.

ELLIE

(spotting him) Daddy. The man shot the bird!

GRAFTON

Not before breakfast, Ellie. I'm thinking.

ON ELLIE: She solemnly lays the bird out at her feet. The
cat, CHE, approaches determinedly. GRAFTON closes his
eyes wearily.
OFF we hear breaking crockery.

And that's Act One—maybe ten minutes or a little more of screen
time.

Act Two will be time for some real action. Now we need a Big
Plot—and then some terrorists or at least a well-intentioned but
useless anarchist or two. Plus a target for them to aim for. What
better one than a huge public event of the sort governments just
love—especially near election time? In *Pushed from the Wings*, the
maguffin, or plot device, involved a visit by King Charles and
Queen Di. Well, we can't do that, but no matter—the world is full
of bigwigs. Think of all those High Concept Hollywood movies of
the late 1990s that featured heroic presidents: Roland Emmerich's
Independence Day (1996), *Airforce One* (Wolfgang Petersen, 1997),
and plenty of others . . .

SCENE 7. MONTAGE. A DUMMY HIGH-BUDGET COMMERCIAL.

*With the full panoply of whizzbang graphics, the COMMER-
CIAL opens with sweeping chopper shots across Brisbane,
Gold Coast beaches, Mirage resorts, Jupiter's and the expect-
ed bikini shots.*

DRAMATIC VOICE-OVER

The world's greatest state welcomes the world's biggest
event: the World Symposium, a dream for the New
World Order. The brightest and the best will be here.

Computer-generated graphics reveal a vast spacey
auditorium and pictures of the world's leaders flash across
the screen. Images from Asian and Aussie feature films flip,
flop and leap across the screen.

VOICE-OVER (cont.)

Combined with the great new Pacific Rim Film Festival,
a Premier's Department initiative, and opened by the
world's most glamorous and caring couple, this is where
the twenty-first century *really* begins!

END ON the PRESIDENT and HIS WIFE, exquisite,
sun-soaked. As these last images appear the film appears to
jam and then smoulder, bursting into flames.

Well, that sets up the target for the plot, but we still need another lot of villains to create the comedic chaos that the novels use so effectively. The novels both end with a real twilight of the gods. The audience will expect no less.

Challenge

Write a short scene breakdown of the next two Acts, making sure that things end with a suitable bang and a bumblingly heroic role for Grafton.

The important thing to remember is that whatever climax you dream up, someone in the film industry will try to second-guess you. It is at this point that you realise that the nuclear explosion you had scripted is not intrinsically more 'correct' than flood or fire. In other words, be prepared to let plot moments go before you sacrifice character. If your characters lose the plot—fine. You should never lose your characters!

Oh, and don't forget that the option on the books runs out next Friday. You wouldn't be the first writer to have a screen adaptation crash and burn before your eyes because you forgot to extend the option. It happened, just like that, with *My Love Had a Black Speed Stripe*—with finance already in place for production, a distributor involved—but the rights had quietly been handed over by the publisher to another producer—and the film was never made!

This brings us at last to the business of writing totally original screenplays.

Original screenplays: *Wireless Dreams*
You've decided to do it all by yourself. Let's say that in your readings you have come across the tales of the old radio studios of the 1930s to the 1950s. They produced literally dozens of serials and dramas for a mass audience across the world. Indeed, you've found out that Australian radio dramas were so highly regarded that they sold into the American markets in the decades before television (not video) killed the radio star.

The time you have chosen is 1960—or thereabouts—say a few years after the instant success of television (introduced in 1956) and only a year or two before most radio studios producing dramas either shut down or turned to the new medium.

Now your research has also turned up some background information that gives you both plot and several potential subplots. The main plot will be the (typical) *Bildungsroman* (coming of age story) of a young man (CHRIS) breaking into the magical world of radio, just as it is about to collapse forever. His backstory is that, as an asthmatic, years of illness, of lying in bed listening to the radio as a magic pathway to the world of storytelling have given him a drive to enter that magical world any way he can.

The milieu is the bohemian world of writers and artists who were émigrés and refugees ('reffos') from the Second World War. This was a period that saw Australia's culture transformed forever by an influx of talented immigrants from all parts of the world. Many were bruised and haunted survivors of Hitler's death camps.

This background will give you subplot, subtext—and a wealth of characters to support the drive of the main story.

Of course such rich material means you could write the story up as a miniseries. But, no—you've settled on a feature film just to make things harder for yourself. Now you have to create a story that will grab an audience.

What other films have dealt with this period or with similar stories? Well, there was *Tune in Tomorrow* (Jon Amiel, 1990), a delightful movie based on Mario Vargas Llosa's novel *Aunt Julia and the Scriptwriter*. It was essential viewing for writers but ignored by the public. Then there was the George Lucas-produced *Radioland Murders* (Mel Smith, 1992), which went straight to video. And Woody Allen's *Radio Days* (1987)—still not quite in profit—but a great take on the great days of American radio in the forties. And so on. It all looks a bit unpromising, doesn't it? But you really want to tell this story.

And, you remember, there was *Newsfront*. It was both a critical and popular success, so maybe there's hope after all if the mix is right. And series about the 1960s like *Kangaroo Palace* (Artist Services, 1997) worked, so perhaps there is an audience out there interested in the period, after all.

So—how to pitch the concept? Here's one way—and it certainly produced a lot of script development money:

WIRELESS DREAMS

THE PITCH
Background

By the mid-1950s many thought Australian radio drama the best in the world. Certainly the actors and writers were among the finest. Ron Randell, Ray Barrett, John Meillon, Ruth Cracknell, Rod Taylor and Peter Finch all began as radio stars. Writers like Morris White, Michael Noonan, Ruth Park, Sumner Locke Elliot and Alan Seymour all turned out fine work. They were heady days.

Australia *was* a big country and loved and needed its radio. But the cities were not that big, and the 1950s saw a wild bohemian mix of recent émigrés (many were respected writers and artists in their lost countries) and local artists and writers, drinking and working together in a vivid and exciting way of life. Among them were the radio folk who'd never had it so good—actors, writers and directors making a patchwork artistic society that was like an underground stream in the dreary conformities of the 1950s.

Television marked the beginning of the end for this loose knit confederation and many writers and actors didn't make the translation.

Wireless Dreams is a story set in that doomed milieu, capturing a forgotten piece of social and artistic history and weaving it through the rites of passage of **CHRIS GREEN**, a young writer, and **ILONA**, a brilliant and gutsy European girl who's determined to make it—and is the real storm centre of the film.

And so the story and the hook are set up.

Here's how we end up meeting the key characters, in a draft of the screenplay. Notice how the backstory discussed (above) for Chris is cut down to just a hint—a classic example of a writer giving up twenty scenes to retain at least part of the key elements of motivation for the lead characters:

SCENE 1. PRETITLE SEQUENCE: KREISLER RADIO ON A VELVET BACKGROUND.

The camera moves on slowly on the brightly lit dial as the first chords of NIGHTBEAT are heard. FADE under.

CHRIS

(as a man)

I couldn't breathe. Every night I hardly slept.

Simple as that. But it was not long after the war and dads didn't like kids to be asthmatic—that meant low moral fibre. Me . . . I just lived my life through the radio, where other kids lived through books, though when the serials and the Lux theatre gave in to the dance bands, I read, too.

Fact is, all I ever wanted was to be a writer. Or a good

liar. I was good at both, and when I was about eleven, it came to me that they were both the same thing.

SCENE 2. NIGHT. CHRIS' HOUSE. MONTAGE.
Wide angle, brightly lit shots of needles, pills, CHRIS tossing in bed, breathing with desperate asthmatic determination.

DAD'S VOICE

(in a calm, tired voice) No, it is psychological, psychosomatic—in his head. All that stuff about allergies is so much mumbo-jumbo. He needs to stop feeling sorry for himself. And all that radio garbage and bookishness, well, he's got to grow out of it.

MA'S VOICE

But he's only . . . eleven.

DAD'S VOICE

Good time to start weaning him. This asthma—it's all in his head.

LEAK IN: Sounds of an aerial dogfight, as parental dialogue continues.

SCENE 3. INT. THE IMAGINARY SPITFIRE'S COCKPIT. DAY. TIMELESS.
The chatter of machine guns crowds in on BIGGLES as he flings his plane across the sky, but we end on BIGGLES firing on a Messerschmidt and bringing it down. He smiles. We hear the classic radio sound effect of the dying fighter.

SCENE 4. (STOCK FOOTAGE)
Messerschmidt 109 peels away in flames.

BIGGLES

(coolly) So long, Fritz.

SCENE 5. (STOCK FOOTAGE REVERSES)
CHRIS (VOICE-OVER)

Actually, I hated to be so reliant on characters out of books and radio serials. I hated the predictability. I didn't just want to write, I wanted to rewrite.

So, Chris is established and the script is away. Who would ever know how many rewrites it took to reach that simple exposition of backstory? How many more rewrites to go when the producers decide to remove the backstory altogether and start with the action in the studios!

Now we meet the other key characters:

PETE

The old hack writer who's seen it all

VOITEK

Central European refugee—a philosophy professor before the war, now reduced to tutorial work and watching out for his beloved

ILONA

VOITEK's Golden Daughter—passionate, a brilliant mind and fiercely protective of her father and his ideas

SCENE 15. EXT. CARSTAIRS. DAY.
CHRIS is gazing at the gold letters reading 'Carstairs Radio Studios' as ILONA, wild hair flying, rushes out, bumping into him. They both recoil, CHRIS embarrassed, ILONA laughing, looking like a gypsy in her bright clothes.

ILONA

(she has a slight European accent) If you're waiting for autographs, sonny, they go out the back door. Near the rubbish cans.

CHRIS

No . . . no . . . I'm here to see Mr Carstairs. I'm a writer.

ILONA

(with scorn, near rage) Oh, sure, you're his nephew, right?

CHRIS

I wrote a script for Doctor Paul . . . he liked it . . .

Now she's furious.

ILONA

I'll just bet . . . How are old are you?

CHRIS

Almost nineteen . . .

ILONA laughs.

ILONA

And seen nothing, done nothing . . . Ha!

PETE rushes out and bumps into her. She turns in spitting rage.

PETE

Easy. Friends . . . remember, sweetie. Pub?

ILONA

(jabbing her head at CHRIS) Who's he?

PETE

How the hell would I know?

CHRIS

Chris . . . Green . . . I'm the . . .

PETE

(delighted) Oh yeah . . . the baby writer. Ilona. . . . this kid is . . .

But ILONA is darting away. CHRIS looks appalled.

PETE

Oh, that's the Jewish princess, kid . . . same age as you but carries a lot more mileage. Brought up in a Nazi concentration camp. Writes like an angel. Coming to the pub?

Seeing CHRIS hesitating, he grabs his arm.

PETE

Think you should, kid . . . Chris. Before you meet Mr Carstairs, there's a few things you ought to know.

FADE.

SCENE 16. INT. TATTERSALLS' PUB. DAY.

Tatts is a classic writers' and bohemians' pub (the two not then mutually exclusive). A large bearded guy is tearing off some blues chords as PETE and CHRIS enter. Briefly glimpsed in the corner is VOITEK, ILONA's father, in his fifties but looking older, a survivor who's kept his wry detachment, murmuring softly to his daughter. PETE and CHRIS can't see them, least of all CHRIS, dazzled by the bohemian paradise in front of him: the fulfilment of a kid's romantic dream. VOITEK catches sight of CHRIS. He smiles dreamily at ILONA.

> VOITEK
>
> Looks like your cynical friend has a protégé . . . what a holy innocent!

> ILONA
>
> What a bloody fool, you mean, papa. He's the new writer I told you about.

> VOITEK
>
> So? He looks younger than you. You hate competition or something?

> ILONA
>
> (looking hard at CHRIS) One difference, papa. He didn't go to kindergarten at Buchenwald.

VOITEK regards her, angrily.

> VOITEK
>
> So we're saints because we survived? Jesu. Ilona, get me a drink before I hit you.

Shocked, she dashes away to the bar, and the guitarist gives her a royal strum as she does.

> VOITEK
>
> (to himself) So now we got another war?

And so the story begins. Before it all ends, Carstairs' empire will totter, Chris will discover his voice as a writer and Ilona, for a brief time, will be his Muse.

And the Resolution—well—how should it all end?

That's up to you. *Wireless Dreams* can end in so many ways. Here's one possibility you could work with:

Chris has written Voitek's own amazing and true personal story of death camps and resistance fighters. Stark realism has replaced soap opera for one night. Chris loses his job—but maybe found his voice as a writer . . .

And just when you think you've reached the end there is always one last battle you have to fight—against the dreaded plot diagram and character arc!

Character arcs, plot waves and other distractions

LIPNIK

You probably walked in here thinking we wanted people who knew something about the medium. Maybe even thinking there was all kinds of technical mumbo-jumbo to learn. You were dead wrong. We're only interested in one thing: can you tell a story, Bart?

(*Barton Fink*, Joel and Ethan Coen, 1990)

Because plot structure involves complicating the lives of your characters, many script manuals and hence also a lot of funding bodies and producers have internalised the notion that some sort of mathematical formula can be applied to a successful script structure. If it fits, then it'll work. You can see why some bureaucracies might find this notion of a kind of World's Best Practice in plot structure pleasing—it makes everything seem so . . . under control.

Certainly you should try to develop the ability to tell when a script has lost its way. This can happen for many reasons, but the most common ones are:

- dialogue scenes that go on too long (or forever);
- subplots that take over;
- flashbacks (or forward) that become the main plot;
- unresolved loose ends (whatever happened to BILL from scenes six to twenty-five?);
- introducing a character or plot action (a sudden death, a mysterious message) that is disconnected from all the other plot lines and characters (in other words, Red Herrings).

But there is no magic mathematical wand or wave form pattern that can help you with this, since the evidence you are looking for is all internal to the script. Other popular schemas that you may read about include peaks and troughs, and even more mathematical derivatives.

All of this should remind us (again) of William Goldman's dictum that nobody knows anything. In the end the only matrix that works is the old one of a beginning, a middle, and an end. As far as the rest, well, Mr Lipnik would say:

> Dammit, if all our writers were like you I wouldn't have to get so involved. I'd like to see something by the end of the week!

Chapter 13
Children's Television and Film

> Far from being a sacred trust, children's programming is now
> a form of revenue raising. With honourable exceptions like
> *Playschool, Adventure Island* and . . . much of the output of the
> Australian Children's Television Foundation, littlies were
> sacrificed to the tender mercies of bad animation and whoever
> station management could force to climb into a bear suit.

('No More Gooey Custard', Philip Adams in The Australian, 2 Jan 1999: 14)

No audience is more important than that for children's programming. And of course that audience includes parents and carers as
well as children. No script forms so demand apparent simplicity
with an essential appreciation, not just of what children want to
view, but what should become a perfect match of good intentions
and good writing. A writer of children's material at times will deal
not only with the aims, hopes (and some regulations) surrounding
work for the children's market, but will also offer some successful
examples of material that works in the international marketplace.

For more detailed insights into specific forms the chapters on
animation and feature and series drama offer detailed structural
and marketing strategies.

A growing field

The days when writing a children's show was merely a matter of
writing some simplistic gags for a character in a giant bunny (bear,
duck, kangaroo, etc.) suit are long gone.

Although the lower-budget children's shows stay afloat to allow
TV channels to maintain a dubious quota of 'children's material',
the general field of children's programs has expanded
dramatically—partly because of government regulation, but more
importantly because the production sector has realised that children are, if anything, more exacting and demanding and, yes, more
profitable than adult audiences. After all, how many kids watch

shows like *Wheel of Fortune* with anything approaching involvement? Marketing, too, has refined its focus on the huge international children's demographic slice.

Bodies like the Australian Children's Television Foundation (ACTF) have moved to broaden and deepen the scope of material available to children. In this they have been aided in part by government and, more recently and to a greater extent, by involved and risk-taking production companies. Production is often aided by government film and television funding bodies, both state and federal in Australia, and overseas by such organisations as the European Media funding matrix of bodies involved in developing new films and series concepts. As a result the healthiest production sector in general program development is children's television. Children's film, however, like the greater feature film industry, seems prey to the usual whims of the free market—and the usual minefields and bear pits await the unprepared writer and financier (see Chapter 12).

It's a kid's world

The relationship between children and television often involves enormous argument and passionate claims and declarations of high principle—not least about the effects of television upon young viewers. Writers should at all times keep up to date with these debates, while never falling prey to unjustified populist claims about Good Taste or Bad Effects! Beliefs about children's television often act as a focus for much broader public hopes and anxieties about the future of society, and about tradition and change.

Television, in general, is constantly scapegoated, blamed as a harmful influence on children that encourages the wrong values and leads to violence or at least anti-social behaviour. However, television is also seen as a potential tool for education and enlightenment, and as a source of great enjoyment.

To quote from the 1995 World Summit on Children's Television:

Television is frequently accused of destroying childhood, yet, in most countries around the world, it offers cultural experiences that children often claim as uniquely their own.

Much of the public debate about children and television focuses on the harmful influence of the medium, and on the need to defend children against it. Television has been seen as a major cause of consumerism and violence, and as a source of negative attitudes and crude stereotypes. Children, it is argued, should not be exploited for commercial gain, or exposed to experiences with which they are ill-equipped to cope.

They must be protected from these harmful effects by adults, who by definition are seen to know what is best.

While we recognise many of these concerns, we would hope to reframe them in the context of a more positive emphasis on children's rights as an audience. The UN Convention on the Rights of the Child, adopted in 1989, makes specific reference to the need to make information available to children through the mass media, and to ensure that this is of social and cultural benefit to the child. It asserts the right of children to express their opinions, and to have those opinions heard in matters which concern them—of which television is certainly a significant one. To insist on children's rights in relation to television is thus to regard the medium as more than simply a means of targeting audiences for products.

(ACTF website, 1998)

This approach, so disarmingly positive, suggests that the writer for children's television may be in for a Golden Age! If critics are now beginning to identify and to promote its positive potential as a source of education, entertainment, and artistic and cultural experience, then the future looks bright for the writers and producers in the rapidly growing field of free to air, and cable children's specialists such as *Nickelodeon*.

The range of children's programs will broaden to include those which are educational as well as those which are entertaining; they will reflect a broad range of artistic styles and forms. Programs like *Round the Twist* (ABC/ACTF, series from 1992+) clearly already engage children's imaginative, emotional, and intellectual capacities. More and more programs of a similar inventiveness and 'relevance' are needed and only committed writers can provide them.

New programs will play a role in encouraging children's awareness and tolerance of cultural diversity and their discrimination of high quality, though this is unlikely ever to be adequately defined. After all, different people, let alone different cultures, haven't yet been able to agree on a universal definition of 'quality', and what is seen to be 'educational' will depend upon how broadly one chooses to define what children can possibly learn from television. This matter of cultural difference is one that writers should always keep at the front of their minds as they develop story ideas for scripts.

Producers from the USA, the country which so dominates world trade in television, always argue that they respect the indigenous cultures of the countries that buy their products. Of course, plenty would challenge this view: notably academics studying children's television! New media technologies clearly offer great potential for more interactive forms of education and entertainment, yet they may also permit easy access to material which some would see as possibly dangerous. Ultimately, these debates reflect very different assumptions about children—about their needs, concerns, and interests as an audience.

Trends in programming and production for children

Dare I say it, children's programs are sometimes just crap.
One of the best defences against the international animation
invasion is strong, original programming. Of course,
animation has its place, children enjoy it but it is a question
of balance.

(John Willis, Director of Programs, Channel Four Television, UK)

In spite of such feeling, there is a wide and growing market for new and daring ideas for children's productions. The field remains the most exciting of all for writers who don't feel that they are necessarily lowering themselves by writing for children. It could be argued that the best and most challenging work lies in this field; certainly leading international writers like Morris Gleitzman and David McRobbie believe that this is so. The areas of work continue to multiply within genres and forms.

Animation
Animation continues to account for much of the programming produced for children worldwide. With the rise of dedicated international animation services such as Turner's Cartoon Network, and the almost universal appeal of animation, the form looks set to dominate children's schedules around the world for quite some time yet.

The growing appeal of animation is not confined to children's audiences either, with animated programs such as *The Simpsons* and *South Park* gaining large audiences internationally across all age groups. Of course, many have realised that *South Park* is not a children's series at all—it may all depend on what sort of children you have in mind!

Animation is popular on the international and multinational services, due to its ease in dubbing into other languages and also as it is usually not so culturally specific as other forms of programming. There are increasing concerns in some countries about whether the level of violence in some animation series is appropriate. Since this argument was levelled at *Bugs Bunny* and Disney cartoons in the 1940s, the debate seems set to rage on.

Animation lends itself particularly well to merchandising opportunities, which is increasingly an important financing consideration for most producers and broadcasters. From *Bananas in Pyjamas* (ABC TV) to the *Teletubbies* (BBC TV) and the global phenomenon of *South Park* in the recent past, the marketing of merchandise associated with such series has yielded at least as much revenue as sale of the shows themselves. Products sell internationally, unhindered by language barriers. As well, animation provides major opportunities in association with newer forms of media, with CD-ROM titles or even interactive websites now accompanying many animated programs. So if you can come up with an idea with built-in marketing potential, producers will look all the more favourably upon your pitch—even if parents and some educators might not!

Animation series based on popular or classic children's stories are popular with producers, as it is perceived that parents will encourage their children to watch programs based around characters and storylines with which they themselves are familiar. As the supply of children's literature classics remaining to be adapted for television dries up, producers are now turning to adapting box-office hits—such as *The Mask*—riding on the wave of the film's publicity. It involves greater risk for producers and broadcasters to commission and/or produce original animated stories, so these are becoming scarcer, with clear implications for the future diversity of children's programming.

Children's drama

While animation continues to dominate program schedules, children's drama series are increasing in popularity around the world, particularly among the difficult-to-target early teen audience. Although children's drama is expensive to produce, quality drama which tells universal stories within a regional context is in high demand around the world. The domination of series based on recent popular short novels by writers like Morris Gleitzman (*Misery Guts*) and Paul Jennings (*Around the Twist*) suggests that buying the rights to a good novel is about the smartest move a writer can make—but you have to be quick!

Children's drama provides an alternative to animation, which is attractive to those broadcasters wanting to distinguish themselves from the animation-specialist channels. Children's drama is also perceived as more sophisticated than the magazine-style formats often aimed at the early teen audience. As well, it is recognised that children's drama has a much longer shelf life than adult drama programs, with repeat screening continuing to attract large audiences of children, and increasing financial returns to broadcasters and producers over time.

Magazines and news programs

Magazine-style programs for children are still popular, particularly on cable children's channels (e.g. *Nickelodeon*), due to their relatively low production costs and their ability to reflect and involve local communities. As program schedules expand exponentially around the world, magazine-style programs—along with game shows—are seen as ways of filling these schedules in an economical way.

Increasingly, children's programmers are involving children in the production and presentation of magazine-style programs so that children have some say in the content of these programs. This is particularly so with the dedicated children's channels, which aim to build viewer loyalty by promoting themselves as the child's own special channel, a concept with which traditional broadcasters, restricted by limited children's schedule time, can hardly compete.

> Over the years, *Nickelodeon* has institutionalised listening. We do more research among kids than anyone else. We conduct countless quantitative surveys and over 250 focus groups a year . . . and we don't just ask them about TV. We ask how they view the world. What are they concerned about? How do they make friends?

> (Garry Laybourne, President, *Nickelodeon*, USA)

In-house production

Some major US broadcasters have begun acquiring or establishing their own animation studios, signalling an increased emphasis on vertical integration throughout the production industry at large. The rise of in-house production around the world poses challenges for independent producers, who have hitherto been able to enjoy great freedom to create some of the most original children's products. Digital production technology will only increase this tendency.

Some independent producers are hopeful that the proliferation of channels will more than compensate for the program opportunities lost through the rise in in-house production, while others are securing output deals with broadcasters to ensure continuity of production. The stability of the independent production sector appears uncertain in those countries where quotas for independent production on terrestrial channels are not set by regulation.

So the future looks solid for aspiring writers and program makers. The biggest obstacle will be the in-house production and increased lock-step between broadcasters and publishers, represented by the growing power and production muscle exercised by multinational companies.

Bringing the book to the screen

Any survey of the field of children's drama reveals that successful novels and short stories are the single most used resource of producers and consistently achieve those all-important pre-sales that ensure a series will be made. In this section we'll look at a few examples of work that has sold into most territories (US/UK/Europe).

Of course, if you can achieve the ideal double of first creating a successful character and then developing the series or movie based on that character yourself, then your future is probably assured. Surprisingly, few writers actually take this route; most novelists are all too aware of the cruel traps and slow development time for TV and film projects, and prefer to stick to the safety and security of the printed word.

One writer who has pulled off the double is David McRobbie. As an ex-producer of educational children's television and radio programs, he was uniquely placed to know what the market wanted, and how to provide for that need with an intelligent leading character, Wayne of *The Wayne Manifesto* (Artist Services, 1998–99). Imaginative, frustrated, hyperactive, Wayne is the sort of kid other kids readily identify with, whatever country they live in.

Once you have your main character, it's up to your imagination to create a social world (ideally a rather dysfunctional one) and the usual assortment of good and bad neighbours, magic, and fantasy. Whether the scripts sing or plod is of course up to you—and your production company!

In the following extract from the revised draft of episode ten of the series, you can see the interplay between Wayne as the 'stable' dramatic centre of the story and his highly eccentric family. The dysfunctional family setting is almost *de rigeur* for contemporary young lead characters, providing the essential foil and plot generator. Nevertheless, in spite of the realism of the dialogue (in other words it sounds like real people talking!), the Asparagus Man and Grandpa's memories bring an element of the magical and the imaginative (for those who refuse to admit that magic exists) into the screenplay from the start.

Note that the action is cleanly and simply described and the layout classically simple (in scripts, as in all matters, the simpler your layout and descriptions, the less chance there is that someone in the production chain will get it all wrong. This is not of course a guarantee—but it is a great help!

SCENE 1. INT. A TYPICAL MUSIC HALL STAGE. NIGHT.
GRANDPA is spotlit on stage, just finishing his act, which has not pleased the unseen audience. There are boos and catcalls.

> WAYNE (VO)

This is my Grandpa, who used to be a comedian.

A barrage of vegetables descends upon the stage while GRANDPA ducks and dodges as the catcalls grow.

> WAYNE (VO)

Then he couldn't think of any new jokes and routines. (pause) But he got plenty of fresh vegetables.

GRANDPA bends to pick up a cabbage and a small pumpkin.

> GRANDPA

(to unseen audience) I thank yew. You're too kind.

GRANDPA bows to left and right, then with the pumpkin on his hand, Yorick style, and the cabbage under his arm, he makes a dignified exit.

SCENE 2. INT. THE BACK VERANDAH. NIGHT.
WAYNE is all alone out on the back verandah, sitting up in a small camp bed. He has the blanket pulled up to his chin and looks scared.

> WAYNE (VO)

Aunty Irene offloaded Grandpa onto us—so he gets *my* bedroom if you don't mind, which is why I'm on the back verandah. (brightens) But it's all right. Dad fixed it so the wind doesn't get in . . .

A gust of wind ruffles WAYNE's hair. He shivers.

> WAYNE (VO)

. . . he says! (pause) But it's scary out here.

WAYNE's eyes widen then we see what's troubling him. In a reverse shot, there is a cabinet-style deep freeze, the lid of which slowly lifts with a creaking noise.

> ASPARAGUS MAN

(sepulchral voice) Wayne, oh Wayne.

Two hands made of asparagus spears appear over the edge of the deep freeze cabinet. WAYNE's expression betrays his fear.

WAYNE (VO)

It's—Snap Frozen Asparagus Man—he's come to get me.

One of the asparagus hands beckons with a finger.

ASPARAGUS MAN

Wayne, come in and join us. It's lovely in here. You can scrape the ice off the sides and make snowballs . . .

WAYNE

(*Agitato*) Go away, go away! If I pop in there, I'll end up deep frozen—with a giblet pack plus extra drumsticks.

ASPARAGUS MAN

Oooooh! Suit yourself, Wayne. Ooh-ho-ho-ho!

The hands recede into the deep freeze and the lid closes. We see WAYNE's face in CU.

WAYNE (VO)

Well, that bit's a lie, but it is spooky out here.

But there is something else that takes his attention. His elders are in the adjoining kitchen, deep in conversation. WAYNE leans closer to the wall to listen.

SCENE 3. INT. THE KITCHEN. NIGHT.
MUM, DAD and GRANDPA are sitting around the table. GRANDPA looks deflated.

MUM

Come on, cheer up, Dad—it's not the end of the world.

GRANDPA

It was the end of my unit. (He makes exploding gesture with his hands) Poof. Up in smoke.

DAD

I blame the chips. (pause) Hot oil and net curtains . . .

DAD shakes his head.

MUM

And not being insured.

> GRANDPA
>
> Well, don't rub it in.
>
> MUM
>
> You're very welcome to stay here, Dad. Wayne doesn't mind giving up his room.
>
> DAD
>
> And I'll have your unit fixed up in no time.
>
> GRANDPA and MUM had brightened somewhat but on hearing DAD's promise, they both slump. GRANDPA sighs while MUM shakes her head.

Compare a rather less successful script layout for the series *Misery Guts* (Steel Stem Poppy/Barron, 1998), based on the very successful novels by Morris Gleitzman, *Misery Guts*, *Worry Warts* and *Puppy Fat*. In this case, a writer more accustomed to stage work has been rather excited by the move to television and the script is typographically—if not structurally—rather overwrought. First, here's part of the synopsis to remind you of the realist origins of this comic novel:

SYNOPSIS:

> Keith Shipley is the only son of Vin and Marge Shipley. The family live above their 'fish 'n' chips' shop in grey South London. Vin used to make the best 'fish 'n' chips' in all of South London but now things are tough.
>
> Keith's parents are 'misery guts' and Keith is convinced that the only way for the family to regain its former happiness is for him to make his parents smile again.
>
> So Keith paints the fish and chip shop orange. This certainly doesn't make his parents smile! It has the opposite effect!

Now the script . . .

SCENE 5. INT. CHIP SHOP. DAY 1. (KEITH, VIN, MARGE)
KEITH *is still trying to explain to* VIN.

KEITH

I thought you'd like it.

VIN

Whatever made you think we'd like a bright orange fish and chip shop?

KEITH

It's not orange, it's . . .

VIN

And what's all this nonsense about cheering us up?

KEITH breaks.

KEITH

I just wanted you to be happy for a change! Like you used to be! You're never happy anymore.

A deadly silence follows this outburst. VIN looks directly in KEITH'S eyes.

VIN

Happy? You want to know why I'm not happy?

VIN pulls open the fridge door and pulls out a tray of cold battered fish. He holds one up.

VIN

What d'you call that?

KEITH

Cold battered fish.

VIN dumps the tray onto the counter.

VIN

Half of last night's fry up not sold. All wasted. Bin fodder!

VIN slaps a piece of raw fish on the counter.

> VIN

What's that?

> KEITH

Um, Don't you know? Come on, what is it?

> KEITH

Piece of raw fish, Dad.

Now VIN plonks down a potato.

> VIN

And that?

KEITH is seriously worried about VIN now. MARGE comes in with a basin of hot water and a cloth.

> KEITH

Mum, Dad's lost his memory! He's forgotten the ingredients for fish and chips!

VIN bangs the potato on the counter.

> VIN

Answer me, what is it?

> KEITH

It's a potato, Dad. Don't worry, we'll get you help.

VIN is getting frustrated now; he plonks a bowl of batter down, splashing it over the counter.

> MARGE

Vin, don't . . .

> VIN

He has to know!

KEITH panics.

> KEITH

Know what?

He sees a conclusion passing and jumps for it.

KEITH

Aaaarrrggghhh! He's got a brain tumour! He doesn't know a potato from a piece of fish! Get a doctor! No, get an ambulance!

VIN and MARGE roll their eyes; they're used to him.

Two things are immediately apparent from the *Misery Guts* extract. The obvious one is that the script is maybe not in this instance written by the original novelist, Morris Gleitzman (a writer who collected many screen credits before opting for the life of the book-writer). The script itself pretty much follows the trajectory of the book itself, in a straightforward way. Apart from the credit sequence, the treatment is rather flat.

You can see this by looking at the script format itself: the descriptions as originally printed in the script are all capitalised, giving the effect of 'shouting', and the scenes in this and all other episodes are rather longer than we might expect—more like stage scenes in fact. But because of the success and wide audience (internationally) of the original novel, *Misery Guts*, the producers had no trouble at all in raising the finance for the series—with no input requested from Morris Gleitzman except a credit as Story Consultant (this title often means that the original writer will not be consulted at all!). Clearly if you want the best result from screen adaptations—the surest way to pre-sales and series finance—then you should write the original books yourself, then do the adaptations. The trouble is, very few writers have the time and David McRobbie, with his sharp, fast-paced adaptations of his own work, remains a fairly unusual case.

Both *The Wayne Manifesto* and the *Misery Guts* screenplays are good examples of successful and easily and quickly (internationally) financed screen adaptations that are proving popular all over the world. Note, too, that that both lead characters are very alike in character and dialogue: feisty, quirky, and very contemporary. Except for this last quality, which depends a lot on little details, these are character traits that age very well and can keep a series current for a ten years or more (like *Round the Twist*, now in its second decade and looking none the older for it). After all, it's the audience that age, not necessarily the characters, who can always find new audiences if they are strongly enough conceived and developed.

Technically and in terms of presentation, though, *The Wayne Manifesto* script has a clean elegance and an easy-to-read quality that makes it that much more attractive to producers (very often form can be as important as content).

Some final thoughts on children's television in the digital age

The advent of new digital technologies, like the advent of television itself, has led to all sorts of wild and overexcited claims about their educational and dramatic money-making potential, and to equally earnest media prophecies about the loss of genuine dramatic values and the digital loss of humanity itself. The 'convergence' that will be made possible by the digital encoding of information is much more than simply a matter of technological change; it is a coming together of television, telecommunications and computers. Whatever the technology, writers with *experience* and *ideas* are still wanted.

Maybe, after all, we have finally arrived at McLuhan's global village, but the old need for innovative stories, children's plots, characters, and ideas is still there, and no amount of technological hype can take that away. No global village idiots will be required.

Soon writers for children of the digital age will also be seen as a necessary and vital part of the creative process. If you become one of those writers, then you will have a lot of power. Just be aware of it.

Chapter 14
Animation: Imaginary Lives

Animators are the true heroes of the media world. Whether producing megahits like *The Simpsons* (as a series: Fox, 1990) or even the less mentally challenging but still engaging pratfalls and ocker thrills of *Crocadoo* (9/Energee, 1998+), they work at the very sharp edge of imagination and risk.

Animation is also, by definition, the ultimate form of High Concept scriptwriting.

Unless you have in mind a career as the in-betweener or inker on a Disney series, the world of animation is a constant challenge to your originality—and the courage of network programmers!

Remember—you don't have to know how to animate to write for animation. Ideas are always more precious than artistic skills until the day of production. And you can always call in a collaborator to help with the design elements of your pitch.

But animation writing has developed from simple gag writing to a complex and highly industrialised art form, and it is now quite rare for animators to cross from one area of work to another. The two key areas of animation work we'll focus on here are Industrial Animation and Freeform; the difference is similar to the distinction between the production line and cottage industry. The new point of connection between all animators (except those scratching onto raw film stock) is that much animation is done on computers; this has led to a change in the role of many trained animators. The new, more complex role is that of creating interactive software, advertising and commissioned design work (producing animated room details and colour schemes for architects)—and these areas need a book all to themselves.

However bizarre they may seem, all animation stories need a plot and structure of some sort. Even the most anarchic of experimental work has to be carefully planned! What the continued success of adult animations such as *The Simpsons* means is that animation has crossed over the boundaries of the world of children's entertainment—and this simple fact alone guarantees a

long and prosperous future for animation. Few would have anticipated this in the mid-1950s when the cinema cartoon, in spite of
many attempts to make it more 'modern' (*Pepe Le Pew*, *The
RoadRunner*, Warner Brothers), gradually disappeared from the
cinema screens of the world.

It was not long before the cartoon reappeared on the television
screen, first in commercials, then as a substitute for live action
comedy (*The Flintstones*) or resuscitated by compilation shows like
The Disney Hour or in the 1960s, *Sesame Street* (PBS/CTW).

The studio-produced animation of the 1940s and 1950s became
increasingly abstract and expressionistic. UPA Studios, begun by
animators who had broken from Disney following a strike in 1941,
rejected the naturalist style in favour of abstract, two-dimensional
drawings inspired by contemporary artists. The company was
responsible for cartoons such as *Hell Bent for Election* (1944), *The
Brotherhood* (1946), *Gerald McBoing-Boing* (1951), and the 'Mister
Magoo' series. These shorts marked the furthest commercial animation studios would ever stray from the Disney model that still
rules today, in spite of the move to computer animation through
Pixar (*A Bug's Life*, 1998) and even Disney itself (*Antz,* 1998).

The commercial animation script

From *The Simpsons* to short children's series for afternoon television, a glance at the end credits will tell you that animation is
hardly the work of one individual. Indeed, increasingly the story
writing and animation functions are now separated. The screen
credits for writers in a series like *The Toothbrush Family* (five minutes long: ABC/Southern Star) and *The Adventures of Sam* (30
minutes: ABC/Southern Star) reveal that writers with previous live
action series experience are often employed, so you don't need to
be a trained animation writer—just a good storyteller.

Most scripts will follow easily recognisable forms in addition to
the dictates of the commercial break. This is true regardless of
length, and excluding *The Simpsons* and *Beavis and Butt-head*,
which obey the structural rules of the familiar sitcom rather than
of animation itself (which at its best has no rules except those
internal to each individual film).

Any experienced animation writer will use the techniques of feature or series plot-building when working on animation series—
not least conflict, complications and resolution. Indeed, animation
film plots conform almost perfectly to such models to allow for a
maximum play of the visual elements. And, of course, there are the
usual internal rules which must obey the narrative logic involved
in the creation of the series—laws of Nature if you like, that exist
only in the world of any particular series. Original animators

(Svankmajer, Priit Parn), as noted above, create a different set of rules for each and every film project.

This is how Chuck Jones sets out the internal logic of the world of the Road Runner:

- The Road Runner cannot harm the Coyote except inadvertently by going 'Beep-beep'.
- No outside force can harm the Coyote—only his own ineptitude or the failure of the Acme products. The Coyote could stop any time, if he were not a fanatic (Jones quotes Santayana: 'A fanatic is one who redoubles his effort when he has forgotten his aim').
- No dialogue ever except 'Beep-beep'.
- All materials, tools, weapons or mechanical contrivances must be obtained from the Acme Corporation.
- Whenever possible, make gravity the Coyote's greatest enemy (apart from himself).
- The Coyote is always more humiliated than harmed by his failures.

(Chuck Jones: 'The Road Runner Rules, or, Seven Steps to the Acme of Perfection')

Except for the embargo on dialogue of any sort, these rules are a model for consistent action within a *wholly invented* universe—which is the secret of any successful (and addictive) film or TV series.

There are some basic common-sense underpinnings to writing series scripts, as well as some essential ingredients. All cartoon series also have a moral (if you want to be old-fashioned about it) or a central theme (usually it's this: Anyone wanting to bring the Hero(ine) or the Universe or both to a Sticky End is Bad and will be dealt with!). This theme, once agreed upon, provides the motor for all actions, however silly.

Next: all such shows are very specifically targeted at particular age groups, from 2–6, 6–9, 9–12 and onwards and upwards. Though of course not only these age groups will watch, the series are marketed internationally on the basis of 'delivering a specific age group audience to the broadcasting network'; thus the level of language for *Lizzie's Library* (2–6, Henderson Bowman, 1996+) which has a full voice-over narration to be read over the action by a 'storyteller', and a fully dramatised series like *Ginger Meggs* (all ages to 16, 7/ICA, 2000+).

The essential ingredients for a series normally resemble some of the 'classic' plot elements that an old-fashioned detective mystery would have:

- a crime (or a plot);
- the Gathering of the Baddies;

- an early clue (normally an attempt, maybe bungled, to get at the protagonist or an innocent part of society: Children in School, The Water Board and so on). Remember that the personal is political—that is, any action aimed at a part of society is a moral affront to the protagonist;
- chases and investigations (self-explanatory; these take up much, if not most, of the screen time, especially in the lower budget or more simplistic series—we needn't name them!);
- collection scene—the good team get together to sort out a way to deal with the enemy, solve the crime, lay a trap, etc;
- the Big Bang! (resolution, climax, whatever);
- the Gloat: the victors gather to have a good laugh about the victory (normally accompanied by some weak joke about one member of the team to set off the laughter—an awful convention! See particularly *The Jetsons*, Hanna-Barbera, 1962).

Whatever the age of your target audience, the action must be under way at least within the first page of your script. After all, the whole point of cartoons is that they are, well, cartoonish. So be animated! Nothing looks more preachy, or more like an old TV commercial, than animation storytelling that insists on only ever telling stories with a moral.

Original series
On the other hand, a visit to the film markets at Milan (MIFED) and Cannes (MIPCOM) shows that the appetite for animation series with a more subtle message is growing, along with the potential audience. As the number of cable channels stabilises or increases, so does the market. A common thread links many successful new players: relative cheapness of production and, increasingly, a 'green' or environmental subtext, often combined with hints of fantasy or science fiction, for example the long-running live action (but cartoonish) *Ocean Girl* (10/Media World). Such programs use exotic concepts and fantastic and beautiful imaginary worlds too—for European series at least. Animal series are also successful; the animated *Silver Brumby* (10/Media World), based on the children's novel by Eleanor Dark but using original storylines, is a typical offering. Generally, what works well as live action may work even better as animation. And what would cost far too much to produce as live action *has* to be animated. For example, *Neon Genesis Evangelion* (Gainax, 1997) would be unthinkably expensive as live action, but works wonderfully well as manga animation.

Any successful pitch for a new series must involve exceptional artwork and artists' characterisations. The storylines are—typically—the last elements looked at by potential investors. But, provided that the traditional interests and demand for action of the audience are borne in mind and the new series concept offers a 'spin' on the familiar, then a well pitched new series for children is the single genre most likely to succeed in the international screen marketplace.

Cosmo Kids: Somewhere in space ...

The script format for animated series is much like that for the feature film, with one important difference. For animation the writer is also the director in that the screenplay should contain all the visual cues for the animation team to follow, unlike the rather spare look of a drama script (nowadays, as we've noted, it's best to leave out all camera directions).

The recent series *Cosmo Kids* (Novālis Animation, 1999) is a classic example of the planning, selling and marketing of the genre at an international conference. The script excerpt that follows is part of a whole package of materials (pitch, character drawings, storyboards, and scripts) which has been to various international markets including Cannes and Milan in the late 1990s. The producers are careful in their pitch to identify and define the audience:

Target audience

Cosmo Kids is aimed at 7–11 year olds. Audience research reveals that young girls enjoy stories with emotional depth whereas boys like action and adventure. *Cosmo Kids* delivers all of this and more. Like a junior version of *Star Trek*, it also delves into social and ecological themes that today's astute children identify with and approve.

The eco-toon genre

Cosmo Kids is a classic human-alien friendship story that belongs to the new entertainment genre called Eco-Toons. These have proved extremely popular with children because they reflect their ideological values and concerns for the environment.

Eco-Toons have a great track record as financial investments and television ratings winners. The Eco-Toon series *Widget* (USA, 1990–91), now in its fifth series, ranks in the top ten of all daily animated shows in US Syndication.

(© Novalis Animation, 1998)

What would you do if your planet is about to be destroyed and your mother is lost in space?

As you can see, the contemporary pitch for even the most simple of shows needs to show an awareness of the audience—only then will the broadcasters' representatives at film markets get around to reading your script. Here's an excerpt from the pilot of the series. Note the very careful visual directions; visual elements are as important as the characterisations. Of course a storyboard and character concept sketches accompany this script. Key elements such as the STRANGE ANIMALS are in caps and will be accompanied by design sketches:

SCENE 1. EXT. UNIVERSE. DAY.
Move through the universe towards COSMO PLANET surrounded by its SEVEN SMALL MOONS, each a different colour. Pass close to a barren yellow moon and close on COSMO PLANET.

VOICE-OVER

Planet Cosmo . . . once a jewel of the Universe.

The land is clothed in lush forests and bountiful plains. Gentle clouds drift across sparkling blue oceans. We pass low across the plains as a herd of STRANGE ANIMALS gallops away.

On the fringe of a forest of weird trees are several family groups of BLUE SKINNED people dressed in primitive robes. A FAMILY of four stand by a large rock watching the animals. The FATHER has one arm over his DAUGHTER's shoulder and the other arm over his SON's shoulder. The MOTHER stands alongside.

VOICE-OVER

Until the day of the giant eclipse . . .

As in *Superman* (Richard Donner, 1978), the little planet is plunged into darkness and chaos. The people now live underground, emerging to build a great city and search the universe for the precious mineral longevium, which alone can sustain life on their planet. Then the mineral runs out.

7. INT. DAR-OM'S LOUNGE. NIGHT.

DAR-OM is standing in his penthouse apartment staring out through the perspex at the lights of the city. He has one arm over his daughter ZENITH's shoulder and the other arm over MAN-DA's shoulder. PLUMA hovers nearby looking out the window.

ZENITH

Father! What will happen to us?

DAR-OM looks down at his children; his face is etched with emotion.

DAR-OM

Zenith . . . Man-Da . . . unless we can find a new source of longevium we cannot survive.

MAN-DA

But Mother and her crew will find some! She's the best navigator in the universe!

There is a poignant pause.

DAR-OM

My children, I'm sorry that I have to tell you this but . . . (beat) . . . there has been no further contact from Probor Explorer . . .

Note the use of the older radio term (beat) indicating a pause as a direction to the actors. Such terms were once a mandatory part

Cosmo Kids! The eco-toon in action.

of screenplays as well, but now survive only in radio drama and animated films where actors record the character voices before the animation is completed.

Cosmo Kids, both as a script and as a marketing package, is an exemplary contemporary series specifically designed for the ever-growing international animation market. The focus of the series on ecological themes and on relationships shows a new maturity in audiences—if not always in program buyers!

You and your imaginary universe

Animation is such an open field that it would be sad indeed—and a waste of a great medium—if you held back on your imaginative vision, so remember:

- With animation there is no limit: set the show in outer space or inside the body of a baby facing the world for the first time. Nothing is so far out that it cannot be produced by animation, nothing so bizarre that the audience will not go along with you for the ride if you dream up the impossible!
- Write visually and use plenty of descriptive writing in your screenplay. The script reader and producer must be able to visualise, animators to draw inspiration and the audience to inhabit the world you have created.
- Leave nothing out, however small the detail. Chuck Jones and Walt Disney may have been vastly different animators, but they left nothing to chance—or to anyone else, where possible.
- The words 'weird' and 'impossible' do not exist in ToonTown™.
- This last point is doubly important now that so much animation is spread around the globe, with Korean animators working on American series, and Australian animators (Disney Australia, Hanna-Barbera, many others) working for everyone, it seems!
- Ssssh! Keep dialogue to a minimum—certainly much less than for any other form of media writing, for the pictures here are the words. Remember the Road Runner! Most dialogue lines can be replaced by physical reactions to physical actions. Pace and space! Each scene or fade out should end with a wipeout—or at least a visual gag. If you have lined up your gags in a short scene breakdown beforehand, all the better because this will help you pace and space the gags.
- Stop laughing—this is serious! Oh no, it isn't. Keep 'em laughing, and never let the script bog down in solemnity. You can be as serious as you wish about your environmental themes or message, but don't be solemn. And keep the characters' speeches 'in character'—even if that just means a catchphrase

like 'Beep-beep'. Simple things get laughs—and keep the audience coming back for more.

- It's still all about character. Like Wile E. Coyote, let the seeds of success or failure be in the established or revealed nature of your characters. No surprises—the same rule as for drama generally. The flaws or mistakes of your creations are what bring matters to a climax—and a resolution.

No-nos in daytime animation series

This is work for a general audience (with a lot of kids) so avoid actions that children might mimic (stairsliding for example). Surely kids aren't silly enough to try to fly off tall buildings like Superman any more—or are they?

If you start to worry too much about possibilities like this you will never dare to write for animation—the constant checking on possible disastrous results will stifle any new gags before they get to the page. But you do have a responsibility, particularly in relation to onscreen or implied violence. Punching, kicking, bashing, shooting, bombing—as the violence escalates so does your responsibility to make it both unthreatening, unattractive (as, say, a way of life) and so 'cartoonish' as to make it clear that this is all meant to be fun (for the viewers, that is).

Check out some old Disney cartoons from the 1930s and 1940s; even for adults the coldblooded violence can be chilling. And Warner cartoons feature characters who have speech impediments (Daffy Duck, Elmer Fudd, Sylvester, and Tweety) and/or who are fuelled by rage and testosterone (Wile E. Coyote, Daffy Duck—'a fully fledged paranoid schizophrenic' said the *New York Times* in 1987) and plain malice (Bugs Bunny—well, all of them really). That's cartoons, folks!

Then again, if you go for broke and damn the torpedoes you may end up writing a film as successful in the risks it takes as *Who Framed Roger Rabbit?* (Robert Zemeckis, 1988), which is as much a satire on the violence of cartoons of previous generations as a spoof on a the private eye genre. Try doing all that without setting a bad example to someone!

What's the big joke? A word from freelance animators

Many animators over the years have claimed that the production industry's belief that animation is necessarily 'funny' has been the curse upon animation from its beginnings. After all, no one suggested that motion pictures themselves had to be a riot of laughs—not after the first years of *What the Butler Saw* and the very first short Edison films (Kines).

The history of animation as an art form is full of films that have been dark, serious, and indeed anything but amusing. The quite startling works of Carolyn Leaf (especially her sandbox animation of the 1990s) and Jan Svankmajer (*Alice*, 1988) are widely considered to be among the finest of all contemporary animation. Such unique films are clear evidence to counter the myth that Disney-style gags are the only future for animation. Some of the best postwar animation was produced in Eastern Europe, mostly in state-supported studios such as Yugoslavia's Zagreb Studios. Outstanding work includes that of Jirí Trnka (*The Emperor's Nightingale*, 1948), Dusan Vukotiç (*Concerto for Sub-Machine Gun*, 1959) in Yugoslavia, and Ivan Ivanov-Vano (*The Mechanical Flea*, 1964) in the Soviet Union.

Like comic books and the funnies (newspaper cartoons), in general *all* animated films have been perceived in America as first and foremost a children's genre, but in the 1970s they began to address an older audience. The perverse morality plays of Ralph Bakshi—*Heavy Traffic* (1973), *Fritz the Cat* (1972) (the first X-rated animated film), and that very odd epic *Lord of the Rings* (1978)—led directly to the public's ready acceptance of Matt Groening's *The Simpsons* and soon, the anarchic and scatological *Beavis and Butt-head* (Mike Judge/MTV), including a successful 'cult' movie (*Beavis and Butt-head do America*, Mike Judge, 1996).

Original animation: The air up there

Original animation work is the Sistine Chapel of film: a world full of condensed wonders of art and invention, largely hidden from the eyes of all but the aficionados of this freest of motion picture forms.

To enter the world of commercial animation there is no better way than to walk in the door with your own personal film. Just as for any other part of the communications industry, the portfolio of work is critical.

As for the growing international animation industry, you can, of course, enter as a scriptwriter, generally starting out as a storyliner. In this case you need to understand animation, but do not necessarily have to be an artist yourself.

But free animation—producing the sort of individual work that is generally seen at festivals and awards nights—is what all animators long to do. Every now and then, one new animator will break onto the scene and then the choice is whether to stay independent or become populist. In the 1990s in Europe, Nick Park with *Wallace and Gromit* made his name with his original creations—and was by the end of the 1990s running his own small studio (Aardman) producing both original work and commercial animation. True originality has a very long life indeed.

In Australia a number of independent animators have gone on to become small industrial studios: Disneys that never quite get *too* big. One outstanding example is Yoram Gross with his series of features 'starring' Dot the kangaroo; *Dot and the Bunny* (1982) is still screening worldwide on cable. Dave Dineen has turned his hand from pure animation to live action commercials. This is a common move for trained animators, who, like architects, form a surprisingly large segment of the film industry.

Other animators keep themselves afloat with commercial and corporate work (Darren Hughes of VisualEyes, Max Bannah, Denis Tupicoff) but still keep their energies intact for the original work that drew them into animation in the first place. Their work is regularly seen at festivals throughout the world, on SBS and ABC TV and internationally, primarily on European and American television channels. Remember animation often needs no subtitling or dubbing—it is the most universal of film forms since the days of silent film. Even plot-heavy manga animation like *Neon Genesis Evangelion* (Gainax, 1997) is easily dubbed but is culturally international. Festivals devoted to animation are the meccas for all animators, even those working for giant multinational cartoon factories. These include the Zagreb World Festival, the Stuttgart International Festival of Animation, the Ottawa International, the Hiroshima International, and the Annecy (France) and Cardiff (alternating with Bristol) Festivals.

Making the personal film: Dennis Tupicoff and *The Darra Dogs*
Melbourne-based but Brisbane-trained (the Queensland College of Art has Australia's only undergraduate degree in animation), Dennis Tupicoff brings a keen sociological and political eye to his stark animations of the dark side of a sort of universal suburbia. His films have regularly won international awards, none more so than *The Darra Dog*s (1993) and *His Mother's Voice* (1997). Both films are based on personal observations, though triggered by vastly differing events.

The Darra Dogs takes as its narrative line a diary-like reminiscence (voiced by Dennis) about a childhood in the Brisbane industrial suburb of Darra, a sort of urban hell for humans and, in this film, the Darra dogs themselves.

The script reads very like a yarn told in a pub. It is laconic, conversational. But the storyboard gives a hint of much darker matters than suburban memories. It was this simple concept document which, along with the voice-over narration script, attracted the finance for the project.

Because of the unique visual style of the film, the script actually begins with a note on these design elements:

A note on design:

The graphic design of this film will reflect the different textures of these events in my memory. Though using mainly cel and drawing techniques, it will not be a 'cartoon' in its representation of dogs and the world. By using different styles, I hope to achieve the expressive truth of each sequence.

(concept document © Denis Tupicoff, 1990)

The early sequences, setting the scene of family and suburb, show a realistic style (originally to be rotoscoped: that is, animated over live video footage already shot).

The script runs alongside the images indicating pacing and the shots to be created.

But lying there in the creek, this rotting dog seemed to float rippling in another world, somewhere between life and death, heaven and earth.

Across from our school there was a weatherboard house much like the others, except for its cheap coloured glass windows. At night it blazed with small panels of red, purple, blue, green and yellow light. We didn't go to church, so we had never seen real stained-glass.

The Darra Dogs

VOICE-OVER

We grew up in Darra in the 1950s . . . Darra was dominated by the cement works where my father worked. Its
chimneys never stopped, pouring tons of grey cement
over the bush, the abandoned dairy farms. And us.

For a later sequence, the style changes dramatically.

Priest and Dog: Almost completely black and completely
white, rather like a lino-cut. Very broadly drawn with
only occasional highlights of colour, e.g. the lights of the
house, the blood, etc.

VOICE-OVER (cont.)

Across from our school there was a weatherboard house
much like all the others except for its cheap coloured
windows. At night it blazed with small panels of red,
purple, blue, green, and yellow light. We didn't go to
church so we had never seen real stained glass. But
when this house stood up against the stars it obviously
had something to do with heaven. I called it the house
of lights.

From this childlike vision and personal memories Tupicoff
draws a terrifying story—the secret of such animation is its ability
to capture the unsayable images of childhood or dreams, as here
when the priest emerges and proceeds to brutally attack a stray
dog.

The dog ran limping past pursued by a priest. The black
figure with the gold cross kept firing as the dog turned
and faced him.

The dog ran limping
past, followed by a
Roman Catholic
priest with a rifle

VOICE-OVER (cont.)

It was all played out before me just like a movie . . .
Since that day I have never liked or trusted either
priests or churches . . .

Tupicoff's work shows the ability of animation to deal with the
'real' world. Other films like *Mr Bohm and The Herring* (Barbro
Hallstrom, cel animation, Sweden, 1996) which tells the magical
tale of a man who decided on philosophical grounds to teach a fish
to walk is both funny and a wonderfully deflating fable all about
human pomposity and muddled good intentions.

The black figure
with the gold cro
kept firing, as t
dog turned and fa
him.

The Darra Dogs. Harsh realism in the outer suburbs.

Winging It: Dinky-di Aussies abroad

The SBS national animation series *Swimming Outside the Flags*
(SBS, 1999–2000) clearly indicates the willingness of producers to
take a view of the potential of animation itself that is broader than
the simple ability to mount screen gags. This rare initiative by SBS
has led to a number of original films by animators that show the
full range of human experience that can be achieved by well-
conceived and well-written animations.

One outstanding example is from freelance animator Max
Bannah, noted internationally for his wry yarns featuring
Australian customs and obsessions. The films also have strong
visual images of the traditional timber and tin dwellings of a
Queensland that is now rapidly disappearing (*Violet and Brutal*,
1982 and *One Man's Instrument*, 1990).

In 1998 Max Bannah was commissioned (from a submitted storyline) by SBS TV to make a short animated film, *Winging It*
(1999), for a unique series of films (the series title was *Swimming
Outside the Flags*) using all media. (Another animator commissioned for a second series was Dennis Tupicoff.)

The script for *Winging It* used both a highly visually detailed
conventional script layout and storyboards to act as a 'style guide'
and an artistic statement of intent for the film.

SCENE 1. EXT. DESERT.

A jagged ridge overlooks an expanse of distant dunes. The
scene, in pastels with strong contrasting areas of light and
shade, depicts a backpacker in his early twenties sitting
high on a ridge sketching. Tighter shots reveal a loose line

drawing on a sketch pad of a high-set Queensland house. This image fills the frame.

SCENE 2. EXT. HIGH-SET TIMBER HOUSE.

Rendered in black line and areas of hatching, a young man stands in a small clinker built dinghy tied to the landing at the top of the stairs. The boat floats in the air. Two parents, two brothers and a sister are assembled on the landing. The mother kisses the young man who then rows away through the hatching into the distance. The family waves farewell.

VOICE-OVER

With a backpack, a degree in Mechanical Engineering and a hastily drawn sheet of practical knots, my family waved me off to see the world.

The family group remains on the landing, staring off in the direction of the departed boat. A sequence of shots illustrate the house alone in the hatching. A small white form enters along the line of the departed boat and flutters through the black like a bird. As it glides close by, the shape displays itself as an aerogram. It flies through the door of the distant house. Several more follow like a small flock. Flapping wings of hinged postcards and envelopes, like pigeons arriving at a coop, they also enter the house. The mother reappears at the door, gazing at the sky.

VOICE-OVER

At first there was regular contact. I sent letters, photographs and addresses of bars I'd worked in . . . but eventually my progress reports slowed until I realised there'd been no phone calls, not even a postcard to my parents for several months.

The mother's view of the hatched sky fills the frame. The black line work blends with dark hues of pastel.

Though this script appears highly poetic at times, the description is, in fact, very precisely related to the following line drawings and enables the commissioning body to make an informed decision as to the exact nature of the finished film. Thus the writing of the script is both a machine document (that is, containing rules for the representation of characters and events) and a form of pitch in itself, presenting an attractive, vernacular and easily accessible outline of the film project.

With a backpack, a degree in Mechanical Engineering and a hastily drawn sheet of practical knots, my family waved me off to see the world.

(© Max Bannah, 1998)

Traditional story telling skills in an animated film.

Animation rules

A decade after *The Simpsons* spun off from *The Tracey Ullman Show* and helped Rupert Murdoch's American Fox Network rise rapidly in pulling power, prime-time animation has never been more visible, or more popular with television accountants.

Now that the cartoons are increasingly aimed at a more adult market, networks and cable alike are finding that animation might just be the medium for the new millenium. UPN and WB, and they're just among the newer broadcast networks, have developed their own animated sitcoms. *King of the Hill* (Mike Judge/Fox, 1999), *Dilbert* (Adams/UPN, 1999), and *Family Guy* (MacFarlane/Fox, 1999) have all raced off the drawing boards with no sign of a glut in the market for quite some time to come.

It's a good time to be an animator—even better if you can develop your own show. *South Park,* along with its two proud

I'd made it to the Rose Red City in Jordan. Sick of sight-seeing, I'd sold my second day's pass to the palaces and tombs of Petra to an English cyclist.

(© Max Bannah, 1998)

The storyboard should be as expressive as possible.

parents, Matt Stone and Trey Parker, has become an animation fairytale all on its own.

Animation stopped being cute pablum for the kiddies an awfully long time ago. Perhaps it never was.

Chapter 15
Scripting Multimedia

Writers wanted!

The weekly scan of newspaper and communications industries jobs advertised shows that writers and IT producers are wanted for multimedia, television, websites generally and of course for CD-ROM game writing.

For as long as we can see ahead, it seems as if information technology (IT) is where all the new jobs will be for young writers and producers. So any writer should understand the basic playing field that is called the 'digital revolution' and know as many of the rules of the game as possible.

In this chapter we'll look at the growing industry, examine scriptwriting for multimedia and leave you with enough homework for the next ten years and beyond. Because the digital revolution never stops—it just keeps on growing like the Internet. And nobody with ideas should be left behind.

Access and interactivity: New democracy or grand illusion?

Fans of the new digital technologies often talk about 'freedom and equity for all'—a new sort of democracy of the digital world. Well, they said that when wireless first came in, and the monopolies are still accumulating newer and greater empires.

Corbis, the image-bank arm of Microsoft, has gathered the rights to almost a hundred million photographic and other images, and the count goes up every week. The promise of the new information networks was that they would permit an unlimited flow of communication. If the current situation is one in which there is a small number of transmitters and many receivers, the age of digital communication will be one in which we all have open access to information. Far from being mere consumers, all of us will have the chance to become producers in our own right.

Well, that's their pitch, anyway.

The reality is less about freedom and more about licence: in the age of modems and digital video, it will no longer be possible to limit and monitor children's access to images of all kinds. In this respect, recent scares about 'cyber-porn' represent only one aspect of what may come to be a bigger set of worries.

Yet for better or worse, an unlimited free trade in moving images may be further away than we think—and indeed may never become a reality. As with radio and television, there is a danger that the flow of information will be dominated by a small number of wealthy nations, and by commercial interests. The superhighway may well turn out to be a one-way street to corporate profit, if it isn't already. Far from improving access for all, the new technologies could simply increase existing divisions between the information-rich and the information-poor: if information and cultural goods are primarily seen as commodities, it is inevitable that poorer people and by extension, poorer countries will lose out.

Much of the selling of digital technologies such as CD-ROMs and the Internet has been based on their potential as educational tools for use in the home—and this strategy has been increasingly successful with wealthier families in more developed countries. After all, those with little ability to buy stuff (once known as 'the poor' or, geographically, the Third World) are obviously less attractive to the advertisers who pay for the services in the first place.

Rich man, poor man
This distinction between the information-rich and the information-poor also has implications in terms of formal education. In the light of the international flow of information and educational provision, the dangers of handing over everything to market forces are becoming more obvious. So the opportunities for writers continue to expand daily, but the responsibility of writers and producers is to be aware of the possible ethical and other dangers.

Finally, not everything is or ever will be altered by these new technologies. If television viewing can be dismissed as simply a 'passive' experience, it would be as big a mistake to assume that using digital technologies such as CD-ROMs and interactive media is necessarily 'active'. In practice, using most commercially-available software is a matter of choosing from among a limited range of options, and following paths that have been laid down in advance: following scripts in other words.

Web World still needs writers!

What is (or are) multimedia, anyway?
Multimedia is not a single technology but rather a variety of ways (newer ones arrive every second day) to use a range of technologies to grab a single user or an audience. Multimedia can combine a number of media which involve a player—or customer, perhaps—

in finding his or her way among (or *navigating*) various types of data in a user-friendly way.

- A laser disk is multimedia;
- a digital video disk is multimedia;
- a CD-ROM is multimedia;
- a video game is multimedia;
- a web page or
- a database is a form of multimedia;

and the way all of these forms are created involves a writer and a production team.

Folks with more traditional reading skills will have to unlearn many habits so as to produce works which use the full potential of information and communications technologies. As you can guess from the following checklist for a new CD-ROM game title, among the challenges for writers is the fact that multimedia brings together a unique combination of questions in the 'what if . . . ' (see Glossary) process of title selection for creators, developers, producers, publishers, distributors and those whose job it is to support or encourage them:

- What will we call this project and
- has this title been taken up elsewhere?
- What research has been done and what needs to be done?
- Who is the market (defined by age group, etc.)?
- How will the materials be used on publication, and many years later?
- Should sound, music, animation, photos, graphics or video be added?
- What are the costs if such things are added?
- How should the rights granted or looked for be valued? (See Appendix 1: Legals)
- What type of protection against copying should or could be incorporated? (Increasingly that protection is harder to maintain.)
- When might the whole production become obsolete? (No one ever asked questions like this about movies!)
- What software and hardware are involved? When might they themselves become obsolete?

Like the film and television industry, the challenges of the multi media business demand enthusiastic, multi-skilled individuals and teams dedicated to the prompt solution of problems. There is an immediate need for both talent with experience or skills and for a re-skilling of established creative, technical, and business teams. Have a look at magazines like *AdNews* or *Broadcasting and Television* (B&T). A typical job description will often feature something like this:

A Mac operator plus with great design sense to work on brochures and our website . . .

or

Wanted: Mac operator able to take work through to film stage . . .

As you can see, skill in multimedia writing and design (normally a matter of learning how to use design packages like Photoshop) are invaluable add-ons for any young writer, director or producer-to-be.You neglect them at your peril—not least because these skills mean you can provide better ways to sell your film or TV series idea.

Who's involved, and what's involved

The phenomenon of 'convergence' involves the industries of com-munications, electronics, broadcasting, publishing and computing all coming together in ways that always seem to benefit the bigger players. By the beginning of 2000, for example, the most visited site was MSN (a collaboration between Bill Gates' Microsoft and Australia's Nine Network owned by media tycoon Kerry Packer). That didn't take long, did it?

However, there's hope for the new player, as the development, production, publication and distribution of multimedia involve pulling together new teams who bring creative, technical or busi-ness skills derived from those industries.

As a useful simplification, it has been observed that the devel-opment and production of multimedia resembles the processes of film or television production but that publication and distribution of CD-ROMs resembles book publishing. But the writing still has to be good! Or as computer folk used to say way back in the begin-ning, GIGO—that is, Garbage In, Garbage Out. In other words, the work is only as good as what you put into it—as ye sow so shall ye reap!

Numerous publications in recent years have been littered with very different and often competing definitions of 'multimedia'. A technical and more complete definition is that multimedia refers to a set of existing computer hardware and software technologies that permit the simultaneous display of data (information) in one or more forms, namely text, audio, video, photographs, illustra-tions, and so on. Products that fall within the definition of multi-media can be found on:

- CD-ROM, laser disc and DVD formats;
- information or point of sale kiosks;
- online multimedia databases (e.g. parts catalogues, travel locations, real estate listings and interactive advertising); and

- video conferencing facilities (e.g. for meetings, shopping or banking).

'Interactive' potential is one of the key distinguishing features of multimedia as a new media form. Within the long historical continuum of technologies used for human expression, there has been a steady shift away from merely symbolic communication and towards sensory communication. For example, illustrations and words in books involve images and words that are symbols of other things. Multimedia can incorporate such symbolic data and do so in a multi-sensory way. It is a screen-dependent experience, involving active coordination between eyes, ears and hands to engage with content. These observations underline the significance of the interactive features of, particularly, video games, the multimedia genre which has excelled the most in using interactivity.

Multimedia: who needs it?

As illustrated by the Australian CD-ROM sampler bundled by Apple with its CD-ROM players (2000), a range of Australian CD-ROM multimedia titles now exists in the market. In particular a concentration of game, training and educational titles is serving the needs of a variety of users.

The computer offers experiences which are characterised by rapid speed of movement, elaborate graphical and sonic elements, fast action which engages active audience involvement, and direct physical and mental complicity in the actions and sounds displayed. Computer entertainment grew in success during the 1980s to the point where today the games industry has outstripped the film and TV industry in popularity and profitability. Narrative has very little to do with this.

Writing a multimedia script

Multimedia is (more correctly 'are') interactive. That means that the user (player) has the illusion—given by your clever scripting—that he or she can control or alter possibilities. Well, he or she *can*—but only to the extent that you've allowed for these possibilities, each of which has to be scripted.

Here are some general points to remember when planning and creating multimedia.

The capacity exists to present various forms of information:
- images
- sound
- moving vision
- lists and
- files

in a navigable and interactive form. As writer you'll decide when and where the player gets a choice. So what does this mean for you as the writer?

For a start a script for multimedia resembles a map rather than the sort of script you're used to. That doesn't mean you can't devise a classic linear story or plot. But the ways you write it down are different and so are the key plot points. Multimedia scripts allow plots to go not just in one direction (linear cause and effect) but—well, any way you want them to.

Take a simple example:

BOB arrives at a street corner to wait for a bus.
SUE approaches the same bus stop.

Now if this was a linear script for a film this is how it would look:

THE TOMB

SCENE 1. EXT. DAY. STREET. BUS STOP.
BOB, a relaxed young guy in his late teens, saunters down the road and stops by the Bus sign. SUE, a funky chick with purple spiked hair, approaches from the opposite direction.

What now?

Well, we know what they look like and the plot can go any way we like—but once BOB starts up a conversation with SUE (for example) the story is set on a path.

Multimedia, however, gives (or can give, depending on how smart your writing is) a bundle of plot choices at any given moment—all decided on by you. So your multimedia script might start to look like this:

THE TOMB

CLICK ON Icon to Start

Meet BOB. He's a cool looking dude—a bit like the European comic hero Dylan Dog—that kind of slightly weird cool. He's heading down a street.

Now what? BOB can:
• turn left and fall down a manhole into TOMBWORLD;
• turn right and meet SUE at which point does he just
• look at her or
• chat her up or . . .
• and so on . . .

In Chapter 10 we looked at the idea of plot as being a binary set of choices a bit like computer code. Here the choices are only going to be limited by your graphics, your CD-ROM design team—and of course your budget.

Story shapes and outlines for multimedia are like this—but with all those extra possibilities. So a linear story moves like this:

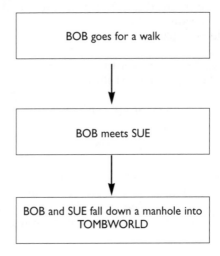

But an interactive story, where your game player can select from options, might look like this:

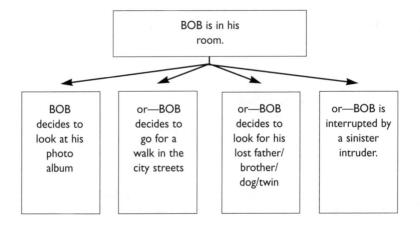

As you can see, each of these possible stories leads to an ever-growing number of others.

Interactive stories

Write a brief (30-word) description of your HERO (male or female). Draw or digitally 'create' them, if you like.

Now place them in a room (workspace, hotel, home, spaceship . . . you decide).

Then write down five optional story directions.

Then offer three new directions to be added to each plot twist.

Multilinear stories

This time you are BOB: You have a problem (What is it? Death of your dad? Strange signals on your PC? You make it up).

So the first story choice will be:

• Read your diary

• or—ring your friend

• or—check your letters

But of course each decision you make leads to other possibilities.
The more options you script in, the longer your reader/player will stay with you!

Multilinear stories like *The Last Express* (Broderbund) or *Titanic* (Cyberflix/Dreamfactory, 1998) which involve the player as a participant are the grown-up versions of the original Shoot-em, Kill-em stuff like *Tomb Raider* which, when you come down to it, are just sophisticated versions of fairground duck shoots (see Appendix 2: Video Games).

Try it for yourself

Choose a simple, well-known story—maybe 'Little Red Riding Hood'—and write it in six straightforward film scenes.

Now write it as an interactive story, just up to the point when Little Red Riding Hood meets the wolf *(but remember there are many ways she can meet the wolf)*.

Beware, you'll have to use diagrams to contain all the 'alternative' story directions. Here are two models derived from classic fairytales that show how important it is to think of your stories as mathematical systems.

Interactive Story

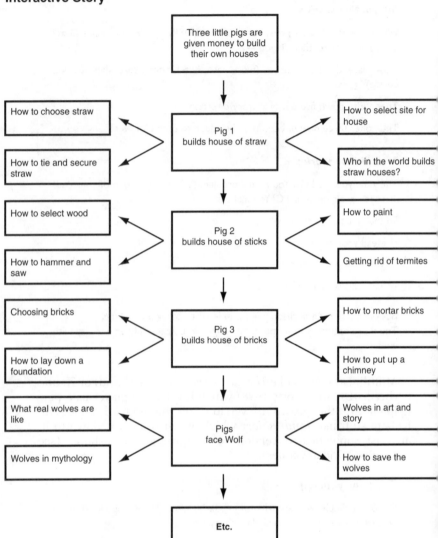

A familiar tale goes digital

© Katherine Phelps, July 1998

Right:
Multimedia means multiple—almost infinite—story possibilities. And choice.

Multi-linear Story

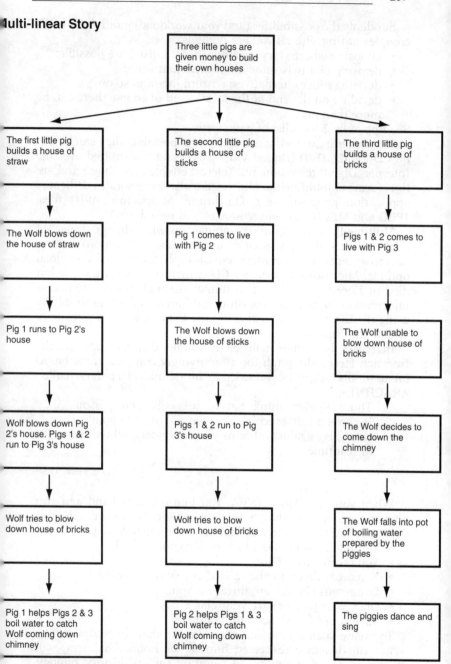

Three little pigs are given money to build their own houses

The first little pig builds a house of straw	The second little pig builds a house of sticks	The third little pig builds a house of bricks
The Wolf blows down the house of straw	Pig 1 comes to live with Pig 2	Pigs 1 & 2 comes to live with Pig 3
Pig 1 runs to Pig 2's house	The Wolf blows down the house of sticks	The Wolf unable to blow down house of bricks
Wolf blows down Pig 2's house. Pigs 1 & 2 run to Pig 3's house	Pigs 1 & 2 run to Pig 3's house	The Wolf decides to come down the chimney
Wolf tries to blow down house of bricks	Wolf tries to blow down house of bricks	The Wolf falls into pot of boiling water prepared by the piggies
Pig 1 helps Pigs 2 & 3 boil water to catch Wolf coming down chimney	Pig 2 helps Pigs 1 & 3 boil water to catch Wolf coming down chimney	The piggies dance and sing

© Katherine Phelps, July 1998

Suddenly the possibilities (and your workload) multiply! It looks complex at first. But all you are doing is:

- choosing where story variations (plot twists) are possible;
- devising plot twists and alternative pathways;
- devising other alternatives: costume lists and so on;
- deciding on the end of the story—and of course there can be more than one.

See Appendix 2 for a list of game genres.

Most interactive media are cheap and portable: they can be put on CD-ROMs, DVD (Digital Video Disk) and transmitted over the Internet. Digital television and Teletext enable user choice and are thus forms of multimedia. Multimedia also incorporates dedicated application programs—e.g. Quicktime, Shockwave, AVID files, JPEG and MPEG—to deliver images and sound.

Multimedia can include combinations of a diverse range of media effects—images, sound, animations, live action, banner advertisements, web counters, e-mail reply forms, and download options. Microsoft's *Cinemania* CD (which won many awards but died in 1999 from lack of a customer base) allows you to access information on thousands of films and film personalities simply by using the CD, but you can also use the CD to log into a website to update information.

Increasingly, games will be available directly through the Internet. Here's the pitch for a terrifyingly complex game based on a totally scientific knowledge of (shudder) spiders, called ARACHNEA.

> Think Spider, think battle, sex, silk and poison.
> Become a spider with your own unique 3-D point of view. Play against other players as spiders, all online, in real time.

(Schizomedia, 1999)

When you play ARACHNEA, you join a spider band and you play as a spider. Note that, however scientific the research, the spiders have had to become very 'human' for there to be a game at all!

- You inherit your clan's history, for good or bad.
- You receive your Fate.
- You are ordered to obey a God you may not respect.
- Dangerous choices are thrust on you.
- Obey your God or save your clan?
- Save your life—or act with honour?

To create such a complex game means that the script by the writer (in this case respected film writer Frank Chalmers) will involve an amazing amount of detail on spiders' history, biology, and behaviour. Because multimedia can contain so much information, the research tasks are more than those normally required for a TV series. It's here that you realise that the interactive creative task, like comedy perhaps, is one best undertaken by a team. At this point every writer needs a collaborator.

But remember—creating the stories is fun. The devil is in the detail!

Multimedia need not be expensive. Multimedia can also lead the user into other interactive sites such as chat rooms and e-mail discussion groups. The project team—the producer, the writers and the programmers—set the parameters of the project and develop a structure for it, and a user interface for the development of the interactive elements.

Information CD-ROMs: making documentary reality sharper

A recent project developed under the Creative Nation initiative gives a clear picture of the many pathways that a good writing and creative team can develop to approach historical materials. In this case the CD-ROM project was based on one of a successful TV Open Learning series running on ABC TV, called *Images of Australia*. The TV series dealt with the various ways in which history has been represented in many media, from songs, cartoons and painting to films, TV miniseries, and drama. It was a big task, and one that stretches across thirteen half-hour episodes with much supporting material (books, guides, etc.).

The CD-ROM project grew out of the theme of one particular program dealing with the Gallipoli campaign in World War One—a campaign that many feel defined Australia in many ways and has come to represent the birth of the modern nation.

After visiting the opening screen:

> ### *Gallipoli*
>
> * The Event
>
> * The People
>
> * The Myth

users could choose whether they wanted to examine the history and causes of the events, meet the people (at war and at home) or check out the thousands of songs, stories, letters, and myths that followed the actual events. Each decision offered a huge range of screens to visit and each screen offered choices from period film (including some Turkish film footage rescued from old nitrate film

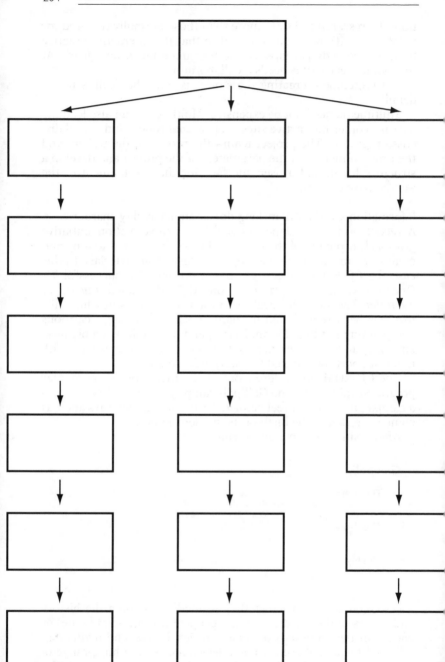

Blank storyboard for a CD-ROM project.

held in rusting tins in the War Museum, and never before seen) as well as hearing songs of the period (off old records and cylinders) and reading real newspapers, diaries, and studying images from genuine photo albums.

When writing the 'script' for such a complex web of materials, a writer (generally several) must use a storyboard form developed for the project, because no single line of words or clip of film footage is unconnected with something else and all the links must be planned from the beginning of the writing. See the previous example of a blank storyboard for a CD-ROM project.

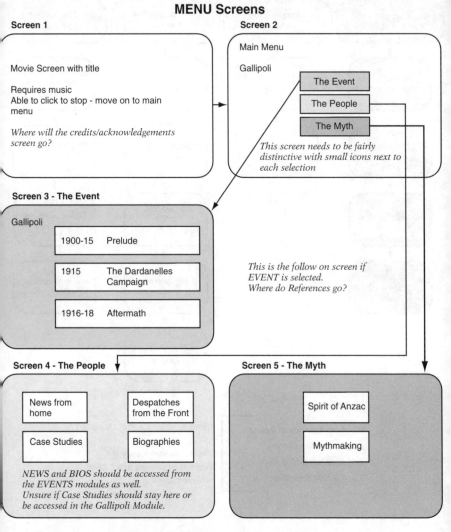

Menu Screens—Gallipoli CD-ROM project.

Here are two screens from one section of the Gallipoli CD-ROM script.

Notice how the writer must foresee or detail all possible transitions and links as the writing proceeds.

No wonder a typical budget for a CD-ROM development can run to over a million dollars.

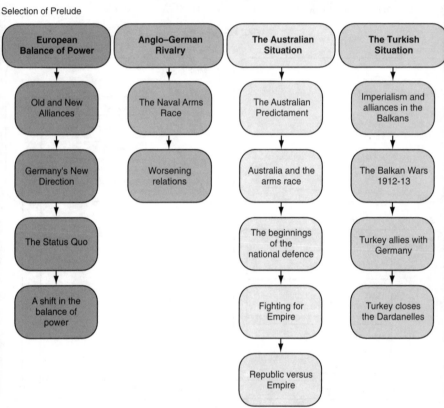

Screens related to Gallipoli - The Event

Selection of Prelude

Menu items for the Prelude screen

The above screens are the information screens which follow on in sequence.

Screens related to Gallipoli - The Event

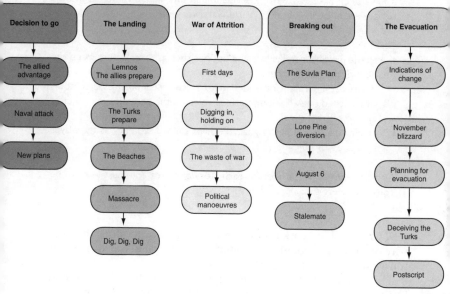

Conclusion: CD-ROMs and interactivity

The advantages of CD-ROM and interactive websites are unlimited—or so it seems—because of the almost magical ability to store and access all sorts of information, from dazzling graphics and music to film to . . . well, whatever you want or can afford! The digital format makes it possible to bring together video, music, photography, cinema, literature, graphics, games, and blend them into new stories as varied and complex as you want to make them.

Digital storytelling constitutes a very different kind of relationship between the reader and the (digital) story. Although a linear 'movie' mode can be included as one of its options, the player/reader can react and join in in all sorts of ways by repeatedly using the mouse ('pointing and clicking' interactive buttons) or clues (marked or hidden) on the screen; in some cases, he or she can also type in messages or make drawings. These activities are often transposed versions of common daily activities:

- Reading diaries
- Looking at scrapbooks (photos, etc.)
- Ringing an informer
- Peeping through keyholes
- Ringing doorbells, pushing handles
- Leaving messages, turning a steering wheel, or
- Pulling the trigger of a gun.

You've been asked to write a script for an interactive game based on a private eye in Berlin just after World War Two.

List:
- all the possible parallel lists and options such as dress, street maps, and historical materials then;
- devices (on screen) for your hero to use—weapons, research tools (dramatised ones, like a mysterious voice on the phone), army contacts and so on;
- finally, what is the hero's goal? (Perhaps there'd be many as the player moves up through degrees of difficulty.)

Name about ten possibilities for each story/plot area. You must learn to be constantly alert to multiple choices.

A CD-ROM artwork often encourages a slower, more thoughtful way of moving through the material, giving plenty of time to stop, return, and even change the results.

This is equally true for the enigmatic virtual worlds embedded in the successful mystery game *Myst* (1993) by Rand and Robyn Miller. Naturally, the opposite is also possible, epitomised by the recent interactive games (and a movie), such as Sony Imagesoft's *Johnny Mnemonic* (1995), which keeps the player constantly on edge, assaulted by surprises—just as the movie based on the game tried, perhaps less successfully, to do.

Interactivity: You and your audience

What does it mean to think electronically? Proponents of electronic culture, and in particular new media, constantly evoke an emergent transformation of the way we think, engage with, and assemble information, as a consequence of the information technologies we have at our disposal. The information economy is booming, virtual communities continue to grow apace, and there is the accompanying 'info hype' to deal with.

New media, by definition, grab the consumer in new ways. Game play has today replaced 'storytelling' as the measure of an entertainment title's success. Unfortunately the life of such games can be much shorter than that of a movie; titles are withdrawn and disappear for ever at a dismayingly fast rate. New games of increasing sophistication or difficulty are developed, designed to capture the smart or 'cool' buyers who are (apparently at least) the perfect target market. Yet every day a quite marvellous, narrative driven, and sophisticated adventure game like *The Last Express* (Broderbund, Germany, 1997) comes to grief. *The Last Express*, appealing to a sophisticated urban market and set in the romantic world of the Orient Express on the eve of World War One was, perhaps, just too clever for a market increasingly wanting *Tomb Raider* simplicity and shoot-outs. *The Last Express* was removed from the market by mid-1999, after barely two years. Most books and certainly all films and TV series are given a much longer chance to survive—normally at least a decade.

Finally, you should always be awake to the inherent contradictions (just as in the movie industry) of the role of the artist and of independent creativity in an industrial world ruled by the lures of commercial potential and managers who are always looking at the profit line.

So, what else is new?

Future challenges for CD-ROM makers and artists

There is evidence that children learn to use new technologies with no problems at all, with ease, for information, for creativity, for pleasure, or all three at once. But, how 'new' actually are these skills? On one level it is clear that the new technologies offer more than just another way of making existing materials more attractive. Some questions you should think about:

- Do computer games offer a new form of non-verbal communication?
- How can the language of signs be used for works with more complex narratives?
- Is sound always at the service of image?
- How does time work?
- What is a reasonable length of time for a fast-reflex game to run as opposed to a role-playing game or a game of strategy? Should an interactive drama take up as much time as a feature length movie or should it be as long as a 400-page novel?

Now get back to writing that CD-ROM script! It may be your last shot at individuality!

And for an endlessly updated glossary of Internet terms and ideas, check out <*http://www.matisse.net/files/glossary.html*>.

Appendix 1
Legals

This little piggy went to market

Everyone has a horror story about an idea that got lost on the way to the film market, only to turn up somewhere else as another writer's idea. Or worse, as the product of the genius of a TV network executive. Is there a writer anywhere who does not believe that at some time or other they have had a Grand Concept pinched?

The problem is endemic to the very nature of a writer's work. An idea, a concept document, a script, all make the rounds of many cities and more offices. In addition, there's something called the Zeitgeist—a raft of ideas whose time has come—so that several writers will believe that it is theirs alone. Look at the rash of Robin Hood movies in the mid-1990s. No one would admit they weren't the first. Perhaps no one was.

The bigger the industry, the more likely it is that ideas, let alone whole series concepts, will be duplicated—and, yes, occasionally pirated wholesale. Ideas are the sole currency of movie towns like Hollywood but they're just as rare in Sydney and London. You let them float around unguarded at your peril. Recent litigation over scripts has seen some wins for the writers. Art Buchwald successfully claimed that the plot line for *Coming to America* (John Landis, 1988) was borrowed from a column of his. Of course, there's not much compensation around, as years later the film has yet to 'go into profit'—almost US$220 million gross is not enough to appear as black ink in Hollywood ledgers, unless it suits. More recently, the key plot elements and some of the visual gags of *Shakespeare in Love* (Gillies MacKinnon, 1998) were 'lifted' from the 1941 novel *No Bed for Bacon* (Caryl Brahms)—long out of print so not the subject of litigation by its (deceased) author). The list is endless, the lawsuits normally quickly lost.

In Australia's small market, where you'd think ideas were more visibly attached to their authors, the problem is no less. The concept documents for *Streets and Rivers* (see Chapter 8) had been sent to all networks, attracted interest, and lay around ignored at one drama department for two years before the amazingly similar *Willing and Abel* series emerged (briefly) from the same stables. Just a coincidence? Maybe. Everyone has a story like that.

It's not that writers are just unlucky or even (as many producers may claim) naive. It's that the industry by its very nature is chatty, discursive, and driven by brain waves and luck. So there are some simple things you should do with any script idea when you start writing. Do it quickly. But if you get unlucky—well, join the club. Almost everyone else is in it!

Register your work yesterday!

Copyright is that most essential relationship between you and your script. Who has it? Who could take it away? Copyright can be defined as the exclusive right to carry out or prevent others from carrying out certain acts in respect of the subject matter (which is protected under the Copyright Act). The subject matter is referred to as 'works', which includes all the traditional creative works of literature, drama, music, and art as well as (the rather vaguely named) subject matter other than 'works' (!). This last, sometimes called 'neighbouring rights', refers to recordings (sound, film, video, and so on) and published editions. They're not your worry—yet.

You have to protect yourself as much as possible, but there's no Patent Office to which you can submit a script, which is a peculiar form of property known as Intellectual Property.

Of course, you can deposit a copy of your script with your lawyer or a bank. But the ideas are still floating around out there. Meanwhile, the Australian Writers' Guild (affiliated with all the key overseas guilds) is the place to go, both to register your idea and then to deposit, for a small fee, your script. This move doesn't guarantee anything—but at least you can argue your case from a position of union solidarity when the inevitable happens! Each property, whether a comedy sketch or a final draft feature of two hundred pages, should be registered separately as should any alternative titles.

Title pinching and recycling is a popular blood sport and some titles (like *Final Cut*) seem to re-emerge every few years. The Hollywood tendency of the last decade to use clichés and popular phrases (*Fatal Attraction, Indecent Proposal, Double Threat, Enemy of the State* and so on) means that any current or past saying or song title (*Pretty Woman* et al.) is fair game in the name of good marketing and brand recognition! You should, of course, join the Guild as soon as possible—the services offered range from script assessment to industry contacts and excellent courses (and wrap parties) on screenwriting for anything from soaps to features.

Since music tracks are now such an important part of the selling of mainstream and alternative movies, song titles may also lead to important narrative possibilities—consider how many opening title sequences use a song as a narrative short cut. *Pretty in Pink* (John Hughes, 1986) was merely the sign of a new and probably permanent fixation by mainstream cinema on the popular song as the key to unlocking the mass audience. The entire opening montage was cut to the Psychedelic Furs version of the song, a strategy that had been foreseen as soon as the title was chosen. In other words, titles are valuable property; insure them if you can. But basically, titles seem to float in the open market of ideas, and you'll be lucky to hang onto your great title idea if someone gets finance up before you do.

Tough luck

Of course, not everything can be protected, however careful you are, and however many sealed envelopes the AWG is keeping in its safe for you. And conversely, just because titles are hard to keep safe, that doesn't mean you can pinch *Top Gun* or *Sliver* as a title just because you have a new spin on a movie that's still in the video stores. The lawyers will descend on you like the Jedi. But where there is no pre-existing movie or series you are on fairly safe ground. There is also a kind of gentleperson's arrangement (let's not call it an agreement) between The Money (producers) who seem to have a mechanism for registering titles with a loose agreement that no other producer or company will snaffle the title. Writers, you'll find, don't have that kind of unspoken accord, loose as it is. But, after all, there's no title so brilliant that it can't be replaced, and in the end it's word of mouth that will get the audience there. Remember the sneering talk about the mega-budget *Titanic* ('It'll sink quicker than Captain Cameron steers towards the iceberg', etc.)? Nobody is laughing two billion gross dollars later! The movie could have been called *Jack and Rose*. After all, it was the love story that hooked them, not the ship.

Ideas also can't be protected. If you rush around the traps telling industry folk about your great High Concept drama set in an Antarctic Station, don't be surprised if there's a script development grant or finance package announced for *White Out* a few weeks later. Nothing is more contagious than an idea whose time has come.

Common sense dictates that you should keep copies of everything you write, every concept you come up with—and date them. Some writers even go so far as to send themselves a copy of the script/idea/title/plotting master-stroke to act as a form of time stamp, witnessed by the Postal Service.

In addition, whenever you receive any correspondence from interested folk—production houses, funding bodies, whatever—keep the letters. Memories can be very short in an industry that can move as slowly as a glacier one week and like a laser the next, depending on the potential profit. That includes keeping rejection letters if the thought does not make you suicidal. Rejection is no proof of a lack of interest in the inherent value of your intellectual property.

Rights and Chain of Title

A screenplay can come from many sources, making the use of the word 'original' vexing and the subject of ceaseless litigation (see above!).

A script for any type of project may be an original work commissioned by a producer, developed from a pre-existing literary work (a novel, play, poem, poster, song, advertising slogan, and so on) or a draft screenplay or outline presented to a producer.

If the screenplay is to be developed from an existing work, the producer will often be the person to take out an option (if you don't do it first) and then the agreement will be between the production company and the author or the author's representatives—or even the publisher. If there's some doubt about just who owns what you should get a 'Quit Claim' from the publisher, relinquishing their rights and making the relationships between original work and your work clearer.

The Chain of Title may not always be clear and it must be. Basically this term describes the invisible legal chain linking you, your producer, and the owner of the original rights. Chain of Title is the biggest tripwire in the rights process, so make sure there are no muddy areas. If necessary, get hold of a copyright lawyer early in the 'chain'.

Deal memos

The basic rule here is: if it's written on a bar bill, then check it out later as soon as possible. Many a film deal is struck over drinks or a meal, and memories being what they are, producers and writers just love the frisson of doing a deal while 'doing lunch'. But things can be forgotten, so check out the fine writing and make sure that scrawl doesn't come back to bite you later.

The point of a deal memo is generally to cement a crucial creative relationship and to define the boundaries of that partnership as soon as possible. It's exciting and addictive stuff—but like most such behaviours it is not a formal contract and never a legally precise document.

- A good deal memo should be re-drafted somewhere quiet—and with all the advice you can muster.
- Make sure everyone involved is identified and their roles spelt out.
- Allow for subsequent events—spinoffs, sequels, even merchandise if you feel that's appropriate. Define expenses—and what the point is at which profit is achieved and hence how you as a writer might share in this. This share is normally defined by way of percentage 'points' after gross, and other actuarial systems that should be watched.
- Spell out all the key deadlines for delivery of everything from first draft (and payments) to on-set rewrites and even post-production involvement.
- Make sure someone sane—and of Good Will—signs and witnesses the whole shebang.

Screen credits

Nothing causes more rage and dispute than screen credits. They're crucial when you consider that they mark out all the stages in your career. No wonder everyone else seems to want a piece of your own personal signature—the screen credit.

- Common tricks include directors 'negotiating' a shared credit when you're not around and every variant on that scenario. Make sure that no credits are negotiated when you're not there—almost every screenwriter has lost (or given up) screen credits at some stage in his or her career.
- Voluntarily relinquishing a credit because you've come to hate the whole deal is one thing. Having credits pinched by former partners is quite dreadful, terminally depressing, and happens daily.
- Always demand the right to see the finished show and to carefully check all the credits.
- Make certain your credit is designed and placed in a sufficiently prominent (or insignificant if you feel that way about it) onscreen position. Producers are not usually responsible for inadvertent 'omissions' of your credits so you should try to have specified, well before the crunch time, what that credit will be—and that it is there at all!
- If in doubt get the help of the Guild. This is what they are for!
- And first and last rule: don't leave town until the credits are done.

Appendix 2
Video Games: A Very Short History

Research suggests the first video game appeared in 1972. Introduced by Magnavox and called 'Odyssey', it was childishly simple by today's standards. The program wasn't clever enough to 'paint' the playing field, so one had to put sticky tape on the TV screen to represent the court. It remained a curiosity and it wasn't until around 1976 that video games became a household item.

Pong was the breakthrough game. Almost all of the hot sellers used ball and paddle (tennis, hockey, handball, squash and catch). Nowadays, cyber-magazines such as *Wired* offer monthly updates, and you can visit Games 'R' Us in most cities any time or just check out the Net—there's something new every day.

With the arrival of video games, CD-ROMs, and video arcades, we have seen kids' obsessions grow, along with extraordinary hand–eye coordination. A teen movie from the 1980s (*The Last Starfighter*, Nick Castle, 1984) sums it all up, featuring a kid who saves the universe with his video game skills. In a very short period of time we have gone from consoles to computer games and now Internet games (like *Arachnea*).

Key definitions
A CD-ROM (Compact Disc Read-Only Memory) is a compact disc that stores computer information. The information can't be changed (rewritten). It is an optical medium which can store large amounts of computer data. The disc is physically identical to an audio CD. CD-ROM players are designed to be much faster than audio CD players because they must be able to access non-sequential data instantly from different parts of the disc.

How is the CD-ROM different from the Internet? The Internet is an 'online' system and the CD-ROM is strictly 'off-line'. However, both of them support the hypertextual principle of organising data. (The term 'hypertext' was first introduced by Ted Nelson in 1965. It refers to a data-based system that makes intelligent links between various linguistic components.)

The Internet, if it isn't crippled by governmental surveillance and censorship, and relentless commercialisation, will provide a powerful way of distributing information and demos about CD-ROM artworks created outside the commercial systems of production and distribution.

CD-ROMs: The basic genres

Genre identification is much more difficult in new media. With rare exceptions, the boundaries for TV and film are well set. Most movies are easy to find on the video rental shelf: 'Thriller', 'Arthouse', 'Sci Fi', and so on.

But interactive entertainments are much more fluid. At the same time, the range of genres is actually narrower than in film and TV.

Sports/Techno

These are based on 'real-life' experiences we all dream of but few get to try, like driving a Formula One car or piloting a Jumbo or a Spitfire. Cricket and Footy are big sellers (sadly many only for PC, not Mac). No drama skills are needed here; just the technologies and reactions needed to 'play'. Examples: *AFL 99*, *Shane Warne's Cricket*, *Flight Simulator*.

Shoot-em-ups

Remember when you went to the fair and stopped at the shooting gallery to ping tin ducks? Well, this is the high-tech version, highly influenced by the *Die Hard*, *Terminator*, and *Lethal Weapon* movie 'franchises'. Because these games continue to sell so well, manufacturers don't feel they need any narrative or character development. Just like, well, *Lethal Weapon* and *Die Hard*. Examples: *Tomb Raider*, *Rebel Assault*, *King's Quest*, *Wing Commander*.

Mystery

This is the Haunted House or Naked City mystery made for the interactive medium. These games are big on exploration, finding and interpreting clues, and making decisions, such as whether to poke around in the old warehouse or the locked room. These games are usually slower-paced and more intuitive and often quite literary, requiring more traditional storytelling tools. *Myst* is the biggest-selling title to date; its 'sequel' is *Riven*.

Tactics/Strategy

Players who love these used to be the sort (and many still are) who played elaborate war games on huge boards or collected and manouevred huge armies of toy soldiers. Examples: *Command and Conquer*, *Warcraft*.

A last thought

The sad thing is, as we noted looking at the fate of *The Last Express* (Broderbund, 1997–99) is that Romance, Historical Drama, and even Comedy are, at the moment, not wanted. What a pity! What a waste of a perfect medium.

Appendix 3
Gallipoli

The images that follow show you, better than many words, the basic building blocks of the Gallipoli project introduced in Chapter 15.

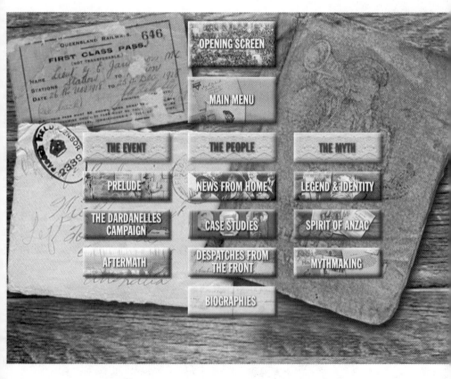

Above: Entering Gallipoli: the options
Facing page top left: Title screen; *top right:* Screen Two main menu
Facing page centre and bottom: Strong visuals of Section Screens of The People and The Myth

DESPATCHES FROM THE FRONT

MYTHMAKING

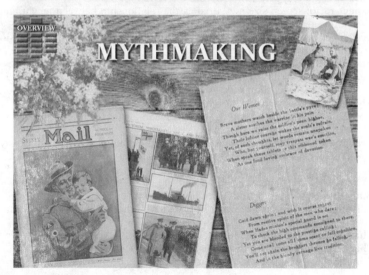

Glossary

Act (in a script): a major dramatic section, often one of three acts in a classic structure

Action: what the camera records; it is also the command from director or assistant director to commence action when the camera is running

Adaptation: a script based on a publication or materials from another medium: a play, novel or even a poem

AFC (Australian Film Commission): the Australian film cultural and development funding body

Agents: representatives for writers, directors and creative personnel in negotiations

Angles: angle from which the camera records a scene or size of shot, such as Wide Angle

Animation: film or video work producing the illusion of movement by stop motion camera techniques or digitally

Answer print: trial print made by the laboratory to check quality of image and other technical considerations

Antagonist: a character who opposes the Hero

Aspect ratio: screen size measured as the relationship between height and width

Audience: the viewers, or in research terms the segment of the public to which your work is targeted

Backstory: an imaginary biography giving motivation to any character

Beat: usually a script instruction to actors to pause, or instruction to directors to take a reaction shot

Big screen: cinema screen (as opposed to little screen, television)

Book: the script also known as the Bible; can also refer to the production schedule

Broadcast standards: can refer to technical details of a tape format (say NTSC for America, SECAM for France, PAL just about everywhere else), and/or government regulated standards relating to program classification (e.g. 'Parental Guidance', 'Restricted' etc.) or to bandwidth

Budget: every cost in a production not counting publicity

Callsheet: daily list of all requirements for a film shoot including props, locations, and actors

Character: a person in your script

Characterisation: all the distinguishing traits given to a character

Clients: those who commission your work

Cliffhangers: normally used of series or soaps—a dramatic climax that leaves characters dangling and, ideally, the audience keen to see what happens next (also used to refer to any unresolved dramatic issue)

Close up (CU): head and shoulders of a character or detail of a small object filling the screen

Collaboration: work undertaken with a partner or partners (see Appendix 1: Legals)

Comedy: a humorous subject of any length, or a general term for sitcoms

Commercials: radio, television, or cinema short works in any genre; TV commercials are commonly called TVCs

Composition: how you place things and people in a frame in relation to each other

Computers: used for scripting, budgeting, and increasingly, digital effects and editing using systems like AVID; increasingly, computers are playing a part in every element of movie-making

Conflict: what causes trouble between characters; can be an emotion, a character trait or external events

Consultants: (and story editors): people called in to edit, prune and refine scripts of just individual scenes

Contracts: legal documents asserting the desired relationship between, say, producer and writer

Copyrights: the right to use someone else's material—anything from music to whole stories (see Appendix 1: Legals)

Corporates: short films or videos selling or highlighting a company or product; normally around ten minutes in length

Concept (documents): short, hard-selling outlines of the program, film, or series, often including key plot lines and character descriptions

Coverage: all the shots including cutaways needed for an editor to compile a full scene

Credits (or Titles): list of who did what in any production; essential career markers for all program and film-makers

Cutaways: an editing term to describe cutting from one shot to another—often to establish a point as in cutting to a clock to show the time

CUT TO: script term (in CAPS) to indicate a cut to another scene or shot

Daytime soaps: serial dramas where logic and causation laws are generally suspended; can and often do run for decades

Development: the phases of script and project development prior to the shoot, normally involving funding writers, script editors, and successive script drafts

Directions (in script)**:** instructions to actors, or suggestions to a director on movement, what is to be seen in the shot and so on. Do not overdo this.

Director: the person responsible for artistic direction on the set, as well as pre- and post-production supervision; if a studio takes over the post-production as can happen, the director does not have 'final cut' (q.v.).

DISSOLVE TO: like CUT, a script reference to a scene or short transition, this time when one shot overlaps and replaces another, quickly or slowly

Documentary: a non-fiction program of any length, based on historical or current events, which may use dramatic techniques

Dolly: a wheeled gadget for moving the camera and operator or in a script; DOLLY refers to any shot where the camera moves alongside or in onto the subject

Draft: a full script, edited and rewritten as many times as required

Epilogue: dialogue or onscreen narration explaining what has happened after the main action (see also **Prologue**)

Episode: one complete program from a series (generally soaps or TV series and serial)

Establishing (of a shot or scene): setting the scene for action as in a wide shot of a city, a room, wherever the action is to be played out

Exposition: what is revealed through onscreen action or dialogue that moves the story plot along or explains a motivation or an action

EXT. (Exterior): in scripts, refers to a scene set outdoors

FADE IN/FADE OUT: script term now falling into disuse, referring to scene transitions where the end or beginning of a scene fades to nothing to indicate the closure of one scene or the beginning of a new scene

Features (or Feature Films): full-length cinema productions (movies); can also refer to longer documentaries intended for cinema release

FFC (Film Finance Corporation): the key federal funding body for film, TV, and documentary production funding; a film bank

Film funding agencies (see **AFC, FFC**): various state bodies and the Media Fund (Europe)

Final cut: the last, finely tuned (or recut to a producer's whims) version of a program ready for broadcast or cinema release

Final (draft): the last draft of a screenplay before the shooting script

Flashback/Flashforward: a shot, scene or sequence (it can be most of a program or movie) which intercuts with the plot to show events that happened before (Back) or lie ahead of (Forward) the main action

Fly on the wall: an observational documentary where the subjects are (it is hoped) so used to the endless presence of a camera that they will reveal all and behave . . . interestingly

Foley studio/Recording studio: studio for (re)recording post-production sound effects, and 'looped' (rerecorded) dialogue

Goals (Character aims): What the heroes or antagonists want (Love, Treasure, a Clue to the Crime and so on); 'motivation' can cover this too

Golden Age (of Film, Television, etc.): for film, commonly refers to the first forty years of Hollywood; for television, the 1950s

Hand held: the camera is held in the hands of the operator without the aid of a tripod or dolly; normally used to inject tension or a nerviness into a scene (cf. **Steadicam**)

Hero or Protagonist: lead character with whom audiences must (in theory!) identify

Hollywood: the town, the industry, the Centre of the Universe, Hell

Home Box Office (HBO): leading cable channel for new release and special movies made for television

Hook: the central exciting idea that will sell a movie to the public

Hour-long (TV forms): actually around 45 minutes allowing for commercial breaks

Inbetweener: an animation artist who works in the studio system providing non-critical 'inbetween' art. An animation slave.

Indent: as in script layout where action and dialogue are indented; you can use a software package to set this up or just set this up yourself

In-house writers: a dwindling breed of writers employed on a salary or, more commonly now, a retainer by a production house

Insert: a shot (normally short) cut into a scene or sequence to highlight something (see also **Cutaways**); a descriptive shot (such as a ticking bomb, wheels spinning in a chase)

INT. (Interior): any filming that is shot indoors (cf. **EXT**)

INTERCUT: to cut between two or even more different scenes to create the feeling that they are happening simultaneously (as in a car chase)

Line spacing: as in layout of a script; you can use a software package to set this up or just set this up yourself

Location: any place (INT. or EXT.) used for filming that isn't setup in a studio or on an open air sound stage

Long shot: depending on what is filmed, refers to any shot covering an area roughly the same as a human figure top to toe (or larger); not to be confused with **Wide Shot**

Low key (in Lighting): dark, shadowed areas predominate (as in *Dark City*)

Markets, Marketplace: international festivals (Cannes, Milan, Los Angeles, Venice) where programs and films are pitched, viewed and sold (see **Pre-sale**)

Master shot: a single set up or continuous shot covering all of the action for a given scene; some directors choose not to film further coverage (q.v.)—or don't have time

Medium shot: between a **Close up** and a **Long shot**—mostly the human figure is framed from the waist up

Mid shot: a vague general term for a looser close up or a tighter medium shot

Montage: a sequence of consecutive shots that, edited together, is created to compress action and convey the passage of time

More ('. . .more' in script page): means that scene is continued over page

Motivation: what is supposed or asserted to drive a character to act in a particular way

Movies of the Week: films made for TV, often with a social theme

Myth: a story or event that has taken on a more than merely historical force—as in the Myth of Anzac, or The Myth of Papal Infallibility

Narrative arc: an abstract system for measuring the emotional journey of main characters in a story

Networks (and markets): associations of related professionals or organisations such as TV stations

Nuance: an idea or emotion; subtly hinted at rather than uttered

Panavision: trade name of a particular film system; the most commonly used for feature films in the past few decades

Pitch: the selling, on paper or in person, of a project to a funding body or individual; the classic scene at start of Altman's *The Player* says it all

Plot: the events of a story, normally in causal/chronological order

Post-production: after the shoot, the editing, track laying, sound design, and all the necessary elements leading to the final (release) print of a film

POV (Point of View): a shot filmed as if through the eyes of a character—or, less commonly, in spoken dialogue as if narrated by that character

Pre-production: before a shoot begins, all the preparations and organisation for that shoot

Pre-sale: where a planned project attracts a promise of broadcast or cinema exhibition before shooting starts; often a condition of financing (see **FFC**)

Principals: the main (featured) actors of a film story

Producers: financial and executive heads of a production (also Associate, Executive and Co-producers)

Production: all the elements, creative and practical, of a film shoot

Prologue: a scene, sequence, or onscreen message that sets up the background to a story; the most recent classic example of this old trick is the opening to the first *Star Wars* film (1975): 'A long time ago . . . '

Protagonist: the key player (or hero) of a drama

Query letters: charmingly polite letters you write to production companies or copyright holders, asking for a job, or copyright, or anything, really

Quest (Hero's): idea put forward by one school of thought, following American writer Joseph Campbell, which claims that all stories involve a hero on a Quest for . . . er, something

Quit claim: publisher's or copyright holder's letter to you advising that the publisher has no copyright claims to the property you're interested in

Residuals: after the initial script payment, there may be further payments due upon replay, international sale, etc. (the Australian organisation looking after this is Screenrights)

Resolution (in plotting): just before The End, everything is wrapped up

Saleability (see **Pitch, Pre-Sale,** and **Markets**)

Scene: any script is broken up into scenes, each of which covers a piece of the action over a defined time span; where each time location, time or style (as in a Flashback) occurs a new scene number is needed

Scene breakdowns: a list of all scenes in a script or of scenes plus cast and locations; used as a way of testing the dramatic viability of a project before going to first draft

Scene number: every successive scene in a script is given a number—a feature film might typically have around 100 scenes; an action film might have several hundred

Schedules (Shooting schedules): the daily rundown normally prepared by the director of all scheduled activity for a given day of filming; it contains details of everything: cast, locations, and even the smallest props

Schtick: a comic turn or performance; often refers to the expected style or characterisation of a particular comic performer (for example Mary-Anne Fahey's regular character monologues as Kylie Mole)

Screenplay: the full script with all scenes in order and properly laid out

Script editor: a writer, generally assigned by a studio or funding body to polish a script for the original writer; a story editor can also commission scripts in the same way as a TV series producer

Sequence (cf. **Scene**): generally, a group of scenes which together make a coherent and larger part of the script—say a number of consecutive scenes covering a life, a part of a life (e.g. a character in wartime) or a related series of events

Shooting script: the final screenplay version, most often compiled by the director, and including all the technical details such as camera shots

Sitcoms: half-hour comedy format, television programs; normally run approximately 22 minutes (*Frontline* represents the satirical end of the spectrum; *Dawson's Creek* or *Friends* the softer 'family unit' style favoured by the American mass audience)

Sketches (comedy): short comedy routines, generally as part of a longer program (e.g. *Saturday Night Live, Full Frontal, The D Generation*)

Slugline: scene header with all relevant scene information:
SCENE 3. DAY. EXT. MAIN STREET. DAY ONE.

Software programs: for writers, these range from full instructional and formatting systems specifically for film and television like *Final Draft* to more general dramatic structuring programs like *Collaborator*

Sound effects (SFX): script advice that a specific sound is required (SFX Revving motorbikes outside in the street)

Specials (TV): one-off TV programs, often documentary or features related to a topic (*Sharks!*, *Australia's Deadly Outback*, etc.); a good way to enter the independent TV field

Steadicam: Garrett Brown's revolutionary camera platform allowing hand-held shots of great length and steadiness; indispensable to modern film-making. Just don't mention it in your scripts!

Stock footage: as opposed to raw or unexposed stock, material sourced from elsewhere, as in newsreel shots of war scenes

Story: the plot events of a script—what the script is really 'about' as opposed to what happens in it

Storyboard: a series of drawings like a cartoon strip showing each and every shot required for a scene, sequence, or an entire film; film-makers like Steven Spielberg hire specialist storyboarders to produce exquisitely detailed boards

Structure (script): story and plot elements of a script as described in a scene breakdown

Synopsis: short script description (compare with Treatment, a longer, more detailed version of the same script without dialogue)

Teaser: short 'trailer' for a television show before the opening credits, designed to 'hook' the audience

Telemovie (Telefeature): film made for TV, not cinema release (though this may happen later as was the case with Spielberg's *Duel*)

Television series: normally hour-long episodic drama with a complete story per episode, normally produced in blocks of 13 or 26 and with a recurrent cast; the staple of night-time TV

Variety (shows): once the showpiece of television and rapidly less popular in the 2000s—a mix of sketch comedy, dance routines, and singers

Videotape: electromechanical recording tape for television; digital tape is rapidly overtaking the fifty-year dominance of tape

Viewers: audience, punters, the masses

Voice-over (VO): the speaker is invisible but the Voice is heard 'over' the picture; can be used for narration, as a character soliloquy, and as a device for hearing the unseen (as when a character is heard inside a closed room, travelling car and so on. Also OOS, a script term which means 'Out Of Shot'—a voice heard 'off' camera

What if?: ideas for scripting that begin with the proposition 'what if . . .' (e.g. 'What if Martians invaded Earth?')

Wide shot: from full human figure to as wide as the universe

Wild sound: any separately recorded sound and thus not in sync with the camera—a bird's cry, a scream, distant thunder; can be used for straight narrative reasons or to create atmosphere

Workshopping: more and more used as intensive pre-shoot rehearsal period for actors—often leading to script changes (The writer should be there!)

Wrap: the end of a day's filming—or of the whole shoot.

References

Allen, Woody, 'The Kugelmass Episode', in *Complete Prose*, Picador, London, 1980, pp. 347–360.

Australian Children's Television Foundation Website: www.actf.com.au/tol/

Eco, Umberto, 'Casablanca, or the Cliches are Having a Ball', in Marshall Lonsky (ed.), *On Signs*, Basil Blackwell, Oxford, 1985, p. 37.

Encore Directory, Reed, Sydney (annual).

Fitzgerald, Ross, *Pushed from the Wings*, Hale & Iremonger, Sydney, 1986.

—— *Busy in the Fog*, Macmillan, Melbourne, 1990.

Goldman, William, *Adventures in the Screen Trade*, Warner Books, New York, 1983.

—— 'Rocking the Boat', *Premiere*, April 1998, p. 78ff.

Goldstein, Patrick, 'Hollywood Squared', *LA Times*, 26 July 1987: Calendar Section, p. 40.

Jeffrey, Tom, *The Film Business*, AFTRS, Sydney, 1995.

Jones, Chuck, quoted in David Dale, 'Animated Argument', *Sydney Morning Herald*, 25 April 1998, Spectrum, p. 5.

Queenan, Joe, *The Unkindest Cut: How a Hatchetman Critic Made His Own $7000 Movie and Put It All on His Credit Card*, Hyperion, 1997.

Simpson, Roger, 'Between the Sheets: an Australian Writers' Guild/Encore Special Issue', vol. 1, issue 1, 19 November 1997.

Williams, Gordon, quoted in Manuel Alvarado and Edward Buscombe, '*Hazell: the Making of a TV Series*', BFI, London, 1978, pp. 46–48.

Wolff, Jurgen and Cox, Kerry, *Successful Scriptwriting*, Writer's Digest Books, Ohio, 1988.

Wyatt, Justin, *High Concept: Movies and Marketing in Hollywood*, University of Texas, Austin, 1994.

Recommended Reading and Viewing

Books and articles

Bart, Peter, *The Gross, The Hits, The Flops: the Summer that Ate Hollywood*, St Martin's Press, New York, 1999.

Corliss, Richard, *Talking Pictures: Screenwriters in the American Cinema*, Penguin, New York, 1974.

Corman, Roger, *How I Made a Hundred Movies in Hollywood and Never Lost a Dime*, Da Capo Press, New York, 1998.

Day-Lewis, Sean, *Talk of Drama: Views of the Television Dramatist Then and Now*, University of Luton Press, Luton, 1998.

Dunne, John Gregory, *Monster: Living off the Big Screen*, Random House, New York, 1997.

Dyas, Ronald D., *Screenwriting for Television and Film*, Brown and Benchmark, Indiana, 1993.

Field, Syd, *Screenplay: the Foundations of Screenwriting*, Dell, New York, 1982.

Frolich, Billy, *What I Really Want to Do is Direct*, Dutton, New York, 1996.

Froug, William, *The Screenwriter Looks at the Screenwriter*, Macmillan, New York, 1972.

Goldman, William, *Adventures in the Screen Trade*, Warner Books, New York, 1983.

Jeffrey, Tom, *The Film Business*, AFTRS, Sydney, 1995.

Knapman, Katherine, *Low Means Low: the Collected Papers from the Low Budget Seminar*, AFC, Sydney, 1995.

Queenan, Joe, *The Unkindest Cut: How a Hatchetman Critic Made His Own $7000 Movie and Put It All on His Credit Card*, Hyperion, 1997.

Rabiger, Michael, *D.i.r.e.c.t.i.n.g: Film Techniques and Aesthetics*, Focal Press, Boston, 1999.

Schickel, Richard, 'Irreconcilable Differences', *Time*, 8 October 1984.

Wyatt, Justin, *High Concept: Movies and Marketing in Hollywood*, University of Texas, Austin, 1994.

Software packages and websites

Collaborator (TM), Collaborator Systems Cal. (Mac/Windows)

Final Draft (TM), B.C. Software (www.bcsoftware.com (Mac/Windows)

Movie Magic Screenwriter (TM), Movie Magic (Mac/Windows)

The Online Communicator (http://www.communicator.com)

Key films/TV series discussed

Films

Barton Fink, Joel Cohen, 1991   59, 157–8
The Big Sleep, Howard Hawks, 1946   104
Breathless, Jean Luc Godard, 1959   90
Breathless, Jim McBride, 1983   90
The Castle, Rob Sitch, 1996   4, 48–9
The Darra Dogs, Dennis Tupicoff, 1993   24, 184–8
Dead Man, Jim Jarmusch, 1996   8
Feeding the Monster, BBC, Nadia Haggar, 1992   58
Full Metal Jacket, Stanley Kubrick, 1987   28
Grey Gardens, Maysles Brothers, 1976   37, 93
His Mother's Voice, Dennis Tupicoff, 1997   184
LA Confidential, Curtis Hanson, 1997   104–5
La Haine, Mathieu Kassowitz, 1995   2
The Legend of Fred Paterson, ABC/Jonathan Dawson, 1996   34, 69–70
Love Serenade, Shirley Barrett, 1996   6, 8, 89
Newsfront, Phil Noyce, 1978   151
One Man's Instrument Max Bannah, 1990   24, 188
The Player, Robert Altman, 1992   5, 82, 223
Playtime, Jacques Tati, 1967   48
Pulp Fiction, Quentin Tarantino, 1994   13
Rats in the Ranks, Bob Connolly and Robin Anderson, 1996   37–8
Reservoir Dogs, Quentin Tarantino, 1992   4, 13, 87, 98
Self Made Hero (*Un Héros Très Discret*), Jacques Audiard, 1996   82
Video Fool for Love, Robert Gibson, 1996   19
The War Room, D. A. Pennebaker, 1996   37
Winging It, Max Bannah, 1999   188–90
Witness, Peter Weir, 1985   100
Year of the Dogs, Michael Cordell, 1997   37

Series

Hazell, Thames TV, 1977-78   84–5
Homicide, Crawford Productions, 1964-74   121–4
Medivac, Liberty and Beyond, 1996-97   131–4
Misery Guts, Steel Stem Poppy/Baron, 1998   168–71
SeaChange, Artist Services, ABC, 1998+   61–2, 116–21
Swimming Outside the Flags, SBS, 1999-2000   188–90
The Wayne Manifesto, Artist Services, 1998-99   165–8
Wildside, Gannon Jenkins/ABC, 1997-9   124–31

Index

act *see* script structure
action 11, 34, 43, 52, 60, 80, 83, 95, 97–113, 127–8, 157, 175–81, 220
adaptation 18, 75–7, 92, 107–13, 144–50, 171
advertising 6, 21–3, 28–32, 75, 118, 195
agents 83, 89, 220
animation 6, 23–6, 159, 162–4, 173–91, 194, 202, 220
audience 1–4, 9, 12, 14–18, 22–32, 41, 46, 52–3, 64, 82, 103, 115–8, 138, 150–1, 159, 161–4, 171–2, 175–8, 181–3, 208, 220 *see also* markets

backstory 48, 54, 57, 83–5, 90–3, 100, 108, 113,116, 138, 150, 152, 154, 220
big screen/little screen 10–21, 220
breakdowns *see* scene breakdowns
budget 4, 9, 19–20, 33, 205, 220

character 7, 13–15, 17–18, 41–4, 46–50, 52, 54, 57–8, 61–2, 66–7, 74–5, 79–95, 98–106, 119, 122, 127–8, 131, 134–6, 138–46, 148, 150–2, 154, 157, 163, 165, 171–2, 177–8, 181–2, 189, 221
character naming 7, 84, 86–9, 146
character traits 84–5, 89–92, 131, 171, 221

children's film and television 24, 159–72
children's programming 60, 159–64, 171–2
comedy 45–58, 134–7, 146, 203, 217, 221, 224
commercials *see* corporate videos and commercials
contracts 104, 214, 221
copyright 107, 144, 211, 213, 221, 224
corporate videos and commercials 26–32

daytime soaps *see* soaps
dialogue 45, 57–8, 66, 74, 83, 91–2, 114–5, 118–9, 124, 131, 135, 139, 142, 165, 171, 175, 181, 222
documentary 19, 21, 27, 33–40, 58, 69–70, 82, 93, 203, 221, 222, 225

feature films 20, 41–2, 95, 138–58, 222, 223
film finance *see* film funding bodies
film funding bodies 2, 16, 42, 59, 66, 77, 116, 137, 157, 160, 220, 222
flashbacks/flashforwards 98, 105, 157, 224
funding *see* film funding bodies

hooks 5, 10, 12, 14, 17–18, 106, 152, 222

markets, marketplace 7, 18,
24–5, 27, 29, 32, 34, 38, 41, 69,
159, 162–3, 176–8, 181, 194,
208, 223, 224, *see also* audience

pitch, the   4–5, 10, 15, 25, 28–9,
58–79, 86, 115–8. 151, 173,
176–8, 189, 202, 223, 224
plot   8–11, 14, 16–18, 41–4, 57,
60, 62, 65–8, 74, 80–2, 85, 89,
91–3, 95–113, 116, 118, 125,
131, 138, 141–2, 145–6, 148–50,
157, 165, 173–5, 197–202, 210,
221, 223–5

registration *see* copyright

scene breakdowns   57, 65–9,
72–4, 139, 150, 181, 224–5
script *see* script structure
script editor   3, 16, 44, 81, 128,
137, 139, 221
script structure   21, 25–6, 34, 37,
45, 60, 74, 80, 95–107, 125,
146, 157, 173, 203, 220, 225
selling ideas *see* pitch

sitcoms   41, 44–9, 53–8, 191,
221, 224
sketch (comedy)   49–53, 143,
211, 224–5
soaps   41, 44–5, 114, 221–2
software programs for screenwriting   92–3, 143, 227
story *see* plot
story editor *see* script editor
storyboards   25, 29, 77, 177–8,
180, 184–90, 205–6, 225
structure, script *see* script structure
synopsis   62, 64, 74, 140, 168,
225 *see also* treatments

television series   59, 61–8, 88–9,
114–37, 145, 225
three-act structure *see* script
structure
treatments   65–6, 69, 74–7, 134,
171, 225
see also synopsis